WALES, THE WELSH
AND THE MAKING
OF AMERICA

WALES, THE WELSH AND THE MAKING OF AMERICA

Vivienne Sanders

UNIVERSITY OF WALES PRESS

2021

www.uwp.co.uk

British Library Cataloguing-in-Publication Data
A catalogue record for this book is available from the British Library.

ISBN   978-1-78683-790-5
e-ISBN   978-1-78683-791-2

Typeset by Chris Bell, cbdesign
Printed by CPI Group (UK) Ltd, Croydon CR0 4YY

CONTENTS

LIST OF FIGURES

ACKNOWLEDGEMENTS

The Merion Friends: figures 4 and 5; Paul Frame: figures 6, 7, 8 and 15; Mrs Gladys Jones Rumbaugh, figure 16; Portmeirion Ltd: figure 22; Wikimedia Creative Commons: figures 3, 10 and 21 (Sxenko); United Mine Workers of America: figure 19; Thomas Jefferson Foundation Monticello: figures 11 and 12.

For my parents and Great Aunt Kitty,
who loved both Wales and America.

Wales, the Welsh and the Making of America

I CAN STILL remember my surprise during a tour of Shirley plantation in Virginia in 1970, when our guide said someone in colonial America hailed 'from a place in England called Wales'. Although the early 1970s saw an outburst of white ethnic assertiveness and pride amongst groups such as Italian-Americans and Polish-Americans, Californian congressman Thomas M. Rees told the US House of Representatives in 1971 that 'very little has been written of what the Welsh have contributed in all walks of life in the shaping of American history'. That statement remains true half a century later.

Why have Welsh and Welsh American contributions to American history been frequently underestimated or ignored? First, Wales is a small country, sparsely populated and long dominated by England and the English. Many Americans have been unaware of Wales or have thought it simply 'a place in England'. Second, although a considerable proportion of colonial Americans were Welsh or of Welsh ancestry, they would soon be greatly outnumbered by immigrants from other nations. Dr Arturo Roberts, founder of a North American Welsh newspaper, pointed out: 'There are 20 people of Irish descent for every one with Welsh descent – that makes a big difference.' Third, the Welsh assimilated relatively easily. 'They bought into the American dream,' said Professor John Roper of the American Studies department at Swansea University. As George Washington supposedly said, 'Good Welshmen make good Americans.' Edward Hartmann, the son of a Welsh immigrant mother and writer of *Americans from Wales* (1967), argued that Welsh immigrants and their descendants were 'not chauvinistic over past wrongs or vengeance-minded over former ill-treatment, they came over quietly, modestly, willing to accept what opportunities the new environment might have to offer'. A possible fourth reason might be the lack of any long-lasting and frequently replenished concentration of Welsh Americans in big cities – there has been no Welsh equivalent of the 'Boston Irish'. Much Welsh emigration took place before the United States became increasingly industrialised and urbanised during the nineteenth century, and those early immigrants tended to settle in small townships in rural areas.

There have been a few studies of the Welsh and America, notably the respected Welsh historian David Williams's pamphlet *Wales and America* (1945). Edward G. Hartmann's *Americans from Wales* was reprinted in 1978 and 1983, and then by the National Welsh-American Foundation (NWAF) in 2001. There have also been more specialised studies of the Welsh in areas such as the Pennsylvania coalfields, Iowa, Tennessee and Wisconsin. Overall, though, as Arturo Roberts noted,

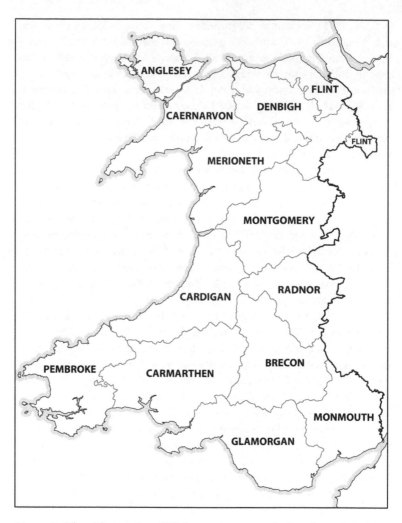

Figure 1. *The old counties of Wales, as they were during the emigration of the Welsh to America during the seventeenth, eighteenth and nineteenth centuries. These county names were changed in the later twentieth century, but this book uses the names familiar to the Welsh emigrants discussed here.*

'The Welsh have low visibility.' Ronald L. Lewis, author of *Welsh Americans: A History of Assimilation in the Coalfields* (2008), used a similar vocabulary when he described the Welsh as 'nearly invisible to most Americans'. Perhaps it is time to try to make the invisible visible, especially if doing so helps illuminate the nature and development of the United States of America.

THE NUMBER OF AMERICANS OF WELSH DESCENT

While 2.5 million Americans said they had Welsh ancestry in a recent US census, most of the 20 million who said they were simply 'Americans' came from the South, to which many Welsh people had emigrated in the colonial period. As a result, the number with Welsh descent may well be greater.

CHAPTER ONE

MADOC: EXPLORER AND DISCOVERER OF NORTH AMERICA?

I N 1979, I attended Professor Gwyn Alf Williams's inaugural lecture at
Cardiff University. He was an unforgettable speaker with a distinctive
appearance – a white mane, piercing periwinkle blue eyes, the short-
est of short Welshmen. His stutter guaranteed attentive and supportive
listeners willing him to get the next word out, and his enthusiasm was
contagious. 'Gwyn Alf' was particularly inspired by his return home to
Wales after years of exile in England, and he lectured on another Welsh
wanderer, Prince Madoc. Legend had it that Madoc established a colony
in North America in the twelfth century. A cynic warned me that my
euphoria would wear off outside the lecture theatre, but it never did,
and so I start with Madoc in attempting to argue Welsh importance in
the making of America.

MADOC AND THE EARLY COLONISATION
OF AMERICA

There is no physical proof that Prince Madoc ever existed, but legend has him as an illegitimate son of Owain, a ruler of Gwynedd in
north Wales. A thirteenth-century Flemish work mentioned a seafaring
Welsh Madoc, but it was in Elizabethan England that the Madoc legend
gained great prominence. The first printed mention was in Sir George
Peckham's *A True Reporte* (1583), which advocated colonisation and
discussed who had 'lawful title' to North America. The account of
Madoc in David Powel's *The Historie of Cambria now called Wales*
(1584) was speedily taken up by other writers, notably such widely
read promoters of English exploration and colonisation as Richard
Hakluyt and Walter Raleigh.

The Elizabethan dissemination of the Madoc story arose primarily
from the English desire to refute Spain's claims to exclusive possession
of the New World by right of Spanish-sponsored exploration and papal
gift. Interestingly, one sixteenth-century Spaniard labelled what is now
the Gulf of Mexico as Tierra de los Gales – Land of the Welsh.

The Elizabethan enthusiasm for Madoc also owed something to the
unprecedented number and prominence of Welshmen at the court of
the Tudor dynasty, a result of Henry VII having had a Welsh grandfather. That prompted the contemporary joke that St Peter, guardian of the
gates of heaven, was so exasperated by the sudden influx of Welshmen
that he got a nearby angel to shout 'Toasted cheese', which led the
Welsh to run out after him and enabled the other residents to shut the
heavenly gates behind them.

Year	Exploration of the Americas	Possible Welsh contribution
10th, 11th or 12th centuries	The first European settlers in the Americas were the Vikings in Newfoundland	A Welsh Prince Madoc possibly landed in the present-day United States in 1170 and established a settlement
1492	Spain sponsored Columbus's voyage. He landed in the West Indies and has been credited with the discovery of the New World	
1497	Henry VII of England was one of the sponsors of the 1497 voyage of John Cabot, who landed in North America, probably Newfoundland	Some claim Richard Amerike (ap Meurig), whose family coat of arms contained stars and stripes, sponsored Cabot's voyage and asked him to name any lands he found 'America'
1507	The name 'America' first appeared on a map. It is generally considered to have originated with Italian/Spanish explorer Amerigo Vespucci	
1523	Spanish-sponsored explorer Ponce de León landed in and named 'Florida'	
1534	Jacques Cartier claimed Canada's St Lawrence River region for France	
Late 16th century	Spaniards explored what is now the south-western USA, which led to seventeenth-century settlements	
1578	The English tried but failed to establish a colony in Virginia, named after the Virgin Queen Elizabeth I	
1607	First permanent and lasting English colony established at Jamestown (named after King James I) in Virginia	Possibly some Welshmen amongst them
1620	The Pilgrim Fathers landed at Plymouth in what became Massachusetts	Possibly some Welshmen amongst them

Madoc's descendants: the Welsh Indians

Some early settlers in the British North American colonies expanded the Madoc legend when they claimed the existence of 'Welsh Indians', supposedly descendants of Madoc's party and the Native American population. In 1608, a group of Virginia colonists thought that an Indian tribe they encountered spoke a language similar to Welsh. The Rev. Morgan Jones claimed that when some North Carolina Indians captured him in 1669, his speaking Welsh caused them to spare his life and enabled him to preach Christianity in Welsh to them for several months. Gwyn Alf Williams was sceptical. However, it seems feasible that Indians, always fascinated and awed by perceived insanity, might be riveted by a garrulous Welshman speaking his strange tongue. Morgan Jones's narrative gained popularity when published in the *Gentleman's Magazine* in 1740, amidst further clashes with Spain over trade in the New World.

PENGUINS AND WELSH INDIANS . . .

Some early explorers found 'proof' of the existence of Welsh Indians when they heard the native population talk of penguins. The explorers thought this must be due to the Welsh words pen gwyn, which translates as 'white head'. Unfortunately, penguins have black heads.

During the seventeenth and eighteenth centuries, the Madoc story was widely believed in Wales and America and both experienced what Gwyn Alf called 'Madoc Fever' in the late eighteenth century.

INDIANS AND NATIVE AMERICANS

In the late twentieth century, descendants of the original inhabitants of North America rejected the use of the word 'Indian' and declared their preference for 'Native Americans'. Arguably, the use of the word 'Indian' might be considered appropriate in coverage of the historical period in which that was common terminology.

'MADOC FEVER' IN AMERICA

Several attempts were made to locate the Welsh Indians, some at the behest of the very powerful. In 1796, Welsh explorer John Evans sought them on behalf of the Spanish, who obviously took the Madoc stories seriously. In 1804 President Thomas Jefferson instructed the explorers Lewis and Clark to find them. Both the Spanish and American governments were motivated by the desire to establish their right to the territories west of the thirteen original British colonies.

The Mandan Indians were the preferred candidates for Welsh ancestry, because they had unusually fair skins (some had blue eyes), lighter hair that turned grey, and villages that bore some resemblance to hillfort settlements of Iron Age Britain. In 1841 the painter George Catlin noted similarities between Mandan boats and Welsh coracles. Mandan girls were celebrated for their good looks, amiability and incessant chatting, even while making love, which some observers considered conclusive proof of Welsh descent. There were other candidates. In 1858, the Mormon leader Brigham Young sent a Welshman to visit the Hopi Indians of Arizona to see if they spoke Welsh. Three Hopi were brought back to Salt Lake City, but were apparently nonplussed when enthusiastic Welsh-speakers attempted to converse with them. Welsh American Mormon missionary Llywelyn Harris visited the Zuni Indians of Arizona in 1878. He said that they told him they were

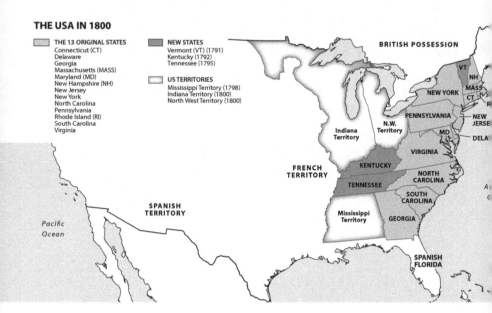

Figure 2. *The USA in 1800. Much of the territory of what is now the USA was the subject of dispute between the USA and Spain, France and Britain in the late eighteenth century.*

descended from 'Cambaraga', white men who had come across the sea before the Spanish. Harris insisted that the Zuni language contained many Welsh words.

Madoc fever in America is easily explained. Americans migrating westward into new territories were interested in unfamiliar Indian tribes, especially when explorers declared their ancient forts and ruins too sophisticated to have been constructed by any 'inferior' Indian race. Furthermore, a prior Welsh colony helped counter Spanish claims to the new lands for which Americans lusted, so it is not surprising that the Madoc legend was perpetually 'proved'. Scores of people claimed to have spoken Welsh with Indians, and several Indian chiefs such as the Cherokee Oconostota claimed Welsh ancestry. It is difficult to understand what Indians had to gain from fabricating an ancient association with the Welsh. Was it the desire for greater respectability, acceptance and advancement amidst contemporary white racism? Or for attention? Or did the Madoc story fit in with their own legends?

A further explanation of Madoc fever in America lay in the significant number of Welsh Americans moving west in America, and the continuing belief in Madoc and Welsh Indians back in Wales, where there was a dramatic Madoc revival in the 1790s.

'MADOC FEVER' IN WALES

Many factors contributed to the Madoc revival in Wales. The story once again benefited from a bestseller: Dr John Williams's *An Enquiry into the Truth of the Tradition concerning the Discovery of America by Prince Madoc* (1791). Dr Williams explained his motivation: 'My design . . . was to show that the Spaniards have not an unquestionable right to the Continent of America.'

Other Welshmen had a variety of motives for reviving Madoc, as can be seen in a manuscript written by William Jones and circulated at a 1791 eisteddfod. Jones urged contact with Madoc's colony for reasons of national pride, noting that 'some modern sceptics . . . deny . . . Madoc . . . because they will not acknowledge that a Welshman is capable of performing any brave or generous action'. Jones came from a depressed cloth-producing area of Montgomeryshire from which considerable numbers would emigrate to America, so it was not surprising that he mentioned the need to escape the 'ungrateful soil' of a mountainous Wales dominated by an avaricious landed gentry. Jones assured 'all indigenous Cambro-Britons' that they would find a promised land in America, that the inhabitants of Madoc's colony 'are at this time a free and distinct people, and have preserved their liberty, language and some traces of their religion to this day'. As the Pembrokeshire-born Rev. William Richards declared in 1791, the existence of Welsh Indians 'greatly interested' Welsh people, because 'if such a nation really exists, and there seems now to be no great room to doubt the fact, it will then appear that a branch of the Welsh nation has preserved its independence, even to this day'. This idea of reunification with an independent branch of the Welsh nation greatly influenced the flood of Welsh emigrants in the 1790s.

For some Welsh people, Madoc fever coincided with considerable disillusion over the English establishment's stance on religion and the American and French Revolutions. Many Welsh had rejected the Anglican Church of that establishment and turned to Protestant nonconformity. Welsh nonconformists such as Baptists, Methodists and Quakers dreamed of a better, freer life in the land supposedly settled by Madoc. Some of these nonconformists sympathised with the American revolutionaries who had rejected the British political system, and the French revolutionaries who had overturned the traditional social order. These Welsh nonconformists resented the English establishment's dismissal of those causes. For example, Morgan John Rhys, a Baptist minister from Pontypool, defended the new American Republic and also advocated a search for the descendants of Madoc, the 'Lost Brethren'. He and many other religious Welshmen hoped for the conversion of American Indians.

OPPOSITION TO THE MADOC STORY

Although the Madoc and Welsh Indians stories were long-lasting and influential, not everyone believed them. During the nineteenth century, people in Wales began to lose interest: the American West had been fully explored and had produced no conclusive proof of the existence of any Welsh Indians, while south Wales was becoming more anglicised and Welsh nationalism was focused more upon education.

The Madoc belief lasted longer amongst Indians (notably the Cherokee) and white Americans keen to emphasise their ancient and ancestral roots. In 1953 the socially prestigious Daughters of the American Revolution organisation erected a plaque at Fort Morgan, on Mobile Bay, Alabama. Their plaque claimed that Madoc had landed in the Gulf of Mexico in present-day Alabama in 1170 and that there had been Welsh-speaking Indians.

One of their cited sources to prove this claim was an 1810 letter written by John Sevier, one of the founders of Tennessee. Sevier wrote of the Cherokee belief that some Welsh-speaking ancestors of the Cherokee had landed in Mobile Bay. In 2008, the Alabama Parks Service removed the plaque, claiming that it wanted to protect it from Hurricane Ike. It was never replaced. There was a similar plaque at Fort Mountain State Park in Georgia, where legend had it that one of the three stone forts constructed by Madoc was located. This plaque met a similar fate in 2015, and the Welsh Indians were excised from the replacement plaque. These removals no doubt originated in a dislike of popular claims that more sophisticated Indian fortifications and dwellings had to have been created by white men rather than Native Americans, and in the belief that the Madoc story was unproved and an embarrassing fiction.

BEWARE THE CLAIMS OF 'RACIAL GROUPS' . . .

In 1971, the eminent American historian Samuel Eliot Morison, warned that 'Canada and the United States seem to be full of racial groups who wish to capture the "real" discovery of America for their medieval compatriots'.

Gwyn Alf Williams gave us cogent reasons to disbelieve the Madoc story, but widespread belief in Madoc persisted for an extraordinarily long time, and while we have no concrete proof of the existence of the Prince or the Welsh Indians, the Viking discovery of America was long disbelieved until archaeological evidence was discovered, and Tim Severin's transatlantic voyage in a vessel similar to Welsh coracles proved that relatively primitive craft could cross the Atlantic.

While the Welsh may not have discovered and settled America in the twelfth century, they certainly played a significant part in the subsequent history of the United States.

CHAPTER TWO

THE WELSH AND
THE COLONISATION
OF NORTH AMERICA

I N 1607, the first successful British settlement in what is now the United States was established in Virginia, and in 1620 the Puritan Pilgrim Fathers voyaged on the *Mayflower* to what is now Massachusetts and founded the Plymouth Colony. While both groups contained individuals with names that might indicate a Welsh connection, a steady stream of known Welsh individuals settled in Virginia and Massachusetts in the second quarter of the seventeenth century.

THE INTOLERANCE OF THE PILGRIM FATHERS

Although the Pilgrim Fathers had emigrated to escape persecution under the established (Anglican) church in England, they were intolerant. The Massachusetts Bay Colony's religious authorities banished Roger Williams, whom some consider to be of Welsh stock, from Massachusetts in 1635. They disapproved of his religious views, especially his belief that church and state should be totally separate. Williams went on to establish the colony that became known as Rhode Island.

In 1662, the first known group of Welsh settlers arrived in North America. They were Baptists, whose preference for adult rather than infant baptism alienated many other Christians. They came in search of religious freedom and were led by John Miles (or Myles), a minister from near Swansea in south Wales. When their religious ideas were rejected as unacceptable in the Plymouth Colony, they moved over forty miles away to south-eastern Massachusetts and christened their settlement Swanzey. However, it was in the Pennsylvania colony that Welsh religious refugees had the greatest influence on colonial life and on what became the United States of America.

WELSH QUAKERS, PENN AND PENNSYLVANIA

The Welsh constituted the largest proportion of immigrants arriving in Pennsylvania between 1682 and 1700 and the legacy of their settlement is evidenced in place names such as Merion and Radnor.

Perhaps the most influential of the Welsh who settled in Pennsylvania were those of the Quaker religion. The Society of Friends (or Quakers) emerged along with other radical sects during the tumultuous English Civil War period, but the restoration of the monarchy under Charles II led to periods of persecution that prompted thousands of religious nonconformists to emigrate to Britain's American colonies.

In 1681, Charles II granted lands south of the New York colony to the English Quaker William Penn. Charles was indebted to Penn's father, but Penn attributed the King's generosity more to the desire to be rid of troublesome Quakers. Quakers rejected the idea of a state Church, emphasised self-government within their community and believed in the equality of those who had the Quaker 'inner light'. William Penn's father was not best pleased when his son adopted the typical Quaker refusal to remove his hat in deference to his father or any other social superior. Unsurprisingly, the conservative authorities in England and Wales perceived Quakers as a danger to the social and political order.

On the voyage to Pennsylvania in 1682, Penn told a Welshman that his family origins were in Wales and that he had thought 'New Wales' an appropriate name for his proprietary colony with its 'pretty, hilly country', but lamented that he had been overruled by Charles II's preference for the name Pennsylvania 'in honour of my father'. Penn then rationalised the embarrassing situation, pointing out that as 'pen' means 'head' in Welsh, Pennsylvania would translate as 'head of the woods'. Welsh Quakers from Merionethshire, Montgomeryshire and Pembrokeshire constituted a substantial number of those who joined Penn in seeking religious toleration and, they hoped, financial gain. In 1754, Lewis Evans would write that the Welsh constituted roughly 'the tenth part of the first settlers under Mr Penn'.

Penn wanted his proprietary colony to have free speech, liberty of conscience and a wider franchise than that in England and Wales and in Britain's other American colonies. He promised the Dutch and Swedes already living in Pennsylvania that they would 'be governed by laws of your own making', but although he wrote that it was desirable 'to put the power in the people', he came from a privileged background and had pronounced elitist and authoritarian tendencies. Penn's royal charter gave him the power to govern the colony in conjunction with a legislative assembly, but he had invested a great deal of money in his colony and expected that he and his chosen representatives should have ultimate control and be obeyed. This led to serious disagreements with Pennsylvania's assertive Quakers.

Thomas Lloyd

When Penn departed from Pennsylvania in 1684 after a two-year stay, he left executive power in the hands of a trusted Council under the presidency of Thomas Lloyd, the son of a noted and affluent Montgomery-shire Quaker. Lloyd was quickly and repeatedly promoted by Penn, but would prove to be Penn's most dangerous and dedicated enemy in the

Figure 3. *Portrait of William Penn, date and painter unknown*
(unknown author, Public domain, via Wikimedia Commons).

Pennsylvania colony. In 1688, Penn was warned that Lloyd and his faction were denying Penn's authority and 'raising a force to rebel'. Interpretations of Lloyd's motives varied. Some said he led the opposition to
Penn's proprietary powers because he thought that the colony could do
better under another form of government. Others thought Lloyd considered Penn's authority unenforceable amongst anti-authoritarian Quakers.
Penn supporters insisted that Lloyd was simply ambitious. However, one
overlooked motive is the likelihood that Lloyd shared the general Welsh
disillusionment with Penn. Lloyd's father, Charles, was a member of the
committee of prominent Welshman who had visited London in 1681 to
negotiate the purchase of a large tract of land in Penn's colony. They had
sought a distinctly Welsh settlement and the right of self-government in

a 'barony' north-west of Philadelphia, 'within which all causes, quarrels, crimes and disputes might be tried and wholly determined by officers, magistrates and juries of our language'. Unfortunately, the committee's agreements with Penn were merely verbal, and this subsequently led to great antagonism. Many Welsh grew angry with Penn because he disputed the committee's claim that there had been an agreement under which the Welsh would collect their own taxes, and he divided their barony into administrative townships, separated their settlement into different counties and opened up their Welsh Tract to settlers of other nationalities.

Thomas Lloyd, like many of the Welsh Quakers in Pennsylvania, was a well-educated member of the gentry, willing to defend his rights in assertive fashion. Indeed, such was Pennsylvania Quaker combativeness that a 1693 dispute between Lloyd's followers and another Quaker faction led to the physical destruction of the Philadelphia meeting house as both sides used axes to destroy the wooden gallery in which the opposing faction sat. Lloyd was fearless, whether in defying axe-wielding fellow Quakers, William Penn or King William III. It was in vain that Penn pleaded with Lloyd, 'For the love of God, me and the poor country, do not be so litigious and brutish.' When Lloyd insisted that Pennsylvania would not contribute to the defence of the colony during King William's war with France, the Crown took over Penn's colony in 1692 on the grounds of Quaker 'animosities and divisions'. 'Thomas Lloyd brought this to pass,' sighed Penn. However, the colony proved so recalcitrant that the King's representative, Governor Benjamin Fletcher, soon asked to be recalled and the colony was restored to Penn in 1694.

In a book written in 1694, Penn had 'Being Deferential to No One' as one of the twelve basic tenets of Quakerism. This lack of deference was well illustrated by the Pennsylvania Quakers' frequent rejection of authority and laws, whether Penn's or those of their elected representatives. Penn found the Pennsylvania Quakers 'noisy' people, so 'open in your dissatisfactions' that 'it almost tempts me to deliver [Pennsylvania] up to the King and let a mercenary governor have the taming of them'. Quakers were the most anti-government in sentiment of all Britons, and they increasingly viewed Penn as a representative of the hated government in London. The Quaker belief in their equality before God frequently encouraged them to reject Penn's authority. They were convinced that their God-given inner light enabled them to recognise if the laws and actions were acceptable to God, and that those that were unacceptable could be disobeyed. Penn himself frequently urged his colonists to ignore and disobey the English government if he thought it threatened his authority or revenue in Pennsylvania.

WELSH PRESBYTERIANS AND AUTHORITY

The Welsh Quakers were not the only Welsh settlers troublesome to those in authority. David Evans was born in Carmarthenshire in 1681. At the age of sixty-six, he wrote a biographical Welsh-language poem that described his experiences as a Presbyterian minister in the American colonies. As a minister in the Delaware Welsh Tract from 1714 to 1720, he found that he and his congregation were 'not comfortable together', and he took up another ministry, this time at Tredyffryn in Pennsylvania's Great Valley, where he served for twenty years. In his biography, he said that the bitter strife and incessant bickering amongst his Pennsylvania Welsh congregation exhausted him, and that he wished that congregations would have more respect for their ministers. In 1740, he bade farewell to his Tredyffryn congregation in a sermon entitled 'Goats I found you, and goats I leave you'. He then became a minister to an English, German and Ulster Irish congregation in New Jersey and he was far happier amongst those nationalities than he had been with his own countrymen.

Figure 4. *Welsh Quaker meeting house in Merion, Pennsylvania, constructed between 1695 and 1715 (engraving dating from 1837). 'Its timber framed roof structure is . . . a remarkable example of early Welsh timber-framing practice,' according to David Mark Facenda's 2002 University of Pennsylvania Master's thesis, to which I was kindly directed by Robert F. Sutton and the Merion Friends.*

Figures 5a and 5b. *The survival of the Merion Friends Meeting House is an example of the physical impact that the early Welsh settlers had and still have on the American landscape.*

WELSH ANGLICANS IN PENNSYLVANIA

After the Quakers established the Welsh barony, a second Welsh settlement was created in Pennsylvania at Gwynedd township, north of
Philadelphia. Most of the Gwynedd settlers were Anglicans (known as
Episcopalians in America). One of their surviving churches is the Church
of St David's, constructed in Radnor in 1715 and serving as another
reminder of the Welsh contribution to the establishment of a thriving
religious life in the American colonies.

David Lloyd

After Thomas Lloyd died in 1694, his relation and fellow Montgomeryshire
Quaker David Lloyd led the increasingly assertive Pennsylvania Assembly.
David Lloyd was a rabble-rouser, a superb writer and an intelligent and
devious politician. He contended that a powerful Assembly could better
resist proprietary or royal authority than any executive Council such as
that which Thomas Lloyd had dominated. David Lloyd had such popular
support that the new Pennsylvania constitution of 1696 gave political control to the Assembly, which remained under Quaker control. David Lloyd
was as willing to defy Penn, King and Parliament as Thomas Lloyd had
been. When the British Parliament passed a Navigation Act (1696) that
established Vice Admiralty courts to deal with colonists who engaged in
smuggling to avoid paying customs duties to the Crown, Lloyd declared
this a worse attack on the 'liberties and privileges of the people' than the
actions of the tyrannical King Charles I.

When Penn returned to Pennsylvania in 1699 after an absence of
sixteen years, he wanted David Lloyd prosecuted for 'high crimes and
misdemeanours', but was advised against it on the grounds that most
colonists favoured Lloyd as their defender against the authority of Penn
and of England. Penn left for England again in 1701, and Lloyd's faction worked further to erode his proprietary powers. Penn reluctantly
agreed to the Assembly's sovereignty, but left Governor John Evans to
look after his proprietary rights. Evans was an Anglican who despised
colonials, and by 1708 the Quakers were considered to be on the verge
of revolt. Penn blamed David Lloyd – 'a traitorous person, a delinquent
and vile ingrate . . . What proprietor and governor would care one jot
what becomes of such foolish, if not wicked people?' Penn concluded
that Quaker antipathy to government made them ungovernable and that
life on the frontier in the 'howling wilderness' had exacerbated that tendency. As with many other immigrants, Welsh Quakers had faced great

upheavals because of their deeply held beliefs and their incessant quest for better land in which to live free and prosperous, and they resented any authority that got in their way.

HAIR-RAISING ESCAPES ON THE PENNSYLVANIA FRONTIER

Welsh Baptist minister Thomas Jones emigrated from the Bridgend area in 1737 and bravely settled on the Pennsylvania frontier in Berks County. Thomas 'mortally hated' the Indians because they had nearly scalped him and had run off with his wig.

The significance of Pennsylvania and the Welsh contribution

Of all the European immigrants of the seventeenth and eighteenth centuries, it was perhaps Penn and the Quakers in Pennsylvania who most shaped what would become the United States. The society they established in Pennsylvania was religiously and ethnically pluralist. It was more committed to political equality than were most contemporary Britons and colonists, and contained individuals who were vociferously assertive and articulate in discussion of citizens' rights. Through the establishment of these principles, the Pennsylvania Quakers, amongst whom the Welsh were so prominent, had a great impact on the beliefs and the national character and identity of the new American nation. The Welsh Quakers, and particularly the Montgomeryshire Lloyds, gave an early and inspirational demonstration of the independence of spirit and the political beliefs that characterised the revolutionary generation in the American colonies in the late eighteenth century, the generation that broke from Britain and established the United States of America.

WELSH SETTLERS IN DELAWARE AND SOUTH CAROLINA

The Pennsylvania colony was far more tolerant of religious diversity than Puritan Massachusetts. However, the Radnorshire Baptists of Pennepek (now within the city of Philadelphia) so disagreed with the views of a group of Welsh Baptists who arrived in 1701 that the new arrivals purchased from Penn a 'Welsh Tract' in what is now Delaware. Baptists, Presbyterians and Anglicans from Wales lived in harmony in this Welsh Tract, although some moved on in 1735 in the hope of a better life at a Welsh settlement on the Pee Dee River in South Carolina.

THE WELSH BECOME 'AMERICANS'

In 1700, one-third of Pennsylvania's 20,000 inhabitants were Welsh, but by the 1770s, most of the 12,000 or so people of Welsh stock in Pennsylvania were losing or had lost their separate identity. This was mostly because the Welsh had been joined and outnumbered by other immigrant groups. In Gwynedd township in 1743, the Welsh constituted 39 of the 48 taxable individuals, but by 1776 it was 24 out of 143. They were experiencing what would become known in the twentieth century as the American ethnic 'melting pot'.

Other immigrant groups often regarded the Welsh as English, so much so that the Welsh were counted as English in the census of 1790.

WELSH NAMES

Americans with typically Welsh surnames might conceivably have Welsh ancestry. Amongst these names are Bowen, Daniels, Davies/ Davis, Edwards, Evans, Griffith, Gwynne, Harris, Hopkins, Howell(s), Humphreys, Jenkins, Jones, Lewis, Llewellyn, Lloyd, Meredith, Morris, Morgan, Owens, Parry, Powell, Price, Pritchard, Probert, Pugh, Richards, Roberts, Thomas, Vaughan, Walters and Williams. Sometimes the colonists had to take special measures to distinguish between Welsh Americans of the same name, so in colonial settlements there might be a John Jones the Shop and a John Jones the Deacon. Much later, in Powell, South Dakota, there was a Hugh Roberts Religion, a Hugh Roberts Ungodly, and a Hugh Roberts Inbetween.

THE WELSH CONTRIBUTION TO EDUCATION IN THE COLONIES

The generation of American colonists who helped lead the colonies to independence from the mother country were members of a highly educated and articulate elite. The development of the American system of education for that elite owed much to Wales and the Welsh.

The Protestant nonconformists in the American colonies established colleges in order to train the well-educated preachers that they desired. Welshmen played a valued part in the foundation of colleges that would develop into three of America's most prestigious universities, Yale, Brown and Princeton. Yale University was named after Elihu Yale, whose family's ancestral lands were in north Wales, at Plas yn Iâl ('Yale' is an anglicisation of Iâl).

Yale

Elihu Yale was born in Boston in 1648. His nonconformist parents had emigrated from north Wales to America, but the relative religious toler-ance of Oliver Cromwell's republican regime encouraged them to return to Britain in 1652. Elihu spent years working for the British East India Company, during which time he made a fortune that owed much to the slave trade. In 1692, he returned to Britain and spent a great deal of time in north Wales.

Elihu's charitable donations attracted the attention of Jeremiah Dummer, a London agent of the Massachusetts Bay Company. Dummer had a friend who was a trustee of the tiny Connecticut Collegiate School established in 1700 in New Haven. He informed his friend that Elihu Yale had no sons and was considering naming a relation in New Haven as his heir and donating money to an Oxford college. The Rev. Cotton Mather of Boston reminded Yale of his New England connections, emphasised the Christian character of the New Haven college and said that if it 'might wear the name of Yale College', it would be a better memorial 'than an Egyptian pyramid'. Although Elihu Yale had not lived in America since he was four years old, he responded to the requests to make a donation towards a new building for the college, and sent 417 books for the library and saleable goods worth £800. Grateful col-lege officials expected even more and named the building and eventu-ally the college after him. However, Yale only sent half of what he had promised Dummer and his heirs contested his will so that Yale College never received his £500 bequest.

A 1999 article in the popular *American Heritage* magazine described Elihu Yale as America's 'most overrated philanthropist' and argued that Jeremiah Dummer was a far more generous benefactor, but that naming a college Dummer College was deemed inappropriate. On the other hand, Yale's was the largest gift from any individual prior to 1837 and he gave it at a time when the college desperately needed it.

Brown and Princeton

Brown University is another educational legacy of Welsh nonconformity. Baptist Minister Morgan Edwards emigrated from Pontypool in south Wales in 1757 and became pastor of the church at Pennepek in Phil-adelphia. During 1767–8, he was in Britain to raise funds for the new college in the Rhode Island colony and raised £900, which he consid-ered a disappointing sum (he blamed it on the bad press that America had in England). Edwards persuaded his Pembrokeshire-born friend Dr William Richards, a minister at Lynn in Norfolk, to donate his library to the college, which would become Brown University. The foundation of the equally prestigious Princeton University in New Jersey owed much to Welsh Presbyterian Minister Dr Samuel Davies.

A SMOKING MINISTER?

After an Atlantic crossing in which his wife and son died, Anglesey-born Goronwy Owen taught at Virginia's prestigious College of William and Mary, but then became rector of St Andrews Church, Virginia, where his salary was paid in 18,000 pounds of tobacco per annum.

CONCLUSIONS

The Welsh who helped colonise America made a considerable contribution not only to the education of many generations of Americans in top-class institutions, but also to a desire for freedom from an unsympathetic government, for the right to practise religion as one saw fit and for the opportunity to be able to move freely to sparsely inhabited regions in search of a better life. These would prove long-lasting characteristics of the people of what became the United States of America.

The very act of leaving Wales was akin to a rebellious statement of religious and political dissatisfaction, so it is not surprising that Welsh Americans played an important role in the American colonists' campaign for independence from Britain and in shaping the character of the new nation.

CHAPTER THREE

RICHARD PRICE
AND THE AMERICAN
REVOLUTION

O N THE EVE of the American War of Independence (1775–83), the population of Britain's thirteen American colonies was nearly 2.5 million. It has been estimated that this number included at the very least 8,000 Welsh-born immigrants and Americans of predominantly Welsh ancestry. According to this estimate, around 6,000 of the 8,000 lived in Pennsylvania, where the Welsh Barony, the Great Valley and Gwynedd contained extensive settlements, and Lancaster County and Berks County contained some smaller ones. It was said that there were so many people with Welsh connections in the city of Philadelphia that the Welsh language could be heard in the streets. An estimated 1,000 others of Welsh stock resided in the Delaware Welsh Tract, 500 in the Welsh Neck area of South Carolina, and 200 in Swansea, Massachusetts.

Much Welsh immigration had been in response to the British government's discriminatory treatment of non-Anglicans. Some of the Welsh Americans and some from other ethnic backgrounds remained suspicious of that government. Relations between Britain and the American colonists began a dramatic deterioration during the 1760s. After a series of disputes centring on British powers of taxation over the thirteen colonies, British troops clashed with colonists during 1775, and the American colonists declared their independence on 4 July 1776. The American War of Independence, also known as the American Revolution, ended in the defeat of Britain and the establishment of the United States of America. While many Welsh immigrants and Welsh Americans played an important part in the fight against Britain in the years 1775–83, the eminent Welsh historian David Williams argued that while Richard Price 'never set foot on the American continent, he contributed far more than any other [Welshman] . . . to the growth and development of the United States'.

The Englishman Tom Paine is usually considered the greatest British friend and inspiration to the American colonists in the Revolutionary War period, but there is a strong argument to be made that Richard Price was of equal if not greater importance. While American Founding Father and future President John Adams described Paine as better 'at pulling down than building', he was a fervent admirer of Richard Price.

Price was born to a family of Protestant Dissenters in Llangeinor, near Bridgend in south Wales in 1723. Although he returned to Wales for annual holidays and swimming at Southerndown beach, his Unitarian ministry was in London. Price was an enthusiastic correspondent and socialiser and on good terms with several of the Founding Fathers of the American nation, especially John Adams and Benjamin Franklin. Price described Franklin as 'a friend that I greatly loved and valued'.

THE FOUNDING FATHERS OF THE UNITED STATES

In 1973, the historian Richard B. Morris listed John Adams, Benjamin Franklin, Alexander Hamilton, John Jay, Thomas Jefferson, James Madison and George Washington as America's Founding Fathers, but others include all the signatories of the American Declaration of Independence in their number.

CAUSES OF THE AMERICAN WAR OF INDEPENDENCE

During 1756–63, Britain incurred great debts defending its American colonies from the French and the Indians in what Britons called the Seven Years War and Americans called the French–Indian War. During 1763–4, the British introduced two unpopular policies in their American colonies. First, Britain sought to prevent further expensive clashes with the Indians by forbidding settlers to go beyond the Appalachian Mountains. Second, Britain tried to combat American avoidance of the customs duties that could help finance the cost of a British army in North America. Frontiersmen such as Daniel Boone and land speculators such as George Washington resented the attempts to halt expansion across the Appalachians, while some colonists argued that customs duties constituted unfair taxation because the colonists lacked representation in the British Parliament.

In 1765, the British Parliament levied the first direct tax on the colonists: Americans were to pay stamp duty on items such as legal documents and newspapers. Mobs in Boston and New York rendered collection of the stamp duty impossible, while New York merchants boycotted British imports and inspired others to do the same. In 1766, Parliament repealed the Stamp Act but unwisely passed a Declaratory Act which laid down that the colonies were fully subject to the authority of the British Parliament. Assertive colonists declared that colonial assemblies alone had the right to tax them.

In 1767, the British imposed more customs duties on the American colonists, and the arrival of 600 British troops in Boston in 1768 led to frequent physical clashes. In what Americans called the 'Boston Massacre' (1770), five Bostonians were shot and killed by British troops whom colonists had pelted with stone-filled snowballs.

When the British repealed all the new customs duties except that on tea, tensions eased somewhat until militant Bostonians boarded tea ships and threw tea overboard in protest against the duty. After that Boston Tea Party (1773), the exasperated British closed the port of Boston under what Americans called the 'Intolerable Acts' (1774), while royal governors dissolved colonial assemblies critical of British policies. The other colonies supported Boston and sent delegates to a Continental Congress in Philadelphia, Pennsylvania, 'to consult upon the present unhappy state of the colonies'. The delegates agreed to boycott trade with Britain and denounced taxation without representation.

In February 1775, the British declared Massachusetts in a state of rebellion. The clashes between British troops and colonists in the Massachusetts villages of Lexington and Concord are generally seen as the opening shots of the American War of Independence. The Continental Congress met a second time and began directing a war against Britain. George Washington was appointed commander of the Continental Army.

Some historians consider the colonists' main motivation to be economic, but they were lightly taxed. Others argue that their prime motivation was political, that they feared that a faraway government in which they were not represented was attempting to increase its power over them. The latter argument seems more persuasive: as the Welsh Dissenting minister Richard Price said, the colonists had grown up.

PRICE AND THE TAXATION OF THE AMERICAN COLONIES

During the 1760s, Richard Price became convinced that an increasingly arbitrary British government was eroding the liberties of Britons and Americans. Benjamin Franklin expressed similar concerns when he visited London in 1765 to voice the colonists' protests against the Stamp Act, under which the British government imposed direct taxation upon its American colonies for the first time. While the British government responded to the colonists' outcry with the repeal of the Stamp Act, it simultaneously issued a Declaratory Act (1766) that said Britain 'has power, and of right ought to have the power to make laws and statutes to bind the colonies, and people of America, in all cases whatever'. Price expressed horror at those words: 'Dreadful power indeed! I defy anyone to express slavery in stronger language.' He likened the British government to 'mad parents' opposing the 'natural law' that children must grow up and leave home. He dismissed the claim that the American colonies were British land, pointing out that the colonists had laboured upon it without help from Britain and that 'no power on earth can have any right to disturb them in the possession of it, or to take from them, without their consent, any part of its produce'.

It was probably Price who encouraged Franklin to publicise parallels between Welsh history and the current position of the American colonists. Franklin pointed out that the Welsh had their own laws and

Figure 6. *Portrait of Richard Price painted by Benjamin West in 1784. Price is holding a letter from his friend Benjamin Franklin, one of the Founding Fathers.*

were not taxed by the English Parliament until Henry VIII brought about full political and legal union between England and Wales (John Adams also said this in his *Novanglus Papers* of 1774). It is possible that Franklin had these parallels pointed out by his acquaintances of Welsh ancestry in Pennsylvania or by his politically radical Welsh friend David Williams, but Richard Price seems the most likely source of the inspiration.

BENJAMIN FRANKLIN'S WELSH FRIEND LEWIS EVANS

Caernarvonshire-born Lewis Evans (c.1700–56) immigrated to Philadelphia in the 1730s. He became a close friend of Benjamin Franklin, who encouraged him to publish maps of the colonies. His *General Map of the Middle British Colonies in America* (1755) was highly valued by the British forces during the French–Indian War.

Figure 7. *Portrait of Benjamin Franklin by Stephen Elmer (1780). Franklin is resting his hand upon a copy of Richard Price's* Observations on the Nature of Civil Liberty.

Price's *Observations on the Nature of Civil Liberty*

As tensions between the British government and its American colonies escalated, Price's sympathies lay with the colonists. In November 1773, he wrote to Henry Marchant, Attorney General of Rhode Island: 'I admire the exertion of the spirit of liberty among Americans ... America is the country to which most of the friends of liberty in this nation are now looking, and it may be in some future period a country to which they will all be flying.' Price's Harvard professor friend John Winthrop wrote to him in April 1775: 'All America is greatly indebted to you

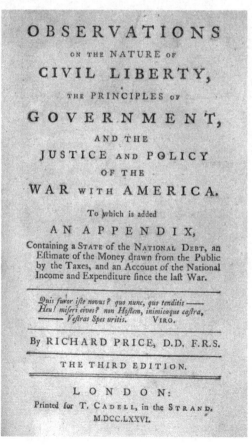

Figure 8. *The title page of Richard Price's*
Observations on the Nature of Civil Liberty.

for the sympathetic concern you express for their distress.' Price even warned his American friends about British troop movements and recruitment on several occasions, as in December 1775.

Price defended the American colonists' opposition to Britain in his *Observations on the Nature of Civil Liberty*, published in February 1776. He thought a print run of 500 copies would be sufficient, but his pamphlet sold 1,000 copies in three days. By late 1776, 60,000 copies had been sold in Britain alone. There were also American, Dutch, French and German editions. The pamphlet's popularity, and the poor sales of the many refutations, convinced Price that 'the sense of the nation is more in favour of America than the [government] are willing to believe'. The City of London, concerned about commercial relations with the colonies, thanked Price for his principled stance and granted him the Freedom of the City.

In these *Observations*, Price argued that every community has the right to 'self direction or self-government' and that man 'without religious and civil liberty . . . is a poor and abject animal'. He believed government originated with the people and that taxation and legislation should be 'conducted under their direction'. Price's arguments in the *Observations* would be echoed in the American Declaration of Independence that the Continental Congress issued in July 1776, which raises the question whether he had any impact on that document.

PRICE AND THE AMERICAN DECLARATION OF INDEPENDENCE

It can be argued that Price had little or no impact on the Declaration of Independence, most of which was written by Thomas Jefferson. Tom Paine's highly influential pamphlet *Common Sense* was available in America three months before Price's *Observations on the Nature of Civil Liberty*, and this earlier availability may have ensured that Price's work lacked the impact of Paine's. Furthermore, the echoes of Price's language found in the Declaration may simply have reflected the fact that intellectuals such as Price and Jefferson spoke the same political language, making it difficult to claim that any one writer influenced others.

On the other hand, leading members of the Continental Congress read Price's *Observations*, which was printed in Boston, Philadelphia, Charleston and New York, and was certainly widely known in America in July 1776. Samuel Chase, a delegate to the Continental Congress, asked John Adams for a copy. Indeed, in 1982, the French scholar Henri

Laboucheix argued that the words 'self evident' in the American Declaration of Independence owed much to Price, who had used 'self-evident' over twenty times in his *Review of Morals* (1758), in which he emphasised that men are naturally moral and that right and wrong are 'self-evident' to us. Whether it was Benjamin Franklin or Thomas Jefferson who was responsible for changing the words 'We hold these truths to be sacred and undeniable' to the more ringing 'We hold these truths to be self-evident', both were familiar with Price's ideas. Price and his American friends certainly shared many ideas and beliefs: he urged the rebellious colonists to focus in their pronouncements upon 'the principles of liberty' rather than 'the practices of former times', and they did – to Jefferson's chagrin. During the French Revolution, Price would write that it was justifiable to rid oneself of a government guilty of misconduct and then to frame one's own government – exactly as the colonists had done.

Price's invitation to America

After the American Declaration of Independence and the escalation of military hostilities, British public opinion turned against the American colonies, and Price wrote to John Winthrop that his continued support for the Americans had aroused frightening levels of abuse against him. American recognition of Price's supportive role in the American Revolution and/or the financial expertise he had demonstrated in several publications was demonstrated when the Continental Congress resolved in October 1778,

> That the Honorable Benjamin Franklin, Arthur Lee and John Adams Esquires or any one of them, be directed forthwith to apply to Dr Price, and inform him, that it is the desire of Congress to consider him a citizen of the united [*sic*] States, and to receive his assistance in regulating their finances. That if he shall think it expedient to remove with his family to America and afford such assistance, a generous provision shall be made for requiting his services.

Price thought this offer 'among the first honours of my life', but declared himself 'not to be sufficiently qualified . . . [and] so connected in this country, and also advancing so fast into the evening of life, that he cannot think of removal'. His refusal was of sufficient significance to merit the publication by the *Morning Post* of a Franklin letter saying that 'Dr Price, whose assistance was requested by Congress, has declined the service'.

PRICE AND THE AMERICAN CONSTITUTION

Price believed from the first that Britain would lose the colonies, and gave much consideration to the form of government appropriate to a new American nation. In 1779 he wrote to Arthur Lee, an American representative in France, that he was 'taking the liberty to communicate' his 'observations' on American constitutional problems because 'the interests of mankind depends so much on the forms of government established in America'. Rather than resent what might be perceived as a Briton's interference, Americans continued to revere him. In 1781, Yale University awarded two honorary degrees – one to George Washington, the other to Richard Price.

Price continued to proffer advice, and the American Constitution echoed his ideas. In January 1783, he wrote to Declaration of Independence signatory Benjamin Rush that it was necessary to balance the powers of the new nation's federal government with the 'liberty and independence' of the thirteen new American states. In June, he wrote of the necessity for the separation of Church and state and for allowing free speech. In his 1784 *Observations on the Importance of the American Revolution and the Means of Making It a Benefit to the World*, he advocated a strong central government but opposed a standing army. He sent copies to many Americans and received favourable responses from four of the Founding Fathers. George Washington wrote to Price that he hoped his 'excellent observations . . . should take deep roots in the minds of the revolutionists'. Benjamin Franklin said the *Observations* would do Americans 'a great deal of good' and gave a copy to John Adams, who was inspired to ask Price if they could correspond.

However, not all Americans were enamoured of Price's ideas all of the time. Some were unenthusiastic when he criticised slavery. Henry Laurens, a South Carolina planter and member of the Continental Congress, peevishly informed him that the British were to blame for having planted slavery in America. When Thomas Jefferson told Price that the need for a strong central government was 'early perceived' by the Americans, he was perhaps trying to let Price know that what he was advising sometimes was simply stating the obvious.

Price remained ever and defiantly proud of his American connections. He was accused of being a 'tool of Benjamin Franklin' during the American War of Independence, but in Benjamin West's 1784 portrait, Price chose to be portrayed holding a letter from Franklin. Americans in turn continued to revere him. In 1785, he became close to John and Abigail Adams, who were snubbed by London society because Adams

JOHN ADAMS (1735–1826)

After a career in the law, John Adams became one of the most significant figures in the birth of the United States. He represented Massachusetts in the Continental Congress (1774–8), and contributed to the drafting of the Declaration of Independence (1776). During the next decade, he represented the emerging American nation in France, Holland and then Britain. He influenced the American Constitution through the Massachusetts Constitution that he wrote in 1780. He was the nation's first Vice President, serving loyally under President George Washington (1789–97), He was then elected as the second President of the United States (1797–1801). Perhaps his greatest achievement as President was his strengthening of the nation's defences while simultaneously defying the popular call for war against France in the years 1798–1800. His least admired action was his support for the Alien and Sedition Acts (1798), under which criticisms of the federal government could be adjudged criminal. This measure was defended on the grounds of national security by the Federalist party, which favoured a strong federal government. Adams's son John Quincy Adams had a similarly distinguished career, and was President of the United States from 1825 to 1829.

While some claim that John Adams had Welsh ancestry, David McCullough's *John Adams* (2001) has Adams descended from Henry Adams of Somerset, who arrived in Braintree, Massachusetts in 1638. John Adams was certainly exceptionally aware of and knowledgeable about Welsh history, as evidenced in his *Novanglus Papers* (1774). He cited Welsh history in order to inspire the Royal Welsh Fusiliers, who had arrived in America in 1773 to help enforce order: he asked them to remember their 'brave and intrepid' Welsh countrymen 'who struggled at least a thousand years for liberty'. He emphasised the similarity between the American and Welsh situations, for 'Wales was forever revolting' against English domination. He was aware that the Welsh celebrated St David's Day, and in Richard Price and David Williams had at least two close friends who were Welsh. When he served as US ambassador to Britain, his leisure visits did not include Wales, but as Birmingham was the furthest point from London that he visited, sheer distance may have been an important factor.

Significantly, when a diplomat in France said he was sure that Adams would be glad to be moving to England as ambassador, as he must have plenty of relations there, Adams replied: 'Neither my father or mother, grandfather or grandmother, great-grandfather or great-grandmother, nor any other relation that I know of, or care a farthing for, has been in England these one hundred and fifty years, so that you can see I have not one drop of blood in my veins but what is American.' Of course, that was England not Wales . . .

represented the new nation. Adams subsequently told Price that there were 'few portions of my life that I recollect with more satisfaction than the hours I spent . . . with you'. In 1785, the corporation of Harvard University thanked him for purchases such as scientific instruments on their behalf and for supplying copies of his works, describing him as 'a patron of humanity, a benevolent asserter of the civil and religious liberties of mankind, and a warm friend to the United States of America'. Influential Americans continued to revere Price's ideas. During 1785–6, Jefferson asked Price to write on slavery and Benjamin Rush asked him to write on education. His *Sermons on the Christian Doctrine*, published in Philadelphia in 1788, sold well amongst leading Americans. George Washington bought four copies, Benjamin Franklin six, and eleven delegates to the Constitutional Convention of 1787 also purchased the book. Price told Rush of his regret that America's disagreements about the form of government and financial problems were 'subjects of triumph' in Britain.

When Price received a copy of the proposed American Constitution, he wrote to Arthur Lee in March 1789: 'the new federal constitution, in its principal articles, meets my ideas, and I wish it may be adopted.' However, he wrote to Ezra Stiles that 'there may be omissions and there must be defects' that would hopefully be dealt with in subsequent years. Americans continued to think of Price as one of their own: in 1789, Franklin told him that the abolitionists of the Pennsylvania Society wanted him as a corresponding member.

RICHARD PRICE: CONCLUSIONS

Price was always more in tune with the American position than with that of Britain. He gave valued and therefore valuable support and advice to the colonists in their resistance to British authority and in their establishment of a new nation. He had anticipated and perhaps influenced the sentiments of the Declaration of Independence and the essentials of the American Constitution. He had rightly argued from the first that the British would not be able to defeat the colonies. He said that for Britain 'to think of conquering that whole continent with 30,000 or 40,000 men to be transported across the Atlantic and fed from hence and incapable of being recruited after any defeat' was a 'folly so great that language does not afford a name for it'. As he rightly pointed out, the American colonists had greater resources, manpower and resolve – a resolve that emanated from their pursuit of greater freedom. In that pursuit, others with Welsh blood had a significance out of all proportion to their numbers.

CHAPTER FOUR

THE WELSH AMERICAN MILITARY CONTRIBUTION TO THE AMERICAN WAR OF INDEPENDENCE

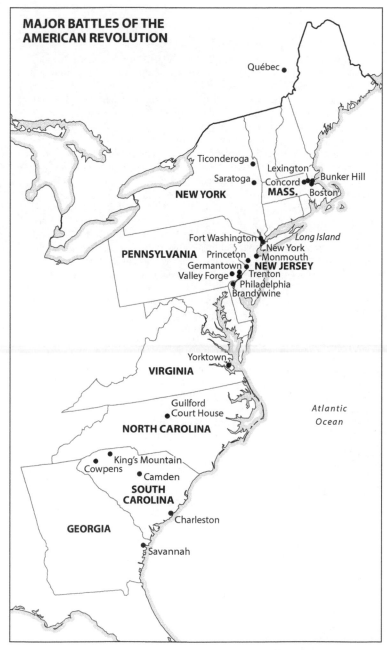

Figure 9. *Major battles of the American Revolution.*

THE COURSE OF EVENTS IN THE AMERICAN WAR OF INDEPENDENCE

In February 1775, Britain declared Massachusetts in a state of rebellion, and the clashes between British troops and colonists at Lexington and Concord are generally seen as the opening shots of the American War of Independence. The Continental Congress met again in May 1775 and began directing a war against Britain. George Washington was appointed as commander of the Continental Army.

In May 1775, General Howe defeated the Americans at the Battle of Bunker Hill, overlooking Boston, but then lapsed into inactivity. Congress then ordered the invasion of Canada in the hope of gaining support from French Canadians. The invasion was a failure and the Americans retreated in spring 1776, but took Boston in March 1776.

General Washington was defeated by General Howe at the Battle of Long Island, New York, in August 1776. 'In general, our generals were outgeneralled,' lamented John Adams. In November, the British captured Fort Washington, New York. With his troops in full retreat, George Washington said, 'I think the game is pretty near up.' However, Howe neglected to press home his advantage, enabling Washington to win victories in New Jersey at Trenton (December 1776) and Princeton (January 1777).

In Pennsylvania, Howe defeated Washington again at the Battle of Brandywine and went on to win another victory at Paoli and to capture Philadelphia in September 1777. Washington launched an unsuccessful counter-attack at Germantown in October, but when General Gates engineered the surrender of General Burgoyne at Saratoga, New York, in October 1777, it encouraged the French to enter the war against Britain.

George Washington's Continental Army struggled through a nightmarish winter at Valley Forge and then made an unsuccessful attack on Monmouth Court House, New Jersey, in June 1778. In July 1779, General Anthony Wayne's victory at Stony Point boosted American morale, but continuing problems with pay and supplies led his Pennsylvania Line regiment to mutiny in January 1781.

Meanwhile, clashes in the southern colonies had escalated after Britain decided it should take advantage of Loyalist support there. The British captured the significant southern ports of Savannah, Georgia (December 1778) and Charleston, South Carolina (May 1780), and General Gates was defeated at Camden (August 1780). However, the turning point in the war in the south, and perhaps in the whole war, was General Daniel Morgan's defeat of Lieutenant Colonel Tarleton at Cowpens, South Carolina, in January 1781. Cowpens contributed to British General Cornwallis's retreat northwards and his eventual surrender at Yorktown, Virginia, in 1781. That surrender was primarily due to the French having temporarily gained control of the seas, thereby cutting off British communications and supplies.

In the Treaty of Paris in 1783, the British recognised American independence.

WHY THE AMERICANS WON

It was difficult for the British to fight a war 3,000 miles away in unfamiliar territory, especially as neither army or navy were in particularly good shape in 1775. The British lacked inspirational civilian and military leaders. General Howe repeatedly failed to follow up military advantage and in 1777 was of little help to General Burgoyne, who was overconfident with regard to Americans and the terrain. The British frequently failed to prosecute the war wholeheartedly for fear of rendering future reconciliation more difficult, as when Howe stopped to negotiate peace while Washington and his vulnerable Continental Army retreated from New York in 1776. On two occasions when Washington was struggling, Howe gave up campaigning for the winter.

The British tried to compensate for their lack of numbers by using Native Americans and rapacious German mercenaries, and by promising freedom to slaves who assisted them. Those measures alienated the colonists, many of whom were already greatly inspired by their 'glorious cause' and by some of their leaders. George Washington suffered several defeats that suggest that he was no great military commander, but he managed to improve the Continental Army, keep it together, deal effectively with the civilian authorities and develop into a popular symbol of an emerging nation. He and his generals won some morale-sustaining victories. Gates and Benedict Arnold defeated Burgoyne in 1777, Morgan turned the tide in the south at Cowpens, and Washington helped bring about the surrender at Yorktown. Amongst the civilians in the Continental Congress, John Adams could rightly boast his contribution in ensuring that '13 clocks were made to strike together'.

European enemies gleefully took advantage of Britain's North American problems. Burgoyne's surrender at Saratoga and Benjamin Franklin's diplomatic skills encouraged the French to enter the war in 1778, and Spain joined France in 1779. Britain then had to divert funds and forces from North America to defend its colonial possessions elsewhere. It was the French fleet's temporary control of the seas that ensured Cornwallis's surrender at Yorktown in 1781.

WELSH AMERICANS contributed to American independence at all levels of the military. Each settlement sent volunteers to fight against British rule, and there were many of Welsh stock amongst them. A disproportionate number of George Washington's generals had Welsh ancestry. Amongst them was Welsh immigrant Frederick Watts, Otho Holland Williams, whose parents were immigrants from Wales, Francis Nash, the grandson of Welsh immigrants, and John Cadwallader, whose maternal grandparents were Welsh-born Quakers who had sailed with William Penn to Pennsylvania. Most famous of all were General Charles Lee, General 'Mad Anthony' Wayne, and General Daniel Morgan.

CHARLES LEE

Born to a gentry family in England, Charles Lee (1732–82) had a Welsh grandmother, Susannah Bunbury (née Hanmer). A professional soldier from the age of fourteen, he served from 1754 to 1760 in the French and Indian War during which the British gained France's North American territories. Lee acquired an Indian wife and fathered twins during that war, but abandoned them when he returned to Britain. By this time, according to a clergyman who met him in England, he was 'famous Colonel Lee, commonly called Savage Lee'. Lee had been greatly impressed by the Indian way of war and believed Indian-style mobile guerrillas, ambushes and targeting of non-combatants was the best way to fight in North America.

Lee spent several years in military employment in east Europe and then emigrated to America in 1773, saying that it was the 'one asylum' where men preferred 'their natural rights to the fantastical prerogative of a foolish perverted head because it wears a crown'. He was welcomed by rebellious Americans such as Samuel Adams and John Adams. He urged the colonists to fight, assuring them in a 1774 pamphlet that they would defeat the British. He hoped to be appointed commander of the Continental Army, but Washington was preferred because he was American-born and offered to serve without pay (but with expenses). The English-born Lee had demanded payment and was also considered alarmingly eccentric.

A queer creature but very clever

John Adams described Lee as 'a queer creature', while General Charles Cotesworth Pinckney thought him 'a strange animal' but 'very clever . . . we must put up with ten thousand oddities in him on account of his abilities and his attachment to the rights of humanity.' Lee was effectively Washington's deputy, and in 1775 they collaborated in Massachusetts on the professionalisation of the Continental Army. There, Lee resided at a Loyalist's mansion, and observers commented on how he was frequently visited by prostitutes and how he let his dozen or so dogs run riot. 'You must love his dogs if you love him,' warned

Adams. In Virginia several years later, Lee would infuriate leading Virginians by letting his dogs wander through the Governor's Palace and its grounds. Despite Lee's eccentricities, Washington respected his military abilities and expertise, and gave him responsibility for the defence of New York in the winter of 1775–6.

LEE AND SPADO

Lee's favourite dog, Spado, was frequently to be found in the saddle alongside his master. John Adams made some rather tactless remarks about Lee's love of dogs in a private letter that was intercepted and then published by the British. When Abigail Adams met Charles Lee, she wrote to her husband: 'the general was determined that I should not only be acquainted with him, but with his companions too, and therefore placed a chair before me into which he ordered Mr Sparder [Spado] to mount and present his paw to me for a better acquaintance.'

Lee described the American War of Independence as 'the noblest cause . . . ever', but he saw the cause in purely military terms and proved less sensitive than Washington with regard to the civilians. In New York, he found the Loyalists and New York authorities difficult to deal with and was horrified that some New Yorkers were supplying the British. When he put pressure on them, the Continental Congress officially censured him lest he alienate moderates. When Congress sent him to command American troops in the south, he kept the wives and children of suspect Virginians as hostages for the head of the family's good behaviour and ordered Loyalists' homes and businesses burned.

In 1776, Lee successfully defended Charleston, South Carolina. The British were both unlucky and error-prone, and the South Carolinians fought fiercely, but Lee deserves much credit for his tactics and for his productive collaboration with the civilian authorities. South Carolina's vice president Henry Laurens said, 'if we don't altogether owe the honor [to him] we are certainly greatly indebted.' The Continental Congress thanked Lee, but Lee was growing increasingly disillusioned with them – and he let many of his correspondents know it.

Lee versus Washington

Lee wrote to his friend General Gates criticising Washington for being insufficiently assertive with the Continental Congress. Lee had become increasingly exasperated with Washington after Washington's failures in the New York campaign. When the British took Fort Washington, officers reported Lee 'in a towering passion . . . so excited, that he tore the hair out of his head'. In November 1776, he wrote to Benjamin Rush that Washington had lost Fort Washington because he had ignored Lee's advice. The New York campaign constituted the low point in Washington's reputation, and many would have preferred Lee to command the Continental Army. Lee was of course angling to replace Washington, whom he described as 'not fit enough to command a Sergeant's Guard'. Lee's ambition probably explains his delay when Washington ordered him to join him in Pennsylvania. Washington's aide-de-camp, Colonel Joseph Reed, wrote to Lee that the New York campaign had made him doubt Washington and said it was 'entirely owing' to Lee that the cause survived. While Washington had 'an indecisive mind', said Reed, 'the officers and soldiers generally have confidence in you.' Lee agreed that Washington had a potentially disastrous 'fatal indecision of mind'. Lee and Washington differed on tactics. Lee favoured irregular warfare and a citizens' army, but Washington wanted professionals and long-term volunteers. Historians tend to side with Washington, arguing that Lee's strategy would have resulted in a brutal and bloody civil war between Patriots and Loyalists that would have increased localism, in contrast to the way in which Washington's Continental Army proved a unifying factor in the nation. Lee may have been the better soldier, but Washington was the better politician.

Capture and fall

When Lee finally joined Washington and the main army in Pennsylvania, he planned a bold manoeuvre that Washington considered unwise and risky. Lee realised belatedly that his army was not fit to do it, then foolishly left it under his second-in-command and spent the night at Widow White's Tavern. The British captured him in his slippers and a dishevelled shirt. Some historians think he had gone there for female company. Lee's capture worried many in the Continental Army. General John Cadwallader said it was 'a misfortune that cannot be remedied, as we have no officer in the army of equal experience and merit'. General Nathaniel Greene said it was 'a great loss to the American states'. Declaration of Independence signatory John Hancock said it was 'really alarming . . . as he was, in a great measure, the idol of the officers, and possessed still more the confidence of the soldiery'. Many ordinary Americans were also dismayed. However, Washington won the battle of Trenton two weeks later, and Samuel Adams hoped that Trenton had shown the British that 'we can beat them without' Lee.

The British officer in charge of Lee during his imprisonment described him as an 'atrocious monster'. During his confinement, Lee offered to broker a British–American reconciliation and drafted a plan to help the British General Howe capture Philadelphia and end the rebellion. Some think these were ploys to save his life or to mislead the British, others consider him traitorous.

After his release, Lee was taken to Washington's headquarters in a small stone house at Valley Forge. Lee spent his first night of freedom with a mistress. The Continental Army officer with responsibility for prisoners was Colonel Elias Boudinot, whose maternal grandfather came from Wales. Colonel Boudinot described Lee's mistress as 'a miserable dirty hussy' and recorded that the other officers had overheard the noisy pair all night and that when Lee appeared late for breakfast, he 'looked as dirty as if he had been in the street all night'.

Lee was becoming ever more eccentric and awkward. He rejected Washington's offer that he command troops in an assault on Clinton and the British in their retreat from Philadelphia, then demanded the command, rejected it again, and finally decided that he wanted it – 'truly childish', said Founding Father Alexander Hamilton.

Lee had many disadvantages when he faced Clinton's army at Monmouth Court House, New Jersey. He was unfamiliar with the local terrain and with many of his officers. He had unclear orders from Washington and he received contradictory intelligence. Daniel Morgan's riflemen misunderstood his instructions and General Lafayette's troops struggled to obey Lee's orders owing to the intense and oppressive heat. Lee therefore ordered a retreat, which infuriated Generals Anthony Wayne, Daniel Morgan and George Washington. Lee then conducted a brave, effective and significant delaying action, for which he expected but did not receive praise and an apology from Washington. The battle ended in a draw and was the last of Lee's field commands. He demanded a court martial and was found guilty of repeated disobedience to Washington's instructions, of an 'unnecessary, disorderly and shameful retreat', and of having disrespected the commander-in-chief in two letters. Lee probably had the stronger case, but it was a political error to challenge Washington. A verdict in Lee's favour would have embarrassed Washington and probably necessitated his resignation, which would have been disastrous for American morale. Furthermore, many officers were exasperated by Lee by this time. They defended Washington during the court martial, and Lee's appeal to the Continental Congress was unsuccessful because his criticisms had made enemies there too. 'Washington is their God,' lamented Lee. Had he been politically more astute, he might have realised that earlier.

Lee then faded into obscurity. In his last will and testament, he wrote that he did not want to be buried in a church or churchyard, 'for since I have resided in this country, I have kept so much bad company, when living, that I do not choose to continue it when dead.'

Charles Lee does not have a very good reputation today, but he was important to the rebel cause from 1773 until the battle of Monmouth in 1778. Even there, he had probably been very useful, but he made too many enemies, and it was a great error to ask Americans to choose between him and Washington.

WELSH AMERICAN LOYALISTS

Amongst the Welsh Americans who remained loyal to the British Crown were descendants of the pioneer ironmasters, the Lennard Brothers of Massachusetts.

'MAD' ANTHONY WAYNE

While Wales may have some hesitation in claiming the one-quarter Welsh Charles Lee, Anthony Wayne (1745–96) is more clearly heroic.

Wayne was born in Chester County, Pennsylvania. His family owned a farm and tannery at which the young Anthony sometimes worked. His mother was Elizabeth Iddings, a Quaker whose maternal grandfather emigrated from Carmarthen to Pennsylvania in 1690. Another of her ancestors had emigrated from south-east Wales. Anthony attended St David's Episcopal Church of Radnor, which his father had helped build and where many of the early congregation were Welsh-speakers. He studied at the Philadelphia Academy of his uncle, who lamented that Anthony was not the ideal pupil as he 'had already distracted the brains of two thirds of the boys under my charge, by rehearsals of battles, sieges, etc.'

Defeats and disasters

By 1774, Anthony Wayne was at the forefront of Pennsylvanian opposition to British policies. He declared himself ready to fight to defend the 'rights and liberties of America' and of mankind. Wayne participated in American defeats in the invasion of Canada and the battles at

Brandywine and Germantown, but his own performance was praised and he was promoted to brigadier general in 1777. His reputation suffered after the surprise British attack at the Paoli Tavern near Philadelphia in 1777. Some of Wayne's men blamed him, but George Washington never did. In 1778, Wayne did most of the fighting at the battle of Monmouth Courthouse and felt betrayed by General Charles Lee's retreat after he had asked Lee for reinforcements that might have won an American victory. Washington blamed Lee, Lee blamed Wayne.

Wayne had much bitter experience of how the American forces frequently suffered from lack of pay and supplies. At Ticonderoga in 1775, his men scraped bones from the soil to use as buttons with which to hold their ragged clothes together. In the freezing winter of 1777–8 at Valley Forge, Pennsylvania, General Washington ordered his officers to find food for the starving army. British Major John André wrote a mocking poem in which he depicted Wayne as a cow chaser (a reference to the foraging at Valley Forge) and loudmouth tanner, who inspired his barefoot troops with rhetorical flourishes and lots of rum. André claimed that Wayne nearly missed the battle of Bull's Ferry because he was chasing a woman into a tavern. Wayne was even mocked on the London stage, depicted in a big leather apron holding a knife – another reference to his having worked in the family tannery.

Stony Point

The high point of Wayne's military career came in July 1779 at Stony Point, where the British had a small fort on a 150-foot rock outcrop overlooking the Hudson River. When Washington asked Wayne if he truly thought he could take the fort, Wayne responded, 'General, if you give me permission, I'll storm Hell itself for you.' The British surrender of the fort provided a much-needed boost to American morale. Congress awarded Wayne a medal, and his friends in Philadelphia told him everyone was talking about him. However, the aftermath illustrated the jealousies, tensions and politics in the thirteen colonies and the Continental Army: some officers expressed anger that he had treated them like 'insignificant beings' and not mentioned them in reports to Washington and the Continental Congress; New Englanders felt he gave too much credit to Pennsylvanians and Virginians; Virginians claimed he had given them insufficient praise. Washington abandoned the Stony Point fort within days and the British regained it – but Wayne had made a great contribution to the maintenance of American morale.

Mutiny

In late 1780, Wayne's soldiers mutinied because of lack of food, clothes and pay. Wayne stood his ground before the mutineers, who shouted, 'We love you, we respect you, but you are a dead man if you fire.' As they pushed their way past him, he begged them not to desert to the British, and they assured him that while they would kill anyone who tried to desert, they were determined to go to Philadelphia to get their pay. Washington told Wayne to stay with the mutineers, so he accompanied them and negotiated with the state government of Pennsylvania for better conditions and an amnesty for them. Washington and Wayne decided to make an example of the ringleaders, and Wayne had twelve mutineers shot. A fifer recorded that 'So near did they [the shooters] stand that the handkerchiefs covering the eyes of some of them [mutineers] were set on fire . . . The fence and even the . . . rye for some distance within the field were covered with the blood and brains.' One firing squad victim lay bleeding but still alive. Wayne ordered a soldier to finish him off with his bayonet. When the soldier said he did not want to kill his comrade, Wayne drew his pistol and threatened to kill him if he did not obey the order. Wayne then ordered the entire Pennsylvania Line to stand around to look at the dead mutineers. Washington agreed with Wayne that such actions were 'certainly necessary'.

How 'mad'?

In 1781, Wayne's battle against Cornwallis at Green Spring, Virginia, won him great praise, but newspapers condemned 'Mad Anthony' for having lost one-fifth of his men. Colonel Henry Lee told Washington that Wayne frequently disobeyed orders, and in his *Memoirs of the War in the Southern Department*, he depicted Wayne as a bloodthirsty warmonger leading drunken Irish Pennsylvanians.

After the British surrender at Yorktown, Wayne was sent to clear Georgia of British soldiers. He was reluctant to return home at the war's end. He wanted to carry on fighting but was forced to resume his political career. The grateful state of Georgia gave him a confiscated plantation, and in 1785 his drunken exploits with other veterans were recorded in a Savannah newspaper.

Wayne was devoted to Washington and bitterly disappointed when in 1789 Washington became President but did not offer him a post. However, when American troops were struggling in Ohio Country in

ANTHONY WAYNE'S CHAPLAIN, DAVID JONES

David Jones was born in 1736 in Delaware's Welsh Tract, to which his grandparents had emigrated from Cardiganshire in 1710. His Welsh grandmother's father and two of her brothers were Baptist ministers in Wales.

Jones became a Baptist minister in New Jersey. He took leave of absence from this first ministry on two occasions in order to preach to Indians in Ohio Country. In 1775, his New Jersey congregation requested his departure because they found him too militantly opposed to British government policies. He relocated to Pennsylvania and became minister of the Great Valley Baptist Church, founded by Welsh Baptists in 1711 – perhaps opposition to British policies was more acceptable there. Jones published a pamphlet, *Defensive War in Just Cause Sinless* (1775), in which he used his biblical scholarship to justify resistance to British tyranny. God, he insisted, was on the side of the Americans and it was their Christian duty to oppose that tyranny.

He was chaplain to Anthony Wayne and his Pennsylvanian troops from 7 April 1776. Jones was credited with inspiring the soldiers on the eve of battle at Ticonderoga, was nearly killed at Paoli, and impressed George Washington with his foraging abilities at Valley Forge. He had studied medicine in early life and was frequently called upon to help with the wounded, removing bullets and performing amputations. He always carried a weapon and was willing to use it. Anthony Wayne wrote to Benjamin Franklin from Ticonderoga in July 1776, saying, 'Through the medium of my chaplain [David Jones] I hope this [letter] will reach you as he has promised to blow out any man's brains who will attempt to take it from him.'

After the Americans had won their independence, Jones returned to Great Valley Baptist Church, living in a farm adjacent to that of Anthony Wayne. He accompanied Wayne as army chaplain in the north-western campaign in 1794–6. At the age of seventy-six, he served as army chaplain in the War of 1812 against Britain. His grandson Horatio served as president of the Philadelphia Welsh Society for over a quarter of a century.

The passionate opposition of so many Americans of Welsh descent to the British government may well have owed something to long-nurtured resentment at the way Wales and the Welsh were treated by the English-dominated government in London.

the Northwest Indian War in 1792, Washington overrode his Cabinet and offered Wayne the leadership of the 'Legion of the United States'. In July 1794, Wayne defeated the Indians at the Battle of Fallen Timbers and negotiated the Treaty of Greenville with them. They accepted the boundary line designated by the Americans and agreed to end their association with the British. Here, Wayne had helped open up the West for Americans.

Washington's Cabinet had opposed the appointment of Wayne because of the 'Mad Anthony' reputation. While President, Washington described Wayne as 'more active and enterprising than judicious and cautious . . . Open to flattery, vain, easily imposed upon, and is liable to be drawn into scrapes. Too indulgent . . . to his officers and men. Whether sober, or a little addicted to the bottle, I know not.' Thomas Jefferson had said that Wayne was 'brave and nothing else', the kind of person who might 'run his head against a wall where success was both impossible and useless'. Wayne's 'mad' reputation seems to have owed much to his fearlessness in battle, fearsome temper, habit of riding around the army camp for hours during the night, and his rousing cry to his men, 'I believe that . . . God is rather thirsty for human gore.' People had said only a madman would climb the steep cliffs below Stony Point. During the Ohio Country campaign, he had wanted 'COWARD' branded on the foreheads of any sentries who deserted, so that even his admirer Major Hamtramck said, 'There is no doubt about it; the old man is really mad.' Mad or not, Anthony Wayne had helped ensure the emergence of a new nation and in his final year contributed to its westward expansion.

DANIEL MORGAN

Daniel Morgan (1736–1802) was born in New Jersey to Welsh immigrant parents who had first settled in Pennsylvania. Daniel left home at seventeen after a fight with his father, then spent wild days on the Virginia frontier 'addicted to drinking and gaming', and involved in 'numerous broils and difficulties', according to the biography written by his great-granddaughter's husband, James Graham. Graham attributed Morgan's behaviour to 'a defective education'.

The French and Indian War

Morgan served as a wagoner in the French and Indian War of 1756–63 and proved fearless when faced with Indians, whom he called 'the red devils'. James Graham described how an Indian bullet caught him:

> The ball which struck Morgan entered in at the back of the neck, grazing the left side of the neck-bone; then passing through into the mouth, near the socket of the jawbone, came out through the left cheek. In its passage, the ball knocked out all of the teeth on the left side . . . The blood ran in a stream from the fearful wound.

That Indian bullet left Morgan with a livid scar above his upper lip, and soon after, he acquired more scars when given 400 lashes for striking a British officer. James Graham recorded that 'the flesh on his back hung down in tags'. Such a punishment could prove fatal and it did not endear the British and their army to Morgan. In 1763, Morgan was further disillusioned by the British government when, keen to avoid further expensive wars against the native population, it prohibited settlement in the Ohio Country.

By the eve of the American War of Independence, Morgan was a very prosperous landowner who viewed Britain's 'intolerable' treatment of the port of Boston in 1774 as proof of British tyranny. Graham recorded that he 'made no secret of his opinions' about 'the tyrannical proceedings of the British government'. He was keen to take up arms against the Crown and would soon use an image of King George III for target practice for his marksmen.

The Canada campaign

In 1775, Captain Morgan and his riflemen participated in the ill-conceived Canada campaign. When they crossed the inhospitable Maine wilderness en route to Canada, some of Morgan's men had to carry heavy boats, and a rifleman recalled that their flesh was 'worn from their shoulders, even to the bone'. There was little or no game, so the starving men ate dog meat, roasted shot pouches and made gruel from shaving soap and lip salve. Although Morgan was captured in Québec, it was through no fault of his own, and Washington advocated his promotion to Colonel. Washington cited Morgan's 'intrepid behaviour' at Quebec and 'inflexible attachment to our cause' while a prisoner, but there was another motive: Washington had to distribute promotions carefully in order to avoid provincial jealousies, and the promotion of Morgan would constitute the replacement of one Virginian by another.

Saratoga

The Battle of Saratoga in 1777 was a great turning point of the war in the north, and Morgan distinguished himself there. According to General Gates, 'Too much praise cannot be given to Colonel Morgan.' The defeated General Burgoyne told Morgan, 'Sir, you command the finest regiment in the world.' John Trumbull may have been recognising Morgan's importance when he put him in a very prominent position in his 1821 painting *Burgoyne's Surrender at Saratoga* – or perhaps it was a matter of composition and contrast to have Morgan at the front in his white buckskins.

General Morgan

In June 1779, Morgan resigned from the Continental Army after Washington said that promoting him to brigadier general could not be justified. However, he was persuaded to return to the fight, and Congress made him General Morgan in autumn 1780. The British had been doing well in the south, but Morgan distinguished himself there. He demonstrated his imaginative approach to warfare when he persuaded a small Loyalist force near New Providence, South Carolina, to surrender in the face of his carefully crafted 'cannon' – a log! However, his greatest achievement was at the Battle of Cowpens.

Cowpens

Stalemate in the north in 1778 led the British to shift their emphasis to the south, where the considerable numbers of Loyalists demanded British help. In 1781, Morgan faced Lieutenant Colonel 'Bloody Ben' Tarleton at Cowpens, South Carolina. Cowpens illustrated both Morgan's military leadership skills and many of the reasons why the Americans defeated the British.

Morgan was determined and aggressive at Cowpens. His men recalled him saying, 'Here is Morgan's grave or victory' and 'On this ground I will defeat the British or lay my bones.' He was inspirational. According to a contemporary, no officer 'knew better how to gain the love and esteem of his men'. He walked around the camp throughout the night before the battle, encouraging the men and joking that they would soon be heroes and free to go home to impress their sweethearts. Militiaman Thomas Young described how during the battle Morgan 'galloped along the lines, cheering his men'. His men liked it that he had come up through the ranks and always wore the rifleman's typical hunting frock, without marks of distinction to demonstrate that he was an officer. There are several possible explanations. Perhaps he always felt like one of them. Perhaps it was because of the poor supply system. He may have been motivated by reasons of safety: one of his own favourite tactics was targeting enemy officers, which the British considered ungentlemanly. When he considered it necessary, he was brutal with friend and foe. He complimented one of his officers, saying, 'You have done well . . . had you failed, I would have shot you.' His tactics and preparation were brilliant, especially his integration of the militia with regular troops and his emphasis on mobility. He positioned his troops on the terrain so as to exploit the British tendency to shoot too high. Of course, like any commander he owed much to his men. Many of them would go West after the war, an act that demonstrated their fearless, adventurous natures.

Morgan boasted that at Cowpens he had given Tarleton 'a devil of a whipping' and that 'a more complete victory never was obtained', for the 'flower' of Cornwallis's army was destroyed. General Nathaniel Greene said no other Revolutionary War battle had been 'more glorious or more timely'. Washington described Cowpens as a 'decisive and glorious victory' that would have a significant effect on the fighting in the southern colonies. Perhaps most significantly, Cornwallis declared the British defeat 'extraordinary' and said it had just about broken his heart. It followed a run of British victories that had suggested total British control of the south, but after Cowpens the British began a retreat from the south that ultimately led to the surrender at Yorktown, Virginia.

A WELSH COLONEL AND COWPENS

Evan Shelby (1720–94) emigrated from Cardiganshire in 1734, and settled in Pennsylvania, then in Maryland, where he worked for a time on a farm called Mountain of Wales. He served in the French and Indian War, then built a trading station in present-day Bristol, Tennessee. He defended Virginia's western frontier during the American War of Independence.

Evan Shelby's son, Colonel Isaac Shelby (1750–1826) distinguished himself in the defeat of the British in South Carolina at the Battle of Kings Mountain (1780). Isaac believed that his advice to Morgan contributed to Morgan's victory at the Battle of Cowpens. Isaac Shelby was elected governor of Kentucky in 1792 and at the age of sixty-two led 4,000 Kentuckians to victory over the British at the Battle of the Thames in 1812.

Years later, Daniel Morgan told George Washington Parke Custis that George Washington had sustained the American Revolution and that without him the Revolution would have collapsed in the field. However, Washington needed generals such as Daniel Morgan. As General Greene said, 'Great generals are scarce; there are few Morgans to be found.'

After Cowpens, Morgan's sciatica caused him to play no further significant part in the American War of Independence, but he had served his country well: he had played a very important part in the crucial battle of Saratoga and his victory at Cowpens was one of the great turning points in the American War of Independence.

DANIEL MORGAN AND THE WHISKEY REBELLION

Significantly, when President Washington considered the authority of the federal government at stake in 1794, he recalled General Daniel Morgan to duty. The greatest opposition to the new tax on whiskey was on the Pennsylvania frontier, so Morgan and his Virginia militia were sent there. The whiskey rebels feared Morgan's coming and were greatly outnumbered. There were no military clashes and Morgan pacified the region effectively. He was a great believer in a strong central government and had helped demonstrate that this was what the United States had under President Washington.

WELSH AMERICAN LOYALISTS, NEUTRALS AND THE CASE OF DANIEL BOONE (1734–1820)

While many who lived in the colonies spoke or fought with passion for American freedom from British rule, some remained loyal to the British Crown. Modern historians generally estimate that out of the two million white American population in the 1770s, two-fifths were active rebels, one-fifth active Loyalists and two-fifths neutral. Somewhat surprisingly, given that he became a legend in his own lifetime, one whose loyalty was debated by contemporaries was the frontiersman and explorer Daniel Boone.

Family background

The Quaker Edward Morgan of Bala immigrated to Pennsylvania in 1691. His daughter Sarah married Squire Boone, a Quaker whose family emigrated to William Penn's Pennsylvania colony from England in 1713. Squire and Sarah met at a Quaker meeting house in 1720 in Gwynedd, Pennsylvania. One of their children was Daniel Boone. Daniel was very close to his Welsh mother, and subsequently told of how she sang Welsh songs to him. In 1750, Squire took the family to settle in North Carolina. One of their neighbours was the Welsh Quaker Morgan Bryan, and amongst the many marriages between Bryans and Boones was that of Daniel Boone to Rebecca Bryan.

Why Kentucky?

Daniel did not want to farm as his father did, preferring to make his living by hunting. His excellent marksmanship made him a useful member of the militia in the French and Indian War. The great expense of that war prompted the British to try to discourage further westward migration because it would lead to further costly clashes with the Indians, but it proved impossible to halt those seeking free or cheap land, adventure, and greater independence from civilian authority. From 1767, Daniel Boone began hunting and exploring in the Cherokee and Shawnee Indian territory of Kentucky. While not the first European to explore Kentucky, he would become by far the most famous.

We are reliant on what others said that Daniel Boone said in order to try to understand what motivated him when he explored Kentucky and led parties of settlers there. One visitor said that 'Boone considered himself an emissary chosen to open the American wilderness'. Boone told someone that he explored 'from the love of nature' and was 'naturally romantic'. He denied that he was motivated by greed, saying, 'I have opened the way for others to make fortunes, but fortune for myself was not what I was after.' That was just as well, because he never made much money. His descendants said he simply wanted to be away from people, but some said that he dismissed that idea. Perhaps the answer is to be found in what a Virginia minister wrote in the early 1770s: 'What a buzz is amongst people about Kentucky. To hear people speak of it one would think it was a newfound paradise.' Daniel Boone surely felt the 'buzz' – Kentucky was indeed a paradise of game where a huntsman might make a living while enjoying the sense of freedom and adventure that characterised frontier life.

The Indian threat

While many on the East Coast were preoccupied with unpopular British policies, those on the frontier focused on the conflict with Indians who wanted to exclude white invaders determined to settle on their land. While Bostonians agitated about British customs duties, Boone led a party of relations and friends to Kentucky in 1773. Exploring and settling the frontier was dangerous. James Boone was Daniel's oldest son. When he and his companions were attacked by Indians, James was shot in the hip and rendered immobile. The Indians slashed at him with knives until he cried for mercy. A Cherokee called Big Jim tore the nails from the hands and feet of James and his companions until they begged for death. James suffered heavy blows to the head and his body was shot through with arrows. One of his companions escaped and told the story of James's agonising end.

Such deaths increased tensions and in 1774, Daniel Boone served as a captain in the Virginia militia in Dunmore's War against the Indians. In 1775, Boone took his family to Kentucky. In 1776, his fourteen-year-old daughter Jemima was captured by Indians, but her father rescued her before she came to any harm. Years later she would recall, 'The Indians were really kind to us.' Indians commonly incorporated desirable captives into their tribe, or perhaps it was the desire for an exchange of prisoners that motivated their capture of Jemima. Frontier tensions rose further in 1777, when British Lieutenant Governor Henry 'Hair Buyer' Hamilton's offer of $50 for a scalp from a settler in the Ohio Valley increased Indian raids and turned many settlers against the British. Daniel Boone's cousin recalled Daniel's anger at this British policy.

In 1778, Daniel Boone was captured when boiling the salt that was vital for the flavour and preservation of food. He persuaded his fellow salt boilers to surrender because the Indians outnumbered them. The Indians gave the salt boilers the option of running the gauntlet between braves or waiting to be tortured by the women and children in the Shawnee town. Women often designed even more unpleasant torture than their menfolk, so Boone ran the gauntlet between braves with their tomahawks and clubs. Although nearly blinded by a cut on his forehead, he got through. After that, the Indians treated Boone well, and the Shawnee chief Blackfish adopted him as a son. Boone's tribal initiation began with the plucking-out of all the hairs on his head except for a 3–4 inch circular tuft. He was then washed and rubbed in the river by women 'to take all his white blood out'.

Daniel Boone – Loyalist?

Daniel Boone's loyalty to the American cause has been questioned because while he was a prisoner of the Indians, he got on well with them and with their British allies. He apparently hinted to the British that he was sympathetic to their cause, and promised the Indians that he would surrender the fort at his settlement of Boonesborough to them. When it was nearly time for the Indian attack on Boonesborough, Boone escaped. He received a poor welcome when he returned to the fort because other escapees reported that he had sold out the other salt boilers and collaborated with the Shawnee, and that he was a Loyalist who had promised to surrender the fort to the Indians.

Boone suggested making peace with the Indians, but the other men in the fort voted for war. Boone then suggested a pre-emptive raid. The raid went well but left the fort undefended, which added to the doubts about Boone's loyalty. Furthermore, when the Indians were ready to attack Boonesborough, Blackfish called for his 'son' to surrender the fort as he had promised. Boone agreed to the request of his 'father' that they parley, and when they sat together, one observer recalled that 'everyone in the fort was then sure that Boone was gone' over to the Indians. It seems that Boone and the other representatives from the fort had just agreed to live in peace with the Indians and swear allegiance to the Crown when fighting broke out between the Indians and the outnumbered whites, who nevertheless managed to scramble back into the fort. Here again it is difficult to know whether Boone (and the other representatives) had been ready to become Loyalists or whether their move was simply a ploy aimed at survival.

GETTING TO THE BOTTOM OF THE MYTHS AND LEGENDS ABOUT DANIEL BOONE

It was reported by a resident of the Boonesborough fort that during the eleven-day siege, a Shawnee brave repeatedly 'turned the insulting part of his body to the besieged and defiantly patted it'. Legend has it that it was Daniel Boone who silenced him with a shot to the posterior. The myths and legends that grew up around Daniel Boone made good stories, but historians struggle with the many contradictory and possibly fabricated accounts of Boone's actions, attitude and beliefs.

Boone claimed that he had promised the Indians that he would surrender the fort because that was the only way to save the population. A visitor to Kentucky during these troubled times noted the condition of the fort at Boonesborough: 'dirt and filth . . . putrefying flesh, dead dogs, horses, cow, hog excrement and human odour . . . with the ashes and sweepings of filthy cabins, the dirtiness of the people'. Another visitor described the population as 'a poor, distressed, half-naked, half-starved people'. Perhaps times like these helped convince Boone that living in harmony with the Indians was the best way of life.

The testimony of two escapee salt boilers ensured that Daniel Boone was put on trial. There were four charges: that he handed over the salt makers to save himself; that while a prisoner he had consorted with the enemy and told the British commander at Detroit he would surrender the Boonesborough fort; that he weakened the fort defences by leading a raiding party out; that he took all the fort's officers out of the camp to make peace with the Indians. Daniel was found not guilty and promoted to major.

So, was Daniel Boone a Loyalist? He had accepted his captain's commission from Lord Dunmore in 1774 even after Dunmore had just dissolved Virginia's critical House of Burgesses. In contrast, one of Daniel's associates refused to accept such a royal appointment. The loyalties of his relations must have been important to him. A contemporary recorded that at a Baptist meeting in the North Carolina area containing many Boones and Bryans, there was little enthusiasm 'concerning the American cause'. The West attracted many Loyalists from the southern colonies, where aristocratic revolutionary leaders such as Jefferson were disliked by many of the backcountry people. One North Carolina man said that when the rebel forces were doing well, North Carolina Loyalists had to run off and a person 'could hardly get along the road for them'. The North Carolina party of a hundred that Daniel led to Kentucky in 1779 was full of Loyalists. It contained many Bryans, including Rebecca's uncle Morgan Bryan, who left his family in Kentucky and returned to North Carolina, where he fought and died on the Loyalist side in 1781. A North Carolinian wrote that Daniel Boone 'married a Bryan, and the Bryans were all loyal to the English'. A Tennessean said Daniel Boone 'was rather unpopular in that section owing to the fact that he stuck to the King during the Revolutionary war'. There is considerable circumstantial evidence that Daniel Boone was not really committed to either side during the American War of Independence – Rebecca Bryan's father said that Boone hedged his bets during the war and was more of a neutral. Perhaps the answer lay in the fact that he was a family and community man. Whatever he was, his descendants were deeply embarrassed by his ambivalence and in denial about it.

Boone's ambivalence may well have been universal in Kentucky. In 1779, a British and Indian army captured 300 settlers in Kentucky, and the British commander said, 'I do not believe we have more than two families really rebels.' He thought people will 'faithfully defend the country that affords them protection'. It is understandable that settlers should be preoccupied with their own safety in the face of the Indian threat and lack any settled preference for government from either London or the Continental Congress.

In 1781, Daniel Boone's allegiance was questioned once again. He was elected to represent Kentucky in the Virginia legislature but was captured by 'Bloody' Tarleton during the British invasion. He was released within days, and this has generated great debate and controversy. His children said he was released on the promise 'not to take up arms any more' against the Crown. Critics claim this is further evidence that he was a collaborationist.

The Battle of Blue Licks

The death of James Boone and his companions had generated ever more hatred and retaliation. When in 1780 George Rogers Clark led an army to counter Indian attacks and Daniel Boone served as his scout, both sides sought revenge for previous atrocities and engaged in further brutality. Americans took scalps, and even scalped bodies in graves. Daniel Boone's brother was killed by Indians in this year.

Although the war in the American colonies was effectively over after the British surrender at Yorktown, the British wanted to keep the area west of the Appalachians. In 1782, the British and Indians were ready to attack the Kentucky settlements and Boone was made a Lieutenant Colonel of the Fayette County militia, which entered into battle with the Indians at Blue Licks. Boone argued that a battle at this time was unwise, but was shamed into action by the taunts of cowardice from another officer. Boone told his son Israel to flee in the face of the superior Indian numbers and position, but seconds after Israel said, 'Father, I won't leave you,' he dropped to the ground, his body quaking, blood flowing from his mouth and his open eyes already glazed over. 'Shot through the neck,' his father said. Daniel Boone blamed himself for Israel's death, but no one else did. Other officers were more culpable, but Boone felt guilty because he had been taunted into an action he thought unwise. There were those who said that Boone goaded his son into going, but others who claimed that he tried in vain to stop him because he had been under the weather. When Boone and others went back to collect the bodies at the Blue Licks, buzzards were circling and animals were gnawing at bodies bloated and blackened in the sun and basically unrecognisable. Some of the bodies were caught on the river rocks and partly eaten by fish. Most were scalped. The Indians tortured the prisoners taken at the Blue Licks. One escapee 'did not know how many they burned but the smell of a human was the awfullest smell he ever had in his life'.

There have been claims that Daniel Boone hated the Indians and killed many of them, but there are signs that he did not share the common contemporary views of the Indian 'savages'. His descendants rejected claims that he killed a great many Indians, and he admitted to only three. Boone shared the Indian emphasis on freedom of movement, independence and clan, and it is not difficult to imagine his having some sympathy for them.

After the Revolutionary War and in old age, Boone described the twenty-year struggle against the Indians in the Ohio Valley as 'a war of intrusion upon them'. Also, he supposedly said that Indians 'have always been kinder to me than the whites' and that they proved to be his most constant friends: 'while he could never with safety repose confidence in a Yankee, he had never been deceived by an Indian,' and if he had to choose, 'he should certainly prefer a state of nature to a state of civilisation'. A missionary recorded of the old Daniel: 'He worshipped, as he often said, the Great Spirit – for the woods were his books and his temple, and the creed of the red men naturally became his.' It may be that Boone simply mellowed in old age, or that those who recorded him as sounding sympathetic to the Indians were moved by romantic visions of the West, but given that such sympathies were unpopular amongst his contemporaries, it may be that those who recorded him voicing these unfashionable sentiments got it right.

There are also indications that Daniel Boone was ambivalent about the speedy 'taming' of the wilderness that had been Kentucky when he first explored it. Within two decades of his exploration, Kentucky's Bluegrass region was transformed. The buffalo were abundant when Boone arrived, but gone by 1790. The settlers had enjoyed the tastiest parts (the hump and tongue) and wasted the rest. One settler recalled, 'Many a man killed a buffalo just for the sake of saying so.' Daniel Boone suggested that local regulations should strive to preserve game through restrictions on hunting, but nothing was done. Legend has it that any time other settlers got anywhere near them, Daniel would say to Rebecca, 'Old woman, we must move on; they are crowding us.' He certainly moved his family around a great deal – even outside the new American nation.

Spanish Daniel

Perhaps it is best to judge where Daniel Boone stood on the Loyalist and 'civilisation' issues by what he actually did, rather than what he purportedly said. In the late 1790s, Daniel Boone and family members moved to Missouri Territory, which belonged at that time to Spain. His descendants were anxious to emphasise that this did not constitute a repudiation of being an American, but the fact remains that he left 'his' country.

There have been several suggested explanations for Boone's migration into Spanish territory. One major 'push' factor was that he was facing non-stop summonses in court over land disputes and accusations of fraud. A surviving court directive from 1798 says that Daniel Boone should be taken into custody for ignoring a summons on a £6,000 suit. However, 'NOT FOUND' was written on the warrant. A relation recalled, 'He was harassed and pestered . . . The bad treatment of those for whom he had located lands . . . was the cause of his leaving his beloved Kentucky and moving into the Spanish Government.' A family friend said he 'was soured against Kentucky'. Boone told his nephew that lawyers were destroying the dreams of people like him. According to his son, Boone swore in 1799 that he would never set foot in Kentucky again 'and if he was compelled to lose his head on the block or revisit Kentucky, he would not hesitate to choose the former'. Some people reported that Daniel told them Kentucky had become too crowded.

There were also 'pull' factors. There was little game left in Kentucky but Missouri was still full of it. Furthermore, the Spanish were encouraging Americans to settle in Missouri in the hope that they would serve as a buffer to the British. The Spanish authorities were very welcoming to the famous Daniel Boone. Subsequently, Boone was said to have claimed that he only went to Missouri because he was sure it would become part of the United States. That might seem a rather dubious assertion, although Thomas Jefferson said something similar. Jefferson said that the more Americans that settled there, the more chance America would acquire the place 'peaceably'.

When asked about abandoning the United States for Spanish Louisiana, Boone would say that 'it was the country and not the government he had gone in pursuit of'. Perhaps it was land and family that motivated him. Given how much land and money he lost during his lifetime, often through carelessness, it seems unlikely that he was motivated by material wealth. In old age he grew uneasy about depictions of him as opening the way to American civilisation and progress. He said he had not thought about 'Empire, or rule, or profit', but that suggested a recognition that he had opened up the West to exactly that. The half-Welsh Daniel Boone had helped make America an expansionist nation that tamed a continent – and his love of hunting, personal freedom and nature might have rendered him a little doubtful about his achievements. On the other hand, he supposedly complained to visitors, 'Nothing embitters my old age [like] the circulation of absurd stories that I retire as civilisation advances, that I shun the white men and seek the Indians, and that now even when old, I wish to retire beyond [the Rocky Mountains].' Maybe the answer is that Daniel Boone was simply not sure where he stood on nationality, civilisation or Indians. He had never had to think about those things while hunting and exploring.

CONCLUSIONS

Those of Welsh descent who fought against the British in the American War of Independence clearly contributed to the making of a new nation, but so too did those such as Daniel Boone who continued the westward expansion that would greatly increase the size and power of the United States.

CHAPTER FIVE

THE WELSH AMERICAN POLITICAL CONTRIBUTION TO THE AMERICAN REVOLUTION

THE AMERICAN war effort required central coordination. This difficult task was attempted by the representatives of the thirteen former colonies in the Continental Congress. That Congress spent much of its time engaged in trying to maintain unity between what were now the thirteen states and in struggling to finance the Continental Army.

In June 1776, a congressional committee drew up the Articles of Confederation. These Articles established a central federal government with limited powers. Although it took until 1781, all thirteen states ratified them. By that time, however, many Revolutionary leaders were coming to the conclusion that a stronger government was needed, especially for foreign affairs and defence. The eventual result was a Constitutional Convention, which met at Philadelphia in 1787. By 1790, all thirteen states had ratified the American Constitution that emerged from the meeting. Several individuals with Welsh ancestry played an important part in these political processes out of which the new American nation was born.

THE SEARCH FOR WELSH AMERICAN CONTRIBUTORS TO THE AMERICAN REVOLUTION

The search for Americans of Welsh descent who made political and administrative contributions to the American Revolution is not a totally straightforward process. Information about the supposed Welsh ancestry of several highly significant American figures has proliferated on Internet sites written by those with a particular interest in Wales. Some sites claim distant Welsh ancestry for Founding Father John Adams, although academic historians and genealogists have not convincingly confirmed this. The *Dictionary of American Biography* had 'financier of the American Revolution' Robert Morris as born in Liverpool to Welsh parents, and this entry was cited in 1967 by Edward Hartmann, Professor of History at Suffolk University, Boston, Massachusetts. However, Morris's Welsh ancestry is not commonly asserted.

Amongst eminent British historians, only Professor David Williams of Aberystwyth sought out Americans with Welsh blood. His motives were clear. He wrote his pamphlet *Cymru ac America: Wales and America* in 1945, after the close cooperation between the United States and Britain during the Second World War, and his foreword showed that he hoped 'to strengthen, if only by a little, the bonds between us and the great American nation'. He also admitted that his pamphlet was 'an attempt to indicate to the youth of Wales the contribution made by our

WELSH AND WELSH AMERICAN CONTRIBUTORS TO THE AMERICAN REVOLUTION

While not amongst the most famous of the American revolutionaries, the following nevertheless made significant political and administrative contributions:

Francis Lewis (1713–1802) was born in Llandaff, near Cardiff. His father was an Anglican clergyman and his mother's father was a minister in either Caernarvon or Newport. Francis Lewis emigrated to New York in 1734 and became a prosperous merchant. He served in the New York Congress, then represented New York at the Continental Congress in 1775 and signed the Declaration of Independence. Francis Lewis's son, General Morgan Lewis, fought against the British during both the Revolutionary War and the War of 1812, and was Governor of New York state from 1804 to 1807. Interestingly, Morgan Lewis said that when his father was taken prisoner by the French at Oswego, the Indians spoke to him in Welsh.

William Floyd (1734–1821) represented New York at the Continental Congress during 1774–6 and was a signatory of the Declaration of Independence. He served in the militia in the American War of Independence and in the US Congress in 1789–91. William's great-grandfather Richard Floyd was born in Breconshire c.1620 and emigrated to New York.

John Nicholson, Comptroller General of Pennsylvania, was a Welsh immigrant, while **Samuel Meredith**, Treasurer of Pennsylvania, was the offspring of Welsh immigrants. Amongst the grandsons of Welsh immigrants were **Lambert Cadwallader**, a Philadelphia leader, and **Abner Nash**, Governor of North Carolina. Amongst those of Welsh descent who attended the Continental Congress were **Allen** and **Willie Jones** of North Carolina (both delegates in 1780), **Joseph Jones** of Virginia (1777–8 and 1780–3), and **Edward Lloyd** of Maryland (1783–4). Also of Welsh descent was George Washington's brother-in-law, **Fielding Lewis** of Virginia, who was a colonel in the Revolutionary War.

nation to the growth and development of the United States'. There lies the key to the many Internet claims of the Welsh ancestry of prominent Americans, and to the writing of this book: the association of Wales and the Welsh with the creation of the most powerful nation in the world fulfils the desire of a small country to retain and promote national pride after centuries of English domination.

Professor Williams cleverly hedged his bets on the political figures in the American War of Independence who had Welsh connections, writing:

Of the fifty-six representatives of the colonies who signed the Declaration of Independence, it has been claimed that no less than eighteen were of Welsh descent. The list of signatures contains such Welsh-sounding names as William Williams, Robert Morris, Lewis Morris, Francis Lewis, John Adams, Samuel Adams, William Floyd, and Stephen Hopkins.

Having carefully noted those 'claimed' to be of Welsh descent, Williams considered only three of the signatories indisputably worthy of inclusion on ancestral grounds. These were Francis Lewis, Button Gwinnett and Thomas Jefferson, but the Pennsylvania House of Representatives would add Robert Morris to their number.

ROBERT MORRIS (1734–1806)

While it is generally agreed that Robert Morris was born in Liverpool, there is no consensus over his ethnicity. However, in 2003, possibly following the *Dictionary of American Biography* and/or local histories, the Pennsylvania House of Representatives declared him to be 'of Welsh descent'.

THE GENERAL ASSEMBLY OF PENNSYLVANIA, HOUSE RESOLUTION NO. 521, SESSION OF 2003

This resolution said that as Pennsylvanians such as 'Revolutionary War financier Robert Morris' were 'of Welsh descent', and as 'large numbers' of people from Wales settled in the state in the nineteenth century, the state of Pennsylvania should observe St David's Day.

Robert Morris's businessman father made his fortune in America and sent for Robert to join him. Robert subsequently made his own fortune in trade and shipping, then played a vital role in the birth of the United States of America. He was a Pennsylvania representative at the second Continental Congress from 1775 to 1778, and his was the second signature on the Declaration of Independence.

The Continental Army

When in 1775 General George Washington was filling barrels with sawdust to disguise the shortage of gunpowder and thereby maintain the morale of his soldiers, Morris smuggled the necessary gunpowder into

America. Morris considered finance 'the crucial factor in the struggle for independence' and his business expertise and knowledge of international trade and shipping made him indispensable in keeping Washington's Continental Army supplied.

A new nation and its government

After the Declaration of Independence, the interconnected questions of the prosecution of the war effort and the nature of an American national government encouraged the Congress to commission a committee to draw up a constitution. Morris was Pennsylvania's representative on the committee and a signatory of the second seminal document in US history, the Articles of Confederation. Ratified in 1781, these Articles provided for a central government in the form of a Congress that could declare war, raise armed forces, make treaties and alliances and borrow and issue money, but could not levy taxes.

Figure 10. *Robert Morris (right), painted by Charles Willson Peale in 1783* (Charles Willson Peale, Public domain, via Wikimedia Commons).

Superintendent of Finance

The embryonic American nation had an empty treasury, worthless currency and struggling economy. It desperately needed a 'superintendent of finance', and in 1781 there was unprecedented congressional unanimity over the appointment of Robert Morris to the post. He accepted on condition that he could continue his private business and have 'absolute power' to hire or dismiss any employee of Congress or the armed forces involved in government expenditure. One critic described him as a 'pecuniary dictator', while General William Irvine noted that 'the most trifling thing cannot be done in any department but through Mr Morris'. Although the Articles had made no provision for an executive branch of government, Morris was in effect the new nation's chief executive.

As superintendent of finance, Morris exploited his own fortune to maintain the Continental Army and to reassure foreign allies about American credit. He established the Bank of America to revive the economy and, he said, to 'unite the several states more closely together'. The Bank's officials repeatedly raised and lowered the same boxes of silver in order to try to convince the public of the worth of their notes.

The Founding Fathers George Washington, Benjamin Franklin, John Adams and Alexander Hamilton were amongst the leading figures who recognised Morris's importance. Hamilton said, 'Mr Morris certainly deserves a great deal from his country. I believe no man in this country but himself could have kept the money machine a-going.' Washington and Morris became close friends and exchanged letters bemoaning the American financial problems. The combination of the reluctance of his countrymen to pay taxes to finance Washington's army, the states' unwillingness to concede meaningful authority to Congress and the inability of Congress to pay the national debt, led the exasperated Morris to resign his post in 1784.

The American Constitution

Morris, Washington, Adams and Hamilton were what would become known as Federalists, a party that favoured a strong central government. Their pressure contributed to the Constitutional Convention, which met in 1787 and was officially opened by Morris. He collaborated with Adams, Franklin, Hamilton, James Madison and Washington in the writing of the new American Constitution, the third landmark document in the birth of the United States (Morris was one of only two men to sign all three). He was optimistic that this Constitution represented something of a triumph for those who favoured a strong central government.

Bankruptcy

Morris indulged in frenzied western land speculation (in 1793 he sent his agent Dr Enoch Edwards to Wales to encourage emigration to his lands). This eventually led to his bankruptcy. Creditors camped out overnight in the grounds of his rural mansion in the hope of his emergence, and at Christmas 1797, Morris and his guests had to take up arms to force the retreat of a constable and six men with pickaxes and sledgehammers who had come in search of his assets. Morris gave himself up in 1798 and spent 3½ years in debtors' prison, where former President George Washington was amongst his visitors. Those who had always claimed that he was corrupt felt vindicated. Morris certainly made a lot of money during the war, but he also lost a great deal through his subsidising of the war effort. As with others on the committees of the Continental Congress, he awarded himself contracts, but his defenders point out that there were no alternatives. He and John Adams often disagreed, but Adams trusted him and so did Washington.

Robert Morris: assessment

In his sympathetic biography *Robert Morris: Financier of the American Revolution* (2010), Charles Rappleye praised 'the enduring contributions Morris made to America's founding and his indelible impact on the life of its people ... His secret agents had supplied the armies of the Revolution, his credit had salvaged its finances, and his faction had fashioned its Constitution.'

A LOST FOUNDING FATHER – BUTTON GWINNETT (1735–77)

Dr Stan Deaton of the Georgia Historical Society once gave a presentation entitled 'How do you lose a Founding Father?' The 'lost' Founding Father was Button Gwinnett, one of the three Georgia delegates to the Continental Congress who signed the Declaration of Independence. He was 'lost' in that little is known about him, he died within a year of signing the Declaration of Independence, and there is controversy over where he is buried.

This lost Founding Father had Welsh connections. Gwinnetts had settled in Gloucestershire when Caernarvonshire-born George Gwynedd or Gwyneth left Wales for England during the reign of Queen Mary. Button Gwinnett was born in Gloucestershire in 1735 to Samuel and Ann Gwinnett, both of whom had Welsh connections. Button's youngest sister, Emilia, owned Penllyn Castle in Cowbridge in the Vale of Glamorgan, while the wealthy family of Ann's spinster cousin Barbara Button owned the Dyffryn estate near Cardiff. Barbara was Button's godmother and he was named for her. She bequeathed Button £100 in her will and he desperately needed it, because he never managed his money well. He was an unsuccessful merchant whose bankruptcy motivated his emigration to America. He settled in Savannah, Georgia, in the early 1760s. His political ambitions demanded that he should be a great landowner, and while he failed to make a decent profit from his land and suffered financial problems that led to frequent appearances in the law courts, he successfully harvested political offices.

Political office

As tensions with Britain rose, Button Gwinnett turned his economic problems to political advantage by blaming his poor finances on British policies. His enthusiastic anti-British rhetoric probably contributed to his election to the Georgia Assembly and to his position as a representative of Georgia at the Continental Congress. He was one of the fifty-six who signed the Declaration of Independence. In many ways, he is most famous for his signature, only fifty-one specimens of which survive. His signature is one of America's most sought-after – hence the sale of his sole surviving private letter for $722,000 in New York in 2010.

After his attendance at the second Continental Congress, Button Gwinnett focused on Georgia politics. He was elected as Speaker, and then President of the Georgia Assembly. Although totally lacking in military experience, he was keen to lead an expedition to Florida, from which territory Loyalists raided southern Georgia. His unrealistic military ambitions contributed to a long-running feud with Continental Army officer Lachlan McIntosh and his family. When McIntosh publicly denounced Button as 'a scoundrel and a lying rascal', Button challenged him to a duel. Button hit McIntosh in the thigh, while McIntosh hit him above the knee (it was good form to aim for flesh wounds rather than a fatal wound). However, Button's wound became infected and he died three days after the duel. His wife was frustrated in her desire to sue the surgeon because Button bequeathed her much debt but little money.

Button Gwinnett: assessment

It is not surprising that Button Gwinnett is a 'lost' and often forgotten Founding Father. He was a bankrupt in England and a generally unsuccessful trader and landowner in America. He was involved in some dishonest financial dealings in order to gain his land in Georgia, and he played a large part in the preparation of the unsuccessful Georgia expedition against Florida Loyalists. A descendant of the Gwinnetts, Colin Gwinnett Sharp, privately published a biography of Button in 2013 and came to a brutally honest conclusion: 'In short he was a mountebank of the first order and that he had reached the highest position in the state [of Georgia] and become a Founding Father probably astounded his political colleagues.' However, Sharp also suggests that an ambitious and experienced politician such as Button Gwinnett may well have contributed something when he attended the second Continental Congress at Philadelphia in 1776, and points out that he definitely contributed to Georgia's new and democratic state constitution.

Given the way in which the Welsh American contribution to the making of the United States is often downplayed, it seems appropriate that the 'lost' Founding Father should be of Welsh stock. On the other hand, Button Gwinnett was no Thomas Jefferson.

THOMAS JEFFERSON (1743–1826)

Thomas Jefferson was the only Founding Father who publicly declared his Welsh ancestry. His mother was of English and Scottish descent and while there is no evidence that her relationship with Jefferson was warm, Jefferson always wrote and spoke proudly of his father, and mentioned his Welsh origins in his autobiography: 'The tradition in my father's family was that their ancestor came to this country from Wales, and from near the mountain of Snowdon, the highest [Jefferson frequently exaggerated] in Great Britain.' Jefferson's political ideas are typical of the Enlightenment, but the Welsh connection may have played a part. Although Jefferson's father worshipped in the Anglican (Episcopalian) church, as did most prominent Virginians, the Welsh ancestor may have been a Protestant Dissenter, which perhaps helps explain some of Jefferson's ideas about Britain, the liberty of the individual and minimalist government.

THOMAS JEFFERSON – CHRONOLOGY	
1743	Born to a wealthy Virginia planter
1760	Absorbed Enlightenment ideas about liberty, progress, religious toleration and the separation of Church and state at the College of William and Mary
1769–75	Served in Virginia's House of Burgesses
1775–6	Represented Virginia in the Continental Congress
1776	Drafted the American Declaration of Independence
1779–81	Governor of Virginia
1783	A Virginia delegate to the Confederation Congress
1785–9	US Minister to France
1790–93	Secretary of State under President Washington
1797–1801	Vice President of the United States
1801–9	President of the United States

'He detests England'

In 1796, the French ambassador declared, 'Mr Jefferson likes us [France] because he detests England.' Several reasons have been suggested for that detestation. Jefferson regarded the British policies after the French–Indian War as infringing the God-given, natural and legal rights of the colonists. Then, British soldiers destroyed his crops and livestock during the Revolutionary War. When he represented the United States in Europe, he suffered vitriolic British press attacks, and George III turned his back on him when they met. Jefferson believed the new American nation was threatened by British troops on its western frontier and by Britain's commercial policy. Furthermore, his own financial well-being was mortgaged to English and Scottish creditors.

Although no historian has suggested this as yet, it may be that Jefferson's Welsh ancestor played a part in his descendant's views on Britain – or at least on the English government that dominated Britain. The Welsh ancestor may well have left Britain because of the British government's policies towards Wales and/or Welsh religious nonconformity. It is possible that residual resentment was passed down the generations of Jeffersons and likely to be activated at times of disillusionment with the mother country. Or perhaps not. Whether the idea came from his Welsh ancestor or not, Jefferson insisted in an early draft of the American Declaration of Independence that the earliest immigrants came to America without any British support and that they considered their move a clean break with Britain. His colleagues excised this interpretation of history from the Declaration, but it was surely true of Jefferson's Welsh ancestor and of many other Welsh immigrants.

The liberty of the individual and minimal government

Although Jefferson was nominally an Anglican/Episcopalian, his belief in the freedom and liberty of the individual and the arbitrary nature of strong government was in the Protestant Dissenting tradition. His sympathy for any form of dissent was evident in his advocacy of religious toleration and the separation of Church and state, and in his occasionally extreme support for those rebelling against the establishment. During Shays's rebellion against unfair taxation in Massachusetts in 1786, Jefferson wrote to Abigail Adams, 'The spirit of resistance to government is so valuable on certain occasions, that I wish it to be always kept alive . . . I like a little rebellion now and then.' In 1787, he wrote to the Adamses' son-in-law, 'The tree of liberty must be refreshed from time to time with the blood of patriots and tyrants. It is its natural manure.' He gave verbal support to the excesses of the French Revolution, but was subsequently embarrassed by that support.

Americans naturally debated the power and functions of central government during the Revolutionary War. Jefferson considered a strong executive essential for foreign and defence policies, but he thought domestic concerns and taxation should be left to the individual states and he grew increasingly critical of Federalists such as President Washington (1789–97) who advocated a strong federal government.

All men are created equal

Jefferson is credited with beautiful words in the Declaration of Independence, words that have made him a beloved Founding Father to many Americans:

> We hold these truths to be self-evident, that all men are created equal, that they are endowed by their Creator with certain unalienable Rights, that among these are Life, Liberty and the pursuit of Happiness.

While it is ahistorical to expect eighteenth-century Americans to share twenty-first-century values, affection for Jefferson has decreased because of his stance on slavery. While he was the author of those ringing phrases about equality and while he repeatedly made it clear in the Virginia Assembly and the Congress that slavery was morally incompatible with the principles of the American Revolution, he nevertheless kept up to two hundred slaves until the day he died. His ambivalence was demonstrated in his early draft of the Declaration of Independence, where he suggested that slavery was an evil institution imposed upon innocent colonists by the corrupt George III, yet simultaneously blamed George III for 'prompting Negroes to rise in arms against us'. Although Jefferson talked and wrote in favour of the gradual abolition of slavery in the early 1780s, and although he suggested to Congress in 1784 that slavery should be ended in all newly created states by 1800 (his proposal was defeated by one vote), he then grew increasingly cautious and advocated very slow preparation of public opinion for the end of slavery.

Figure 11. *Jefferson's Monticello home, which he designed himself.* (Copyright Thomas Jefferson Foundation at Monticello)

Figure 12. *The recreated slave quarters at Jefferson's Monticello home. Sally Hemings did not live in the slave quarters. She had rooms in the Monticello house* (Copyright Thomas Jefferson Foundation at Monticello).

Several reasons account for Jefferson's change of position on slavery. His denunciation of slavery and suggestion that planters were already moving towards emancipation in his *Notes on the State of Virginia* (1781) had aroused controversy, and he sought to avoid further annoyance. He was also increasingly aware that his own wealth depended on the monetary value and work of his slaves, and he was beginning to realise that he had no answer to the question of what should happen once the slaves were free. Jefferson consistently declared that black and white Americans simply could not live alongside each other. He explained this in his *Notes*:

Deep-rooted prejudices entertained by the whites; ten thousand recollections, by the blacks, the injuries they have sustained; new provocations; the real distinctions that nature has made; and many other circumstances, will divide us into parties, and produce convulsions which will probably never end but in the extermination of one or the other race.

He voiced his suspicion that people of African descent were less intelligent than whites, and that any racial interaction resulting from emancipation transgressed against 'the real distinctions that nature has made'.

The Missouri Question

In 1820, there were heated debates about whether slavery should be allowed in the new territory of Missouri. Jefferson said this Missouri Question alerted him to danger 'like a fire bell in the night'. He contended that ending slavery would not be a problem if the slaves could be emancipated and expatriated, but considered this impossible because many slaves would refuse to go to Africa or the West Indies. He feared that limits on the westward expansion of slavery were a prelude to making slavery illegal throughout America, so he thought that it might be wise for white Southerners to flee before it was too late or for the South to secede from the union of the United States. He confessed that he had given up the search for a workable solution, saying, 'I leave its accomplishment to the work of another generation.'

Jefferson's response to the Missouri Question can perhaps be defended. He was old, ever more in debt, frightened by the Missouri Question, surrounded by anxious fellow Virginian plantation owners and correct in anticipating that the race issue would prove problematic. Perhaps less defensible is the story of his slave Sally Hemings.

Sally Hemings

Jefferson's dying wife Martha supposedly made him promise that he would never remarry. He never did, but a 1998 DNA study finally confirmed beyond reasonable doubt that he had several children by his slave Sally Hemings, who was thirty years his junior. Although contemporaries made many unflattering references to Sally's race, she was apparently very light-skinned, being of three-quarters European ancestry, and she was the half-sister of Jefferson's wife.

Jefferson's avowed views on racial intermixing make interesting reading. When the Virginia House of Delegates had asked him to propose revisions to Virginia law in October 1776, his Bill No. 51 included the provision that any white woman having a child by a black American or mulatto had to depart from Virginia or be out of the protection of Virginia's laws. 'Amalgamation with the other colour [*sic*] produces a degradation to which no lover of his country, no lover of excellence in the human character can innocently consent,' Jefferson wrote in 1814 to a Virginian who freed his slaves as a result of being inspired by Jefferson!

For whatever reason, Jefferson never acknowledged his relationship with Sally. He freed several members of the Hemings family in his will, but his other slaves were sold to the highest bidder.

> ## Unprepared for Gender Equality
>
> In 1807, Treasury Secretary Albert Gallatin suggested that President Jefferson appoint women to federal office. Jefferson replied, 'The appointment of a woman to office is an innovation for which the public is not prepared, nor am I.'

Native Americans

Jefferson had a more positive attitude to Indians than to black Americans, saying, 'I believe the Indian . . . to be, in body and mind, equal to the white man.' A whole chapter in his *Notes* celebrated Native American culture and he designated the Indians a noble race, innocent victims of forces beyond their control. However, if they were to prove uncooperative over white settlement, he wanted them deported to the west of the Mississippi: 'I would never cease pursuing them while one of them remained on this side [of] the Mississippi.' He said this in the knowledge that white Americans would eventually take the land west of the Mississippi too. While he never urged the assimilation of black Americans, he favoured Indian assimilation into white America, 'to intermix, and become one people'.

Why did Jefferson consider Native Americans worthy of assimilation, while black Americans were not? It might be because he had less contact with Native Americans, or because of the contemporary sentimentality towards the 'noble savage', or because he was determined to refute the ideas of Europe's leading biologist, the Comte de Buffon, who insisted that animals and humans degenerated in the Americas.

Thomas Jefferson: the greatest of Welsh Americans?

Although some regret Thomas Jefferson's position on race, he helped found the new American nation and inspired generations of Americans with his ideas about liberty and government. His purchase of the Louisiana Territory from France for $15 million in 1803 doubled the size of the United States and opened it up for westward expansion. Many consider this his greatest achievement as president. In 1802, he commissioned his private secretary Meriwether Lewis to organise an expedition to explore the West, to seek a direct water route to the Pacific and to stake a US claim to vast new territories. In Meriwether Lewis, another American of Welsh descent would play a vital role in the shaping of this new and dynamically expansionist nation.

CHAPTER SIX

MERIWETHER LEWIS, JAMES MONROE AND THE AMERICAN WEST

B Y 1803, the thirteen original states (the former colonies of Connecticut, Delaware, Georgia, Maryland, Massachusetts, New Hampshire, New Jersey, New York, North Carolina, Pennsylvania, Rhode Island, South Carolina and Virginia), had been joined by Vermont (1791), Kentucky (1792), Tennessee (1796) and Ohio (1803). President Thomas Jefferson knew that no European power or Native American tribe would be able to stem further American expansion into the vast and almost empty territories of the West, and in 1803 he sent US Army Captain Meriwether Lewis to explore them.

MERIWETHER LEWIS'S BACKGROUND

Welsh ancestry

Welshman Robert Lewis emigrated to America in 1635 equipped with a royal grant of 33,000 acres in Virginia. In 1769, his grandson William Lewis married his cousin Lucy Meriwether. The Meriwethers were another prosperous family of Welsh descent who frequently intermarried

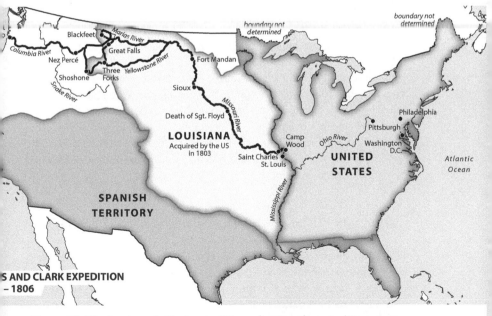

Figure 13. *The Lewis and Clark expedition, charting the expedition route from St Louis to Fort Clatsop.*

with the Lewises. William and Lucy's son Meriwether Lewis was born in 1774. Thomas Jefferson noted admiringly how his neighbour William Lewis then 'left all to aid in the liberation of his country from foreign usurpations'. Like George Washington, William Lewis served without pay in the Revolutionary War. Unlike Washington, Lewis served without expenses.

Army career

Meriwether Lewis rejected the planter's life and in 1794 volunteered to help put down the Whiskey Rebellion 'to support the glorious cause of liberty and my country'. Perhaps he also hoped for adventure or a Western land grant such as those given to Revolutionary War veterans. When the rebellion collapsed, he volunteered to stay on with a small occupation force under another of Welsh ancestry, General Daniel Morgan. Lewis joined the regular army in 1795 and was at the headquarters of yet another with Welsh blood, General 'Mad' Anthony Wayne, when the tribal chiefs of the Ohio region signed the Treaty of Greenville.

Jefferson's secretary

On the eve of his inauguration, Jefferson wrote to Captain Meriwether Lewis that he needed a secretary for 'private concerns [. . . and] to contribute to the mass of information which is interesting for any administration to acquire. Your knowledge of the Western country [and] the army . . . has rendered it desirable that you should be engaged in that office.' Jefferson invited Lewis to live in the President's House, 'as you would be one of my family'. The President had long favoured Western exploration and in 1802 he put Lewis in charge of a transcontinental expedition, of which Lewis insisted that his army friend William Clark be considered co-commander.

THE AIMS OF THE LEWIS AND CLARK EXPEDITION

Jefferson instructed Lewis and Clark to find 'the most direct and practicable water communication across this continent ... The object of your mission is to explore . . . for the purposes of commerce.' The President also hoped for an 'empire of liberty' in which the principles of the American Revolution would be planted across the continent, so he wanted to know about the West in order to establish and confirm American claims to it. Jefferson feared the presence of rival powers in the West, where France had acquired the Louisiana Territory from Spain in 1800 and Britain also had territorial ambitions.

As Lewis prepared the expedition, Jefferson purchased the Louisiana Territory from France in April 1803. This acquisition was home to many Indian tribes, and the safety of American citizens and the expansion of US territory and trade required knowledge of them and a working relationship. Jefferson told Lewis to be 'most friendly and conciliatory' while nevertheless informing the Indians of the great power of the United States. Jefferson also discussed Welsh Indians with Lewis and told him to look for them.

THE LEWIS AND CLARK EXPEDITION TIMELINE

1783–93	Jefferson tried to organise expeditions to explore the West
1802	Jefferson learned that Spain had given France the Louisiana Territory
	Jefferson asked Lewis to lead an expedition to the West
1802–3	Winter: Jefferson obtained congressional support for the Louisiana Purchase
1804	March: Louisiana became part of the United States
	Spring and summer: Lewis and Clark's expedition went up the Missouri River; the Indians of the Kansas prairies were generally friendly
1804	October: The party reached the Mandan Indian villages and wintered nearby
1805	March: The Missouri River thawed and the expedition reached the Shoshone Indians and the Rocky Mountains in spring
	September: The expedition crossed the Continental Divide
	October: The party began floating down the Columbia River
	November: The expedition reached the Pacific Ocean, constructed Fort Clatsop and wintered near the Pacific
1806	Spring: The party began their return journey; Nez Percé Indians guided them across the mountains to the prairies
	July: Lewis divided the party into several exploratory groups
	August: The expedition was reunited
	September: The party arrived at the rambunctious frontier town of St Louis, where most people had thought them long dead.

THE EXPEDITION'S RELATIONS WITH THE INDIANS

Good relations with the Indians and Indian recognition of American superiority were essential for American commerce and future settlement, and for the safety, food supplies and route of the expedition.

Gifts and trading

Gifts and trade goods were important to good relations. The party gifted or traded items such as beads, brass buttons, tomahawks, axes, scissors, mirrors, tobacco, vermilion face paint and whiskey. Indians often valued what they received, as when the Shoshone appreciated metal knives (they had a few Spanish axes but remained mostly reliant upon flint cutting tools).

Some tribes were particular: the Pacific Northwest Indians rejected Lewis's watch in favour of blue beads, and the Teton Sioux declared medals and a silly hat worthless and were reluctant to let the expedition depart unless they received more tobacco. Many tribes appreciated alcohol, although the Arikaras declared themselves 'surprised' that the Great White Father in Washington would offer them whiskey that would make them behave like fools. It was dangerous to be without offerings: by the time they left Fort Clatsop, the party was out of trade goods, and as the Indians grew increasingly surly, Clark had to resort to 'magic'. When he threw a match into the fire, the Nez Percé begged him to take what he wanted from them and extinguish the resultant large flame.

Dangerous Indians

Indian hostility could endanger the party. The Nez Percé, the biggest Indian tribe of the Pacific Northwest, considered killing the party for their weapons until an old Indian woman to whom the party had given gifts spoke out in their favour. Lewis recorded his suspicions of the Indians during the winter at Fort Clatsop:

> Notwithstanding their apparent friendly disposition, their great avarice and hope of plunder might induce them to be treacherous. At all events we determined always to be on our guard . . . and never place ourselves at the mercy of any savages. We well know that the treachery of the aborigines of America and the too great confidence of our countrymen in their sincerity and friendship, has caused the destruction of many hundreds of us.

He considered his men insufficiently wary during frequent visits to the Indian women that winter, but he too could be lax. On the return journey, Lewis's five-man exploratory party met warriors from the famously fierce Blackfoot tribe. The party camped overnight with a group of Blackfeet who stole horses and guns while Lewis slept. In a rare instance of bloodshed on the expedition, Lewis shot an escaping Indian thief.

Lewis always made American superiority clear. In the prepared speech he gave to the frequently uncomprehending Indians whom the party met, he said that while the Great White Father back in Washington would provide protection and presents, it would be unwise to displease him. On the return leg, Lewis urged Indian chiefs to visit Washington in order to 'have an ample view of our population and resources, and on their return convince their tribes of the futility of an attempt to oppose the will of our government'.

Observing the Indians

Future relations made knowledge of the Indians desirable and Lewis made detailed notes and observations about appearance and behaviour. This did not mean that he really understood them. Several tribes proudly showed him enemy scalps, while a Chinook chief showed a medicine bag containing fourteen forefingers belonging to enemies killed in battle. Although it was obvious that wars were frequent and that chiefs were required to have demonstrated warrior skills, Lewis repeatedly urged the different Indian tribes to live at peace.

Lewis looked out for the 'Welsh Indians' and three of the expedition thought they had probably found them. Lewis wrote down many Indian words phonetically in order to compare them with Welsh words on his return. He took special care to note the vocabulary of the Salish Indians because their throaty, guttural speech sounded Welsh to him.

It was with amazement that Lewis often recorded Indian customs, as when the expedition met friendly mountain-dwelling Flatheads. The Flatheads would put a baby in a trough, place a pillow of wool and feathers upon its forehead, and then press a piece of wood down hard on the forehead for a year. The result was a flattened and broadened forehead, which the tribe felt improved appearance. Sometimes, Lewis was both amazed and disgusted. During the winter at Fort Clatsop, he frequently observed the Indians naked below the waist. This was because they were in water much of the time. The Chinook Indian women wore short tunics that horrified Lewis because they revealed so much in certain postures. 'I think the most disgusting sight I have ever beheld is these dirty naked wenches.'

Lewis grew impatient with Indian thieving, which increased as the party moved further west. He described the Pacific Northwest Indians as 'mild inoffensive people . . . but will pilfer.' When the party began the return journey, Lewis noted starving Indians 'constantly hanging about us'. Multiple attempted thefts caused him to complain that 'these are the greatest thieves and scoundrels we have met with.' Tomahawks and knives disappeared in the night because the Indians valued metal. When Lewis's dog Seaman was stolen, he sent three men to retrieve it with orders to fire if the Indians proved difficult. He contemplated 'instant death' to punish any further thieving. When some Chinooks stole a saddle and robe, Lewis sent men to burn their houses to the ground, but his men found the goods and the Chinooks escaped punishment.

Of course, not all Indians were thieves. Indeed, the Indians frequently helped and fed the expedition. Lewis described some Wallawalla Indians who returned a steel trap belonging to one of the party as the 'most hospitable, most honest' he had ever met. However, there were some aspects of Indian hospitality that shocked him.

Sexual relations with the Indians

The expedition's virile young men were well satisfied by the Indians. The party spent the winter of 1804–5 with the Mandan Indians, who believed that power transferred from one man to another through sexual intercourse with a woman. The Mandans considered whites very powerful and therefore gave the expedition free access to their women. Lewis noted that one Mandan woman was 'extremely solicitous to accompany one of the men of our party, this however we positively refused to permit'. He wrote disapprovingly that among the Shoshone, 'The chastity of their women is not held in high estimation . . . [but they were] not so importunate that we should caress their women as the Sioux were.'

Lewis doled out mercury for the syphilis from which his men suffered. He recorded that 'I was anxious to learn whether these people have the venereal,' and when he found the Shoshone already had venereal disease, he thought that 'this seems a strong proof that these disorders . . . are native disorders of America.' However, he also noted that the Shoshone had the smallpox – 'which is known to be imported'.

While Lewis and Clark spent the cold, wet winter at Fort Clatsop writing up their notes, their men frequented a nearby brothel run by an old squaw with six 'nieces'. Lewis was amazed that the Indians 'will even prostitute their wives and daughters for a fishing hook or a string of beads'. A Clatsop chief offered Lewis and Clark a wife each, but they refused, which Clark said left the women 'highly disgusted'. They had also declined a Sioux Indian chief's offer of some 'handsome squaws' for the night some months before. Were they repelled by the Indian women? Anxious to demonstrate to the men that their leaders had different standards of behaviour? Willing to record their men's liaisons but not their own? Or was it fear of 'the venereal'? Lewis recorded, 'Once this disorder is contracted it . . . always ends up in decrepitude, death, premature old age.'

While Lewis was rather ambivalent about Indians, sometimes calling them 'savages', at other times shooting several deer for 'poor starved devils', he and Clark greatly valued Sacagawea.

Sacagawea

When the party wintered near the Mandan villages, they accepted an offer of help from a French trader called Charbonneau. He had several wives, including the pregnant sixteen-year-old Sacagawea, a Shoshone who had been captured and enslaved by another Indian tribe. Fearing a difficult birth, Lewis followed the suggestion of a French trader and gave her a part of a rattlesnake's rattle to drink with water. The baby appeared ten minutes later, but Lewis recorded himself uncertain 'whether this medicine was truly the cause or not'. A few months later, he worried about Sacagawea's health again (a modern medical specialist has suggested she was suffering from venereal disease). Lewis had apparently made her feel better and given her strict instructions as to what she could eat, but when she ate some unripe apples, her fever returned. 'I rebuked severely,' he noted.

Sacagawea was useful. She spoke Shoshone and gave directions to Shoshone lands. Her brother's position as a Shoshone chief contributed to good relations with the Shoshone, and as Clark noted, a woman with a party of men indicated friendly intentions to other tribes. On one occasion, Charbonneau nearly capsized one of the boats. Lewis wrote: 'The Indian woman, to whom I ascribe equal fortitude and resolution with any person on board at the time of the accident, caught and preserved most of the light articles which were washed overboard.' Those articles included important journals, maps and instruments.

Sacagawea's personality and Lewis's indulgent attitude to her emerge from his journals. When restored to her Shoshone homeland, he noted that 'if she has enough to eat and a few trinkets to wear I believe she would be perfectly content anywhere.' While they wintered at Fort Clatsop, some members of the expedition went to see a dead whale, and Lewis noted,

> The Indian woman was very importunate to be permitted to go, and was therefore indulged; she observed that she had travelled a long way with us to see the great waters, and that now that monstrous fish was also to be seen, she thought it very hard she could not be permitted to see either.

When the expedition returned from the Pacific, Sacagawea and Charbonneau stayed with the Mandans. Clark wrote to her husband saying that Sacagawea 'deserved a greater reward for her attention and services on that route than we had in our power to give her'.

OTHER PROBLEMS ON THE EXPEDITION

Indians were but one problem. Amongst the others were food, health, friendly fire and unfriendly flora and fauna.

The flora and fauna

The expedition came across animals and plants with which they were unfamiliar and by some of which they were greatly inconvenienced. Lewis declared Western grizzly bears 'much more furious and formidable' than the black bears of the eastern United States, and thought he 'had rather fight two Indians than one bear ... It is astonishing to see the wounds they will bear before they can be put to death.' It took eight balls to kill one bear – the eighth ball got him just as he was about to attack a member of the party whom he followed in a 20-foot jump from a riverbank into the river. Bears were not the only dangerous animal. Once, Lewis awoke from a sleep to find a rattlesnake ten feet away and ready to strike. He killed it.

Dangerous accidents were probably inevitable. Clark recorded that Lewis nearly fell from a 300-foot bluff overlooking the Missouri River but 'saved himself by the assistance of his knife'. After they departed from Fort Clatsop, Lewis was hunting elk with the boatman, Cruzatte. Lewis felt a sharp pain when a bullet hit him just below the left hip joint, then passed through his buttocks and came out on the right hand side, leaving a wound 3 inches long and the depth of the bullet. 'I instantly supposed that Cruzatte had shot me in mistake for an elk as I was dressed in brown leather and he cannot see very well ... I called out to him, "Damn you, you have shot me."' Luckily, no bones had been hit. Cruzatte denied culpability, but as the bullet was a US Army issue bullet, Lewis did not believe him. However, Lewis wrote, 'I do not believe that the fellow did it intentionally.' Lewis put rolls of lint in the gaping holes in his buttocks so that the wound would stay open and new tissue would grow from the inside outward. The pain was such that he could not bear to be moved and had to lie on his stomach for several days. A poultice of Peruvian bark (cinchona) eventually halted his high fever and luckily the wound did not get infected when Clark washed it in the murky Missouri River water.

Sometimes the hazards were unpleasant rather than life-threatening. As they travelled up the Missouri in 1804, malarial mosquitoes were rampant and the men's bites frequently became infected. In the summer of 1805, three charging buffalo forced Lewis to run through a carpet of prickly pear, the long sharp spikes of which went through the men's double-soled moccasins and left up to sixty thorns to be picked nightly from their feet. That same summer, Lewis also bemoaned how barbed seeds of needle grass

penetrate our moccasins and leather leggings and give us great pain until they are removed. My poor dog suffers with them excessively, he is constantly biting and scratching himself as if in a rack of pain . . . Our trio of pests still invade and obstruct us on all occasions, these are the mosquitoes, eye gnats and prickly pears.

While at Fort Clatsop, the Chinook Indians gave the party a gift of dried fish on straw infested with fleas that proved faithful companions throughout the winter. In summer 1806, Lewis noted 'mosquitoes excessively troublesome ... my dog even howls with the torture'.

Diet and health

The expedition rarely had a balanced diet and frequently suffered irritating health conditions. On the journey up the Missouri in 1804, they were 'much afflicted with boils and dysentery'. That was probably due to the lack of vegetables and fruit, the dirty river water they were drinking, and meat that was most likely contaminated. In the spring of 1805, Lewis noted, 'sore eyes is a common complaint among the party.' He blamed this upon the fine sand, as 'we are compelled to eat, drink, and breathe it very freely'. It may also have been due to the venereal disease from which most of the men suffered, or to the glare of the sun on the water.

When they crossed the Bitterroot Mountains in autumn 1805, they were reduced to eating three of their colts. After a period of starvation, Clark warned against overeating, but the others could not restrain themselves. Lewis suffered violent diarrhoea and vomiting for a week (Clark gave the sufferers laxatives which exacerbated their condition). Clark then recorded: 'Captain Lewis and myself ate supper of roots boiled, which filled us so full of wind, that we were scarcely able to breathe all night.' Lewis recalled: 'I suffered a severe indisposition for 10 or 12 days, sick feeble and emaciated.' While at Fort Clatsop from December 1805 to March 1806, they were short of food again, but Lewis declared himself 'perfectly reconciled' to eating dog. In the early summer of 1806, the party gave the Indians the brass buttons off their uniforms in order to acquire desperately needed food. The Indians were generous on many other occasions and gave the expedition food even when short themselves.

When a member of the expedition was sick, Lewis did most of the doctoring. Before the expedition departed, he consulted with Dr Benjamin Rush, a signatory of the Declaration of Independence. Rush gave him purging pills, popularly called 'Thunderclappers', containing six parts Mercury to one part chlorine and jalap. Lewis ordered fifty dozen for the expedition. Amongst the other drugs taken along were opium and laudanum. Lewis dispensed thirty drops of laudanum to make an unwell man sleep, zinc sulphate and lead acetate for sore eyes, and his 'emollient poultice' for the boils and pustules that were common in the party and probably due to scurvy. While the men were at Fort Clatsop, many were sick and injured. Using one of the four brass penis syringes in the medical chest, Lewis treated their venereal disease, saying, 'I cured ... by the use of mercury.' The early deaths of many of the expedition may have been due to the venereal disease – or to Lewis's plentiful doses of mercury.

Lewis and Clark gained a reputation amongst the Indians for their doctoring. After leaving Fort Clatsop, they eased the paralysis of an old chief by putting him in a clay oven, lighting a fire below it, and making him sweat profusely. He was able to wash his face the next day. The grateful Nez Percé gave them food. Lewis expressed the wish that he was back in Philadelphia where Benjamin Franklin had experimented with electric shock treatment to treat paralysis – 'I am confident that this would be an excellent subject for electricity.'

Lewis and research

Before the expedition had set out, Lewis had consulted experts on subjects such as astronomy and botany. Jefferson wanted to know all about the flora and fauna, so Lewis made copious notes and undertook small-scale scientific investigations. For example, when going up the Missouri and entering Indian country in summer 1804, Lewis killed a bull snake, noted its length (5 foot 2 inches), its 'circumference' (4½ inches), and its markings, etc. Soon after, the expedition suddenly found the river full of white feathers and then discovered pelicans preening and moulting on a sand bar. Lewis killed a pelican and found that its pouch could hold five gallons of water. While wintering at Fort Mandan, he sent live specimens back to Washington, including a prairie dog. In April 1805, the expedition went where no American white man had gone before, which perhaps explains why the buffalo, elk and deer often came up to the members of the party to investigate them. Lewis wrote that the buffalo were 'so gentle that the men frequently throw sticks and stones at them in order to drive them out of the way'. Jefferson and his interests were always on his protégé's mind. Lewis took cuttings from a creeping juniper to send to Jefferson, noting presciently, 'This plant would make very handsome edgings to the borders and walks of the garden ... [It is] easily propagated.'

Lewis also made careful note of the geography of the areas through which they travelled. In the spring of 1805, he wrote of 'a desert, barren country' with 'astonishingly dry' air in which a tablespoon of water would 'evaporate in 36 hours'. He was much impressed by the White Cliffs and the Great Falls, and he bathed in the Yellowstone hot springs for nineteen minutes, taking a scientific interest in how long he could cope with the great heat.

LEWIS'S ACHIEVEMENTS

Meriwether Lewis had prepared meticulously for a dangerous journey into the unknown. With great generosity and wisdom, he had insisted upon sharing command with William Clark, and for the most part had chosen the members of the expedition well.

Lewis made some strategic errors especially towards the end of the expedition. It was dangerous to split the expedition into five groups in order to facilitate more exploration. Not one of the five groups had sufficient firepower to see off a determined Indian attack, and Lewis further divided his group to pursue Blackfoot thieves. However, he managed good relations with the Indians for most of the time and persuaded several Indian chiefs to visit the Great White Father in Washington.

Lewis's expedition was the first to cross what is now the United States of America. He had found a route across the continent – perhaps not the best, but he did not know that. He had meticulously acquired and recorded a great deal of information about the zoology, botany, ethnology and geography of hitherto unexplored regions. He discovered and described 178 new plants and 122 species and subspecies of animals.

Contemporaries valued and recognised Lewis's achievements. In December 1806, Jefferson sent a message to Congress, saying: 'Lewis and Clark, and their brave companions, have by this arduous service deserved well of their country.' One Thomas James of Missouri wrote that 'their accounts of that wild region . . . first excited spirit of trafficking adventure among the young men of the West'. Lewis had basically opened up the continent to the expansion of the United States and he could justly be called one of the discoverers of the continent.

THOMAS JEFFERSON'S EPITAPH ON LEWIS

'Of courage undaunted, possessing a firmness and perseverance of purpose which nothing but impossibilities could divert from its direction, careful as a father of those committed to his charge, yet steady in the maintenance of order and discipline, intimate with the Indian character, customs and principles, habituated to the hunting life, guarded by exact observation of the vegetables and animals of his own country, against losing time in the description of objects already possessed, honest, disinterested, liberal, of sound understanding and a fidelity to truth so scrupulous that whatever he should report would be as certain as if seen by ourselves, with all these qualifications as if selected and implanted by nature in one body, for this express purpose, I could have no hesitation in confiding the enterprise to him.'

LEWIS'S LIFE AFTER THE EXPEDITION

After the expedition returned, President Jefferson appointed Lewis Governor of Louisiana Territory, which Governor James Wilkinson had reported as 'raging with personal animosities' in 1805. Acting Governor Frederick Bates said the Territory was virtually ungovernable and declared himself desperate for Lewis's arrival. The Territory's problems included disputed land grants and trading privileges, clashes between old and new residents, restless Indians, and British traders entering US territory.

Lewis was quick to demand his salary as Governor but slow to get to St Louis to take up his post, for which some have criticised him. The best-selling historian Stephen Ambrose described him as preoccupied with partying, adulation, alcohol and unsuccessful courtships (Lewis had declared himself 'determined to get a wife'), while Jefferson pressed him to prepare his journals for publication and employed him to report back on a several-week-long treason trial.

When Lewis finally arrived in St Louis, there were complaints about his silence from the Secretary of War and from President Jefferson, but the mail was notoriously unreliable. In the winter, it could take up to two months to arrive in St Louis, and some mail simply got lost. Most historians recognise that Lewis achieved something in his first year in St Louis. He did a lot of routine government business, managed Indian problems reasonably well, and initiated reforms and improvements such as road building. However, Ambrose described Lewis as drinking heavily and regularly taking medicine that included opium, morphine and mercury for his malaria. Lewis certainly failed to establish a good working relationship with Frederick Bates, but Bates's correspondence suggests resentment of Lewis's heroic status and close relationship with the president. Some believed Bates wanted Lewis's job. He certainly lost no opportunity for criticism: he and a former Indian agent complained about Lewis's participation in a private commercial venture financed by government funds and approved by Jefferson.

During 1809, Lewis found himself under increasing pressure from all sides. In May, James Madison became President. Madison was less enthusiastic about westward movement than Jefferson, and his administration was financially embarrassed and impatient with Lewis's expenditure. In July, Bates reported Lewis as talking of leaving the job, and Bates anticipated that it would be soon. In August, Lewis was shaken when the Department of State refused to honour his draft (a promise of money) for the translation of the Territory's laws into French for publication. The Secretary of War then wrote to him that his department had reluctantly approved Lewis's contract with the Missouri River Company (in which Lewis and Clark had invested) but would no longer honour his drafts. A rejected $500 draft now became Lewis's debt. William Clark wrote to his brother that Lewis's credit was 'ruined' by the rejection of his drafts and insisted that Lewis was honest. Lewis's attorney William Carr described the Governor as 'a good man, but a very imprudent one', with 'his private [financial] affairs

altogether deranged'. Meanwhile, Bates was damaging Lewis's reputation and was perhaps responsible for spreading the story of how
the government had refused to honour Lewis's drafts. A land commis-
sioner in the territory wrote that it was Bates's 'barbarous conduct'
that caused 'the mental derangement of the Governor'. Criticism from
former President Jefferson would have contributed greatly to Lewis's
distress: Jefferson told Lewis that he was personally embarrassed by
Lewis's slowness in producing his journal.

Suicide?

In 1809, Lewis travelled east to see to the publication of his book and to
try to clear his name with regard to his accounting. He was in pain, and
the general consensus is that he was depressed. He wrote his will. The
crew of the Mississippi riverboat on which he travelled twice stopped
him killing himself. The riverboat's Captain Russell kept a twenty-four-
hour suicide watch, but then noted that after a week 'all symptoms of
derangement disappeared and he was completely in his senses'. Russell
said that Lewis 'acknowledged very candidly to me that he had been
drinking too much and vowed never to drink again', but he was soon
back on the bottle and bemoaning the fate of his drafts. It is possible
that Captain Russell subsequently felt he had to defend himself against
accusations that he had taken insufficient care of a sick man, and he
may have misrepresented Lewis's alcohol intake, for alcohol was cus-
tomarily used to disguise the bitterness of the Peruvian bark that Lewis
was taking for his malaria.

While lodging in Grinder's Inn, Lewis shot himself in the head in
the early hours of the morning and collapsed to the floor. The shot
had only grazed his skull so he shot himself in the breast, then stag-
gered around and collapsed. At first light, according to some subsequent
accounts, the Grinder's servants found Lewis 'busily engaged in cutting
himself from head to foot' with his razor. A year after Lewis's death, Mrs
Grinder recalled how her servants had

> found him lying in the bed; he uncovered his side and showed
> them where the bullet had entered; a piece of the forehead was
> blown off, and had exposed the brains, without having bled much.
> He begged they would take his rifle and blow out his brains . . . He
> often said, 'I am no coward, but I am so strong . . . so hard to die.'

Finally, death took him.

Some believe that Lewis was murdered. Some have suggested that the Grinders mistakenly thought that his closely guarded boxes of documents and diaries contained items of monetary value. However, his friends Clark and Jefferson would surely have investigated if they had thought it was murder. They knew him best and they thought that it was depression and suicide. Within days of Lewis's death, Jefferson wrote to Captain Russell that Lewis 'was much afflicted and habitually so with hypochondria. This was probably increased by the habit into which he had fallen.' Three years later, Jefferson wrote that when Lewis lived in Washington he suffered 'depressions' of mind, in the Lewis family tradition. Jefferson guessed that the expedition would have 'suspended' them but 'at St Louis in sedentary occupations they returned upon him with redoubled vigour.' It is of course possible that Jefferson felt that he had given Lewis the wrong job or had overburdened him, but preferred to blame Lewis's death on the depression.

Interestingly, Thomas Danisi and John Jackson contended in their 2009 biography that malaria drove Lewis to destruction. After mosquito bites, parasites invade the liver and hatch in the blood, causing expansion of the liver and spleen, severe anaemia, delusions, chills, fevers, delirium and even death. Danisi and Jackson cite contemporary doctors telling of patients with malaria suffering 'derangement', trying to wound themselves, and wanting to die during malarial attacks. Lewis self-medicated. He favoured Dr Rush's pills containing calomel over the Peruvian bark, thereby slowly poisoning himself with doses of mercury. Historians can be overfond of their subjects, and it may be that Danisi and Jackson have too many new answers to criticisms of Lewis and the accounts of depressive tendencies that led to his suicide. Whatever the truth, Lewis's last days are a reminder that the making of America, to which he contributed a great deal, was a very demanding and often highly destructive process. It was also a process that depended greatly on the interest and initiative of the President.

JAMES MONROE AND THE AMERICAN WEST

Historians generally rate James Monroe (1758–1831) as one of the better presidents of the United States, and it is rather surprising that so many Welsh writers fail to emphasise or mention his Welsh ancestry. Perhaps this was because Monroe himself lacked interest in it.

Monroe's maternal grandfather was a Welsh immigrant who built up a considerable estate in King George County, Virginia. After the death of Monroe's parents, his mother's brother, Joseph Jones, in effect adopted him.

James Monroe is interesting not only because he was half-Welsh, but also because he illustrates advantages and disadvantages arising from the expansion of American territory. While expansionism made America more powerful, it aroused potentially dangerous tensions with other nations and what would prove to be devastating divisions over slavery.

Military service in the American Revolution

During his military service in the Revolutionary War in 1776–7, Lieutenant Monroe fought under Washington in New York and participated in Washington's retreat across the Hudson and Delaware Rivers and in the battle at Trenton. As aide-de-camp to Brigadier General William Alexander, Lord Stirling, the newly promoted Major Monroe recalled spending most of his time 'keeping his Lordship's tankard plentifully supplied with ale and listening to his long-winded stories'. When Washington's army wintered at Valley Forge, Stirling and many other officers went home, but Monroe chose to remain. Virginia had an abundance of officers but too few soldiers, so for several years Monroe repeatedly tried but failed to enlist sufficient men to command.

Advocate of expansion

In 1778, Monroe returned to civilian life, where his uncle's connections enabled him to become a protégé of Thomas Jefferson. Monroe was elected to the Virginia General Assembly (1782), the Confederation Congress (1783) and the US Senate (1790). He became known as a leading advocate of American expansionism, suggesting to the Confederation Congress that the United States should annex Canada.

The anti-federalist Monroe proved a surprisingly activist Governor of Virginia (1799–1802). He persuaded the Virginia legislature to establish state-supported systems of education and public roads, and greatly exceeded his gubernatorial authority when quashing a planned slave uprising, 'Gabriel's Rebellion'. Monroe was closely aligned with Jefferson and James Madison and the developing Democratic-Republican Party, but President Jefferson rejected Monroe's suggestion that discontented slaves be placed far away in the American West.

President Jefferson sent Monroe to Europe, where, possibly in conjunction with Ambassador Livingston, he acquired the Louisiana Territory from France. While Monroe's instructions were to offer a maximum $9 million for New Orleans and West Florida, he instead obtained the Louisiana Territory for $15 million – one million square miles at four cents per acre. Jefferson was delighted, but rejected Monroe's suggestion that he send troops to acquire Florida.

In 1812, after the desperate British Navy had been impressing American citizens to serve in the Napoleonic Wars and the British were allying with Indian nations in the disputed western territories, President Madison declared war on Britain. Madison became so obviously dependent on Monroe for the prosecution of the war and negotiation of the peace that Monroe emerged from the war as a national hero and was elected as the fifth President of the United States in 1816.

President Monroe (1817–25)

In his inaugural address, Monroe promised to promote national unity, the economy and the defence of the nation. He proved quite successful in doing so.

'Madison's War' had caused considerable disunity, so Monroe chose Cabinet members of all political persuasions, and undertook a tour of the nation in which he was ostentatiously friendly towards Federalists such as John Adams of Massachusetts. The tour proved a great success with the general public and contributed to his unopposed re-election in 1820.

Slavery was another great threat to national unity. Although a slave-holder himself, Monroe said, 'The God who made us, made the black people, and they ought not to be treated with barbarity.' When the question of whether Missouri should be admitted to the Union as a slave-holding state arose in 1819, Monroe wrote to Thomas Jefferson that this issue constituted the greatest threat yet to the peace and continuation of the Union. While Monroe told his Cabinet to keep out of the Missouri Question, he personally favoured the American Colonisation Society's suggestion that slaves should be emancipated and then emigrate to Africa. When Congress financed the Society's purchase of what became the African state of Liberia in 1821, Monroe's support was acknowledged in the naming of Liberia's capital as Monrovia.

GENDER EQUALITY

Monroe was more enlightened about women than most of his contemporaries. He visited the Nashville Female Academy on his national tour, at a time when the education of women was highly controversial.

President Monroe contributed to general prosperity by his promotion of the construction of a National Road that facilitated westward expansion, and his support for the abolition of internal taxation (the federal government was financed by the sale of lands in the West). As yet, though, the president had no power to intervene in events such as the economic downturn of 1819.

It was in the area of what Monroe called national defence that his presidency was most significant. He worked hard and successfully to clarify, secure and expand the borders of the United States. During 1817–18, it was agreed with Britain that the forty-ninth parallel was the boundary between the United States and Canada and that the British and Americans would demilitarise the Great Lakes. Another problematic frontier was that with Florida, which Spain was struggling to control. Florida-based pirates and Seminole Indians were raiding Georgia, so Monroe sent General Andrew Jackson to solve the problem. Jackson in effect occupied Florida. There was some unrest in Congress because Jackson had disobeyed the orders of the Secretary of War and undermined Congress's constitutional authority to declare war, but Monroe encouraged and supported Jackson and most Americans were delighted when the United States negotiated the acquisition of Florida from Spain in 1819. Spain also ceded all claims to the Pacific Northwest.

Spain's decline was further illustrated in 1822, when several Latin American republics declared their independence. When France threatened to help Spain recapture them, Monroe (and, some say, John Quincy Adams) warned the European powers against trying to recolonise Latin America or establish new colonies in the western hemisphere. Most Americans approved of this 'Monroe Doctrine'. In a final securing of US borders, in 1824, the Monroe administration obtained Russia's agreement to abandon any claims on the Pacific Northwest Coast south of the borders of present-day Alaska.

During Monroe's presidency, the frontiers between the United States and British, Spanish and Russian possessions were settled and the territory of the United States greatly increased. This was accomplished with minimal expenditure and military exertion. Overall, given his service to the nation, it seems highly appropriate that the date of Monroe's death in 1831 was 4 July.

While the expansion of the United States owed much to famous individuals of Welsh descent such as Thomas Jefferson, Meriwether Lewis and James Monroe, it perhaps owed more to the tens or even hundreds of thousands of Welsh and Welsh American individuals who settled on the ever-moving frontiers of the new nation.

CHAPTER SEVEN

❧

THE WELSH GO WEST

WELSH PIONEER farmers helped tame the frontier and make it productive. They shared and contributed to the perpetuation of the values of courage, hard work and religiosity that were important in the making of a wealthy and expansionist America.

The late eighteenth century saw the first surge in Welsh immigration to the new nation. Farmers in Wales had long suffered at the hands of landlords who raised rents and enclosed common land, but the 1790s were a particularly painful time. That decade saw frequent crop failures, heavy taxation to finance the French wars, the persecution of those who sympathised with radicals such as the French revolutionaries, and the revival of belief in the Madoc legend. These factors fuelled a desire to create a new and better Wales in America. In 1795, according to the self-styled America expert William Jones (who rarely left his Llangadfan parish), 'Emigration is now become almost epidemical.'

Leading Welsh preachers such as Christmas Evans criticised those who left the traditions and land of their fathers, but Welsh emigration to America continued through much of the nineteenth century. The motivation, experiences and achievements of the Welsh emigrants are well documented in the many surviving letters written by the emigrants to family and friends back home in Wales and in the contemporary publications about Wales and Welsh Americans.

GETTING TO AMERICA

The determination of Welsh emigrants is well illustrated in an account written by George Roberts. Roberts was one of a group that came from the Llanbrynmair area in Montgomeryshire and was led by the clockmaker Ezekiel Hughes.

In 1793, Hughes led a small group of would-be emigrants to Liverpool. They found a ship bound for America, but were hauled off it under the law forbidding the emigration of skilled craftsmen. That prompted an American sea captain to shout, 'There is your boasted British liberty!' In 1795, Hughes arranged for the *Maria*, a vessel from Salem, Massachusetts, to transport his party from Bristol to Philadelphia. His party of ten walked from Llanbrynmair to Carmarthen, which took four days. The *Maria* was too big to sail up the River Towy, so Hughes commissioned a smaller vessel to take the party to Bristol. Britain was at war with France and desperate for men, so when the party learned that a press-gang was at anchor in the river, the men decided it would be safer to walk to Bristol. That walk took them eight days. After three weeks of waiting in vain for a suitable wind for sailing from Llanstephan, the women started the walk to Swansea. They found a ship bound for Bristol and one month after they had first walked from Llanbrynmair, the party was reunited. Their vessel carried fifty emigrants, all but three of whom were Welsh. It arrived in Philadelphia ten weeks later. There they made contact with the Glamorgan-born Rev. Morgan John Rhys, who was organising a new Welsh settlement in America.

Along with Bristol, emigrants also left from Welsh ports such as Swansea, Caernarvon, Newquay and Cardigan, and from the English port of Liverpool. Sometimes the shipowners struggled to meet the demand. Hugh Pugh, from Castell Hen, Bala, described people from Merionethshire devastated to find the Liverpool ships full in 1847 – 'Thousands are coming here and are having to return without a place.'

EMIGRATION STATISTICS

The population of Wales was 587,000 in 1801, 1.6 million in 1851 and 2.4 million in 1911. Statisticians suggest that emigration was relatively unimportant in the context of the total Welsh population, especially in comparison to somewhere such as Ireland. However, Welsh emigration depopulated whole rural communities. In 1857, Samuel Roberts recorded in his magazine Y Cronicl, 'Of those born in Llanbrynmair during the last half-century there are more presently residing in America than there are in Llanbrynmair.'

Just a few examples of voyages suggest large numbers: one vessel left Caernarvon with 300 emigrants in 1796; the North Wales Chronicle reported that the Chieftain left Bangor in 1846 with 200 emigrants bound for Wisconsin; the Welsh American publication Y Cenhadwr reported that 200 (another source said 400) emigrants left Aberystwyth in the 700-ton Tamerlane in 1847; the steamship Jamestown arrived in New York with 274 Welsh people and 90 others on board after a four-week voyage in 1849.

The transatlantic crossing averaged six weeks in the days of sail, but the advent of steamships in the mid-nineteenth century cut the time to around two weeks. There were many fatalities aboard the sailing ships, and religious services were often held on the quayside. In 1839, hundreds congregated at Aberaeron harbour to pray for and bid farewell to the 170 Welsh people leaving on their long and perilous journey to the United States.

From 1840, emigrants could access printed guidebooks containing practical advice on how to prepare for the voyage, such as,

Figure 14. *The* Tamerlane, *upon which 700-ton vessel several hundred Welsh emigrants left Aberystwyth in 1847.*

> It is best for the Welsh to prepare bread, and oatmeal, butter, cheese and meat before leaving home. Tea, coffee, sugar, treacle and salt can be obtained in Liverpool. Food for six or eight weeks needs to be prepared; too much is better than too little, but the remainder will be useful after reaching New York.

Food and water were often scarce by the end of the voyage. It took the Rev. Jenkin Jenkins's vessel three months to cross the Atlantic in 1841. Towards the end of the voyage, Jenkins recorded, 'For eight days we were living on one biscuit a day along with a little water.' In 1844, John Pugh wrote of how 'we are making every effort to catch the rainwater'. The advent of steamships and shorter journeys did not solve all the problems: Rowland Brees of Ohio wrote to his mother in Wales in 1852 that the worst part of the voyage was that the 900 passengers had only twelve places where they could prepare food.

Conditions below the deck of a sailing ship were extremely unpleasant. When the hatches were closed during the frequent Atlantic storms, the air grew suffocating and stale, and stank even more than usual. In 1794, the Rev. Morgan John Rhys described a storm:

> The wind turns and all the people, men, women and children begin to sicken . . . The women begin to howl, and the dishes begin to roll, the children begin to cry, and the men began to waver, and my bowels begin to fight with all the food that is needed to support nature.

Below deck was crowded, confined and unhygienic. Jim Warner was one of the 249 Welsh Mormon passengers on board the *Buena Vista* in 1849. He described the 6 foot by 3 foot berths for two as 'our "dog kennels"'. Dysentery was common, and cholera and typhus also spread on these 'coffin ships'. In 1801, George Roberts recorded that 48 died on a Baltimore-bound vessel, and 53 out of 102 passengers on his sisters' ship died at sea. In 1849, one-fifth of the *Buena Vista*'s passengers died of cholera. Conditions on sailing ships were so bad that from the 1840s, the British government promoted legislation to try to ensure more room, food and accommodation for the sick. Even then, there were too few inspectors to enforce legislation. There were inevitable accidents: throughout her many years of life in Ohio, Mary Davies never recovered from the death on the voyage of her youngest daughter, caused by burns from scalding hot coffee.

Some ships were barely seaworthy. The grandparents and mother of the famous architect Frank Lloyd Wright suffered a traumatic transatlantic voyage in which their ship was hit by gales, lost its mainmast and had to return to Liverpool. It eventually arrived in New York with its sails in shreds and its hull leaking. The trauma did not end there. Frank Lloyd Wright's grandfather, Richard Lloyd Jones, was fleeced by a money changer in New York, to whom he had been introduced by a Welsh-speaker. Appalling weather then forced the Lloyd Jones family to spend the freezing winter of 1844–5 in the Welsh community in Utica, New York. When they set off too early in the spring, their three-year-old daughter Nanny caught cold and died.

WHY EMIGRATE FROM WALES?

In 1841, after twenty years in America, one Welsh emigrant wrote: 'In going to America there are many difficulties to overcome – leaving one's native land, travelling over the sea, learning a new language, new customs – in a word, to go to America, is a revolution in a man's life.' The emigrants wrote freely of their economic, religious, political and social motivation in undertaking that revolution.

Cheaper and better land

Many Welsh emigrants were motivated by economic considerations. Most of those who emigrated in the 1790s and the first half of the nineteenth century were farmers. Many of them found America to be the land of plenty and opportunity for which they had hoped. In the early years of Welsh emigration to Paddy's Run, Ohio, land could be purchased for as little as $1.25 per acre. Welsh emigrants worked hard, so that by 1852, according to the Welsh-born Congregational minister the Rev. Robert D. Thomas, Paddy's Run contained 'Welsh settlers worth thousands of dollars'. J. R. Daniel, an early Welsh settler at Proscairon, Green Lake County, Wisconsin, said in old age, 'A question asked of me many times was: what advantage was there in settling in a place so new and disadvantageous. Our answer was, cheapness of land.' Back in Wales, there was little or no available land because most was already possessed by landlords who demanded exorbitant rents from their tenant farmers. In sharp contrast, large quantities of free or cheap land were available in America to those who developed a farm under the terms of legislation such as the Pre-emption Act (1841) and Homestead Act (1862). Furthermore, much of the available land in America was more fertile than in much of Wales. In 1872, Joseph Jones of Arvonia, Kansas, declared that the Welsh had been 'foolish to remain under the thumb of their landlords, fighting for old, stony farms, hilly and brambly, when there are hundreds of good farms here'. Ironically, though, the very poorest in Wales could rarely afford to emigrate, and it was those with a little more money who did so. 'Myriads would emigrate if they had the money,' wrote William Richards in Newcastle Emlyn in 1801.

In 1850, the Rev. John Phillips preached to the 375 Welsh on board the steamer *Forest Queen* as it left Liverpool. His sermon, summarised in the Congregationalist monthly *Y Cenhadwr Americanaidd*, demonstrated the combination of economic and religious motivation of many emigrants. He lamented how in Wales, 'Rents are high, taxes are high, tithes are repressive and the prices of [the products of] the soil are remarkably low.' He also urged them to hold fast to their religion.

Religious and political freedom

Many emigrated for religious reasons. Most Welsh people belonged to Protestant nonconformist denominations and resented paying the tithe to support the established Anglican Church. One emigrant wrote, 'The only time that people mention the tithe is to give thanks that no such oppression exists in Ohio.' George Roberts emphasised the religious motivation behind Baptist minister Morgan John Rhys's Welsh settlement of Beulah in western Pennsylvania: 'Our end in establishing this settlement was for the general good of the Welsh, particularly that they may have the privilege of hearing the gospel in their own language.'

Morgan John Rhys (1760–1804) was one of the many with both religious and political motivation for emigration. He explained that he fled the British government's 'persecuting spirit' towards political and religious dissidents who advocated the separation of Church and state, criticised the monarchy and lauded the French revolutionaries. In a 1794 Welsh-language pamphlet, he urged emigration to America, 'a new world in which justice dwells', and recommended that those left in Wales should 'Quit the little despotic island which gave you birth, and leave the tyrants and slaves of your country to live and die together'.

A WELSH FREEDOM FIGHTER AT THE ALAMO?

If the historical detective work of journalist John Humphries is to be believed, Tredegar stonemason John Rees fought in the 'People's Army' in Texas, defending the Alamo during the struggle for independence from Mexico in 1836. According to Humphries, Rees then returned to Wales and participated in the Chartists' unsuccessful Newport Rising of 1839 (the Chartists sought political equality). Humphries then traces Rees's escape to the United States, his contribution to the building of a church in Brooklyn and his gold mining in California, where he died aged 78 in 1893.

Social equality

In 1816, Hugh and Catherine Thomas of Oneida County, New York, assured acquaintances in Wales, 'The ordinary man in America will get respect according to his deserts [sic] not according to his wealth.' The Bala-born Congregationalist Rev. Benjamin Chidlaw said his father had heard tell of America as a 'free and virtuous country, with neither monarchy nor title and where poor people could buy farms'. David Watkins worked down a coal mine near Youngstown, Ohio, during the American Civil War. He said:

> It is wonderful to live in a free country where the rights of men are upheld, one weighing as much as the next in the scales, with no difference between rich and poor and if you happen to meet

the two on the street it would be difficult to say which was the gentleman. There is none of the pride or the inferiority of the workmen here.

Henry Davis immigrated to Wisconsin, where he was delighted to find 'snobbery. . . far less evident'. He then settled in Illinois, and in 1871 wrote approvingly that 'there is a feeling of equality stronger than in Wales. There is less snobbery and less servility.' Welsh-born Captain David Evans happened to find himself seated alongside President Ulysses S. Grant in Washington's Metropolitan Methodist Church. Evans felt 'it does one good to see the chief magistrate of a great nation like another human being, not putting on some artificials [sic] to endeavour to make himself something above human.'

America fever

The people in Wales were bombarded by enthusiastic letters from friends and family who had emigrated and now urged them to do the same. In 1910, Welsh-born J. Edno Roberts of Oshkosh, Wisconsin, recalled how the Welsh came to Wisconsin in the 1840s and 1850s: 'It was a hard time in Wales in those years and many enthusiastic letters came from America . . . This was the main reason according to my dear mother, namely the positive letters from those who came here first.'

In 1865, Morris Peat wrote to his brother Edward of Llanbrynmair of the joys of life in Ohio: 'Whoever comes here of the same age as I was when I came will surely be sorely regretful. Not for coming here but that they did not come here sooner.' Edward duly emigrated in 1868 and wrote home from Gomer, Ohio, that life was much easier in America, where people were 'full of food'. In sharp contrast to Wales, he said, the drive to get on in America was such that 'nobody here dreads being in debt . . . This country shows men that there is such an opportunity to "make oneself rich" that not many drown while getting on in the world.' A letter that Welshman Thomas Evans wrote home in 1844 was published in Wales. He wrote that Wisconsin had 'plenty of farmland . . . There is no work to be done cutting down large trees . . . One can have [land] for a year without paying through pre-emption rights and many have lived on farms here for four years without paying a penny.' John and Margred Owen emigrated from near Dolgellau in Merionethshire in 1845–6, stopped for a while in Ohio, then settled in Baraboo, Sauk County, Wisconsin. 'We are only sorry that we did not come earlier,' they wrote to relations in Wales.'

THE 1850 US CENSUS

This census recorded 29,868 Welsh-born living in the United States, 89 per cent of whom were in New York, Pennsylvania, Ohio and Wisconsin. The number was probably inaccurate, for these were the early days of recording a far-flung population and many Welsh were considered 'English'.

The role of the clergy

The nonconformist clergy were probably the most respected group in Welsh society, and many of them urged emigration. During 1840–60, scores of Montgomeryshire Welsh emigrated to America, and many of them were tenant farmers inspired by the anti-landlordism preaching of the Congregationalist Samuel Roberts. Roberts compared the 'fruitless slopes' of north Wales to 'the wealthy valleys of Ohio and Missouri'.

Another great recruiter was the Rev. Robert Chidlaw. Raised in Ohio by his Welsh immigrant parents, Chidlaw made lengthy visits to Wales in 1835 and 1839. His preaching encouraged further Welsh emigration. Edward Pryce recalled how

> I came to Columbus [Ohio] in 1840 . . . A lad of seven years. The Welsh in that period were nearly all from Montgomeryshire. Reverend B.W. Chidlaw put us in the notion of coming to America. Chidlaw told us of the great advantages for raising children in America. My mother took it all in . . . and she decided then and there to come here. Father objected, but mother prevailed and we came . . . arriving in Columbus in June 1840.

In 1840, Chidlaw published *Yr American*, which gave practical advice to would-be immigrants.

Between 1835 and 1850, an estimated 3,000 emigrants from rural Cardiganshire emigrated to 'Little Cardiganshire' in south-eastern Ohio. Many were responding to the advice of the Cardiganshire-born Calvinistic Methodist Rev. Edward Jones, who in 1833 recommended Jackson and Gallia counties for Welsh settlement. Jones also praised Licking County, Ohio, where there were around 800 Welsh in the Welsh Hills settlement by 1843, as 'an excellent place for serving-men and workmen', where 'some who had failed to get enough milk, potatoes, and barley bread in Wales, had their fill and to spare of wheat bread and other fruits'.

The Congregationalist minister Robert D. Thomas, born in Llanrwst, Denbighshire, toured the Welsh American settlements in 1851–2 and emigrated in 1855. In 1872, his *Hanes Cymry America* (*History of the Welsh in America*) was published in Utica. It contained practical tips for immigrants and sold well in Wales.

The best-known of the Welshmen who dreamed of establishing a new and better Wales in America, were the Baptist minister Morgan John Rhys and Congregationalist minister Samuel Roberts.

Morgan John Rhys and Cambria, Pennsylvania

So great was the number of emigrants that Morgan John Rhys struggled to find a ship. He eventually sailed from Liverpool in 1794, and arrived in New York after an extremely unpleasant ten-week crossing. He was welcomed by the Welsh Baptist network which then aided his travels in search of suitable land for a new Wales. During his travels, he began to spell his name Rhees.

Rhys was greatly impressed by the freedom of worship that he observed in America, for 'even a Baptist here may preach in an Episcopalian pulpit without polluting it. The curse of religious establishments has been banished from the land.' However, when he toured the South, he was shocked to find slavery flourishing and decided that no self-respecting Welsh settlement could live in this region. He wondered how George Washington, that 'great defender of liberty', could keep slaves. 'This is a Land of Liberty full of slaves . . . My God! Is this the land that thou hast consecrated to liberty? . . . O America be ready to meet thy God.'

Rhys felt more comfortable in the North. As he travelled through the Northwest Territory, he was very conscious of the Madoc story. He visited an old hilltop fortification alongside the Ohio River and said it was an exact likeness of old castles in Wales. He inspected an ancient barrow and concluded, 'If the Ancient Britons did not live here, people of similar custom have.' He found badly broken-up stone and thought the inscription on it was most likely Welsh.

Rhys met General Anthony Wayne, observed the signing of the Treaty of Greenville, then preached a controversial sermon to an audience of soldiers. He urged 'purchase of the soil from the Indians' and their conversion to Christianity. He lamented that 'the frontiers of America' contained 'a great number of white as well as red savages'. That went down badly with Wayne's Baptist chaplain David Jones. Jones noted in his diary that the sermon was 'not well suited to our ideas on the foundation of American rights to the soil. Men should avoid speaking on subjects they do not understand or they will give offence to men who know better.' Jones always considered himself more Welsh than such 'new' Welsh as Morgan John Rhys, and his hostility seems to have contributed to Rhys's decision that he had better 'retreat' to the east. This was unfortunate, as Rhys had considered the Ohio area suitable for Welsh settlers owing to its fertility and proximity to what he believed were the Welsh Indians.

In the end, the pressure of the great numbers of Welsh immigrants pouring into Philadelphia and Rhys's friendship with Dr Benjamin Rush combined to encourage him to purchase land from Rush. The land was 200 miles west of Philadelphia and beyond the Allegheny Mountains in western Pennsylvania. In 1798, Rhys established his Cambria ('Wales') settlement, centred upon the township of Beulah ('heavenly place'). He advertised the availability of land lots in Beulah for those 'who have an enterprising spirit and are willing, for a few years, to undergo and surmount difficulties in the acquirement of independence'.

The 'difficulties' in Beulah proved great: harsh winters, stony ground and some factious individuals. Rhys noted, 'Mrs Phillips has followed her husband down the country . . . we all hope she never will return.' Rees Lloyd, a Carmarthenshire-born Independent minister, eventually conceded that

> it is too hard for poor people [to] make a living upon this land on the account of its heavy clearing and slow producings. It require[s] a great deal of money and a strong team and to buy their provisions the twice or thrice first years. I cannot with a clear conscience to encourage my poor countrymen to depend much on this place.

Lloyd encouraged an exodus from Beulah to Cambria's other township, Ebensburg, and Beulah did not long survive Rhys's death in 1804.

Samuel Roberts and Brynffynon, Tennessee

On a single day in 1852, Dissenting minister Samuel Roberts of Llanbrynmair saw ninety-nine people leave Llanbrynmair for America. One of the many who had left there was his uncle, George Roberts, who settled in Ebensburg, Pennsylvania. Samuel Roberts declared oppressive landlords to be 'our main reason for leaving'. The sustained Welsh exodus inspired him to try to encourage all Welsh emigrants to settle together in a new Wales in the United States. He bought 100,000 acres in eastern

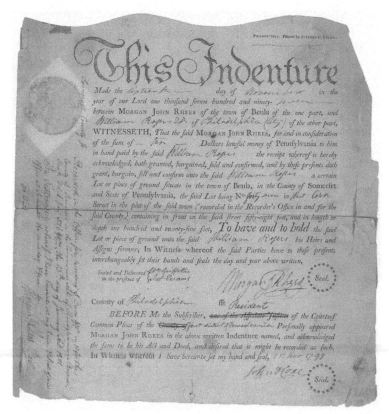

Figure 15. *A 1797 grant for land in Beulah, made out to one William Rogers of Philadelphia, and signed by 'Morgan John Rhees'.*

Tennessee in 1856 and in 1857 sailed from Liverpool on a vessel carrying around 150 Welsh people.

One of Samuel Roberts's cousins was William Bebb, Governor of Ohio from 1846 to 1848. His father, Edward Bebb, had accompanied Ezekiel Hughes from Llanbrynmair to America and eventually settled at Paddy's Run, Ohio. William purchased land in Tennessee for Roberts to establish a Welsh settlement to be known as Brynffynon.

However, there were problems over land rights and the ground was difficult to cultivate. As a result, the Brynffynon settlement failed to flourish, and within a year two families from Llanbrynmair had departed and joined relations in Ohio. John Roberts Jones of Ohio wrote to his uncle Samuel Roberts:

> I should be pleased if I had never seen Mr Bebb . . . and if I had
> never heard of Tennessee . . . it cannot be denied, we have all been
> disappointed in our venture . . . Mr Bebb was very wicked, urging
> us to buy land in Tennessee without knowing more about it, and
> the Titles so uncertain. He should have been the first to settle there
> . . . I do not and have not seen him fulfilling any of his promises,
> and it is my studied opinion that he had nothing more in mind
> when he drew our attention to the land but his own pocket.

Perhaps Bebb had been distracted. A shooting incident had taken place in his Illinois home in 1857 and he was faced with a long trial and retrial on the charge of manslaughter. Whoever was to blame for the difficulties, they were great. Samuel Roberts's brother Richard explained to an admirer of his poetry that farming a densely wooded area had so drained his creativity that he had stopped writing his Welsh verse.

When Tennessee was much fought over during the American Civil War, Samuel Roberts's dream was finally destroyed. He was a pacifist and his opposition to what he called 'the raging madness of the Civil War in America' turned both Confederates and Unionists against him. He returned to Wales in 1866.

THE WELSH ON THE EAST COAST

Until the late eighteenth century, Welsh emigrants congregated relatively close to the Atlantic coast. Most spoke only Welsh, so they stuck together in close communities such as those in Pennsylvania, in New York City, and in Utica, Steuben and Remsen in Oneida County in upstate New York, where the settlers were mostly from north Wales.

The Welsh in Oneida County, upstate New York

Several families arrived from Wales in 1795 and settled in Steuben. In 1801, around one hundred immigrants from south Wales settled in Utica and Steuben. The Welsh in Oneida County had told people back home that land was cheap and fertile, and large numbers of Welsh immigrants arrived in the years 1817–21, when Britain experienced great economic problems following the Napoleonic Wars. By 1832, John Lewis of Utica recorded the presence of 'hundreds of our brethren from the North [of Wales]', most of whom were farmers.

Those who focused on dairy farming gained a reputation for excellent butter. Some families combined farming with the unlimited road and canal construction jobs that Lewis noted were available for them. Another influx was triggered by the great famine of 1848. In 1859, an estimated seven-eighths of the population of Remsen and Steuben was Welsh. Most had come directly from Wales, but some came from Welsh settlements in Pennsylvania where land was more expensive. An estimated three thousand Welsh lived in Steuben and Remsen in 1872, although the Rev. R. D. Thomas recorded that this number was lower than before, because the Homestead Acts had encouraged many to go in search of cheaper land in Iowa, Kansas, Minnesota and Wisconsin.

THE WELSH IN NEW YORK CITY

The Rev. William Davies Evans recorded in 1880 that 'many Welsh people live in New York and the surrounding area'.

Many Welsh prospered in New York State. The potential for upward mobility was demonstrated by the descendants of Jenkin Evans. Jenkin was born near Cilcennin, Cardiganshire, in 1830. He was the son of a labourer and was working as a servant when he met Gwenllian Rees in 1849. They emigrated to America in 1870 and joined other members of their family in south-western New York State. They lived in Freedom and Farmersville, Cattaraugus County, and Hume, Allegany County. Their son Evan Evans, born near Lampeter in south-west Wales, became a Presbyterian minister after having studied at the prestigious Princeton University, amongst other institutions. His son Paul Evans obtained his MA and Ph.D. at Cornell, taught at Yale amongst other places, and in 1914 wrote an account of the Welsh in upstate New York.

EMIGRATION? FORGET IT!

In 1856, Evan Evans wrote from Turin in Lewis County, New York, to his uncle back home in Merionethshire. The transatlantic voyage had made him seasick, and he thought the land seemed very barren and 'unpleasant'. He lamented the absence of any nearby Welsh chapel and amidst his overwhelming homesickness he advised his brother John to stay in Wales, or he would live to regret his emigration scheme.

FROM THE EAST COAST TO THE WEST COAST

The traditional areas of Welsh settlement in states such as Pennsylvania and New York continued to attract Welsh immigrants during the nineteenth century, but as the United States expanded, a steady stream of new Welsh immigrants and many Welsh Americans moved westward where the land was far cheaper. When Morgan John Rhys visited Pencader in Delaware in 1794, he noted, 'This is part of the Welsh tract formerly inhabited by some of our countrymen. There are but few even of their descendants there at present. The soil was perhaps too poor . . . they have removed to the South and West, and scattered over the continent.' In 1838, Evan Davies wrote to his brother in Wales that the future lay to the West: 'A family can make more profit here in three years than can be made in 20 years in the eastern states ... there is nothing to do but enclose the land with a hedge and then plough and sow.' Similarly, Owen Williams of Olney, Illinois, wrote home to Wales in 1851:

> The craftsmen and merchants who have plenty of money and settle in the states of New York, New Jersey, Pennsylvania, Virginia, Ohio, etc, can do well. But ordinary workmen, like those in Wales, would be better off emigrating to Wisconsin, Iowa, Indiana, Illinois, Michigan, etc.

'THOMAS OWEN SAVES CHICAGO'

Ezra Owen was born in Virginia in 1770 to a Welsh immigrant. He followed the frontier to Kentucky, fought alongside Daniel Boone, then settled in Illinois in 1810. His son Thomas Owen was elected to Congress in 1830, helped establish the prestigious Catholic Notre Dame University, and was appointed Indian Agent. As such, he staved off a potential Indian War in 1832, so that in *Thomas Owen: Chicago's True Founder* (1934), J. R. Haydon's second chapter is headed 'Owen saves Chicago'.

Ohio

From the early nineteenth century, many Welsh farmers settled in Ohio. Ezekiel Hughes and his cousin Edward Bebb camped out for four years while waiting for the government to put the land west of Ohio's Great Miami River on the market. The land they bought in 1801 became the community of Paddy's Run in Butler County in south-eastern Ohio. They were probably the first Welshmen to settle in Ohio, but other

Welsh settlements were soon established in the Welsh Hills (1801) and Radnor (1804) in central Ohio, in Jackson and Gallia Counties (1818) in south-western Ohio, and in Gomer (1833) and Venedocia (1848) in the north-west. By 1850, there were over five thousand Welsh immigrants in the state. Most were engaged in agriculture and some were exceptionally successful. Thomas Jones immigrated to Ohio in 1823 and became a leading stock raiser. Some moved on from farming. John R. Hughes emigrated from north Wales in 1848. At the age of nineteen he was working as a farm hand in Granville, Ohio, but he soon set up a business making trunks and eventually became a leading banker and investor in Columbus. Some of the Welsh immigrants were craftsmen. Cardiganshire-born shoemaker Thomas B. Jones, who immigrated to Ohio in 1856 'without means', eventually employed fourteen others in the making of boots and shoes.

'SHE HATED HER WELSH FATHER'

The Welsh played a considerable part in making America religiously conservative. In 1983, seventy-five-year-old American journalist Harrison Salisbury wrote in his memoirs that his mother hated growing up amongst the puritanical Welsh Calvinists in Jackson County, Ohio. Her father, Evan Evans 'Straightback' (he rode exceptionally upright upon his horse), had come to Ohio as a child from Cardiganshire. 'She hated her Welsh father, the Welshness of him, his hymn-singing, his Sabbath-keeping, prayer meetings, hellfire and damnation.'

Wisconsin and Minnesota

Among the many small Welsh farming settlements in Wisconsin were those in and near Racine on Lake Michigan, in Iowa County in the south-west, and in the Spring Green settlement, which would produce America's greatest architect, Frank Lloyd Wright. In 1847, John and Isaac Cheshire wrote from Racine to their parents in Wales, 'There are about five hundred Welshmen living in this town.' In the 1850s, some Welsh settled in Iowa County, while in 1855–7, around 150 Welsh people migrated from Jackson and Gallia Counties in Ohio to the rich Minnesota farmlands of Blue Earth and Le Sueur Counties. The much-admired Montgomeryshire-born preacher, the Rev. Richard Davies, encouraged them in their search for better and cheaper land.

Minnesota sometimes disappointed the Welsh. Edward Morris emigrated from Llanddeiniol to Ohio in 1837, then went on to Minnesota in 1856. However, his family spent only a few weeks in Blue Earth, and blamed the mosquitoes for driving them out. Another Welsh settler described Minnesota's mosquitoes as 'the size of geese'. Nevertheless, Blue Earth and Le Sueur Counties attracted so many Welsh immigrants that by the 1880s there were nearly three thousand attending Welsh American churches in the area.

PIONEERING WOMEN IN WISCONSIN

Jane R. Jones of Iowa County, Wisconsin, was widowed in 1863 but went on to establish a cheese factory as dairy farming gained in importance in the state. She subsequently diversified, opening a dress shop selling 'Millinery and Dress Goods of the latest fashions' in Barneveld in 1881. This eventually morphed into a general store.

Frank Lloyd Wright's aunt by marriage, **Esther Lloyd Jones**, was interested in women's rights and attended a Women's Congress in Madison.

Rachel Davies (1846–1915) was born in Anglesey. A preacher from the age of twenty, she immigrated to the United States in 1866 and married Cardiganshire-born Edward Davies of Waterton, Wisconsin. At the age of forty-four, she became the first female ordained as a minister in Wisconsin. On a lengthy visit back to Wales, she campaigned on behalf of David Lloyd George. Her son Joseph E. Davies was US ambassador to the Soviet Union and did much to maintain the uneasy Second World War alliance between the two countries.

'GENUINELY RELIGIOUS WELSH'

The 1947 Centennial Report of Oshkosh, Wisconsin rather puzzlingly declared that 'Wisconsin is recognized as one of the most Dutch and German states in the Union, but to supplement them, God led a strong delegation of genuinely religious Welsh to the state.'

From Missouri to the Pacific Northwest

When in 1862 the Lincoln administration passed an act granting 163 cheap acres to settlers, many Welsh farmworkers raced to Minnesota and further west to acquire land. In 1864, the Rev. R. M. Evans urged Welsh Americans to go to 'the Welsh settlement in the northern part of Missouri'. He rejoiced that 'so many' of them had 'cheaply' acquired land and homes in the New Cambria settlement in the 'rich and fertile land'. Between 1864 and 1870, over 240 Welsh families settled in Missouri.

Figure 16a and 16b. *A postcard of Bethel Welsh Church, Wymore, Nebraska, built in 1879. In 1910, this postcard, reproduced courtesy of Mrs Gladys Jones Rumbaugh, was sent by Mr and Mrs Robert E. Jones of Wymore, Nebraska, to Mrs Eunice Davies of Crawfordsville in south-eastern Iowa, an area that contained many Welsh settlers. Wymore, Nebraska, is home to the Great Plains Welsh Heritage Project, the only museum on the North American continent dedicated to the settlement of Welsh immigrants on the Great Plains.*

Not all of them focused on farming. John T. Davies wrote home of New Cambria in 1870, 'Many here working on the railroad are from the neighbourhood of Pontypridd and Llantrisant.'

In the 1860s and 1870s, Welsh settlers arrived in Kansas: around two thousand immigrants from Wales and nearly six thousand second-generation Welsh Americans farmed there, especially near the towns of Arvonia, Bala and Emporia. In 1868, an Emporia newspaper noted: 'The Welsh in this vicinity are both an exceedingly industrious and also a religious people, bringing their principles with them from the mountains and the mines of the fatherland, and constitute a very valuable element in our community.'

In 1869, however, the Rev. Hugh Hughes lamented that some Welsh in Arvonia had 'bought very poor land from the land sharks'. He noted that 'the Welsh hire themselves out to other races' and wished that they would 'be more pushing and not let other races get ahead of them'.

Some went further west to Nebraska or South Dakota. Some moved to Oregon and Washington state, where a group of Welsh American fruit growers pioneered orchard industries. In 1891, William D. Davies found one Wisconsin Welsh settlement 'most deserted', because many had migrated further west to Minnesota, Iowa, South Dakota and Washington. Meanwhile, the flood of Welsh farmer emigrants had been reduced to a trickle as conditions had improved in agricultural areas in Wales – partly because so many farmers had emigrated.

Gold in California and Nevada

While many of the Welsh emigrants were lured by cheap American land, some went in search of gold. Nineteenth-century America experienced multiple gold rushes. The California Gold Rush (1849–51) attracted Welsh miners and shop owners. In 1852, eight men left the Wisconsin settlement of Proscairon to search for gold in California. By 1863, one correspondent estimated that there were fifteen thousand Welshmen mining for gold there. In 1862, John Davies wrote from Sierra County that there were 'more Welshmen than any other nation', but in 1864 he wrote from Sacramento County, 'There may be Welshmen but nothing in comparison with other nations.' Still, he said, 'The Welsh and Cornish earn higher wages than other nations because they are better at working loose earth.' There is no doubt that considerable numbers of Welsh settled in northern California, especially in the Sierra Nevada and the Sacramento Valley. As a result, one-quarter of Amador County residents have Welsh ancestry. As late as 1871, Welshmen were operating fifteen large-scale gold mining projects in California, the most successful of which was the long-established Snowdon Hill Mine.

Nevada made at least two Welshmen fairly affluent. Lewis Humphreys was born in 1835 in Penybanc, Carmarthenshire. He emigrated to America in 1855 and lived in Youngstown, Ohio, then in Kentucky. In 1859 he joined an expedition to Pikes Peak in what is now Colorado. A newspaper reported that the expedition was organised by a Welsh company in search of gold. Humphreys recorded with distaste how on his journey west 'we were forced to cook our food on dried animal dung that is called by those who cross the prairie *buffalo chips*'. The expedition met people returning home disappointed because they had not found any gold, so Humphreys turned back before reaching Pikes Peak. In 1860, he was working in the coal mines. He hoped to fight in the Civil War (1861–5), but a bad knee confined his service to the Home Guards. In 1866, he travelled west by steamboat and then stagecoach to Virginia City, Nevada, where he mined for gold. In 1869, while in Lawrence, Kansas, he sent his gold to the US Mint and received $6,000 for it. He heard that there was a Welsh community in Arvonia, Kansas, and settled there. Aberystwyth-born lead miner John Jones also struck it rich in Nevada. As there were several others named John Jones, he called himself 'January Jones'. He eventually employed over two hundred men in his eleven Nevada gold mines.

Utah

In 1840, Flintshire-born Dan Jones emigrated to Illinois and became captain of a vessel that transported settlers along the Ohio and Mississippi Rivers. While transporting Mormons in 1843, he met Joseph Smith, founder of the Church of Latter-day Saints (also known as the Mormon Church). Captain Dan Jones visited Smith in jail the night before Smith was killed, and had Smith not sent him on an errand, Jones too might have died. In his famous 'final prophecy', Smith urged Jones to go to Wales to convert the Welsh, so Jones made missionary tours in 1845 and 1852. He concentrated on the iron- and coal-producing area in and around Merthyr Tydfil. As this was a time of high unemployment, Jones's boast that he had converted over 900 by 1847 and 4,654 by late 1848 appears feasible. One of the most important of recent Mormon leaders, Gordon B. Hinckley, asserted that Jones 'must certainly be included in the half dozen or so most productive missionaries in the history of the Church'. Amongst Dan Jones's many writings were a Welsh-language *History of the Latter-day Saints*, published in 1846, and a Welsh-language edition of the *Book of Mormon*, the Mormon bible.

Over three hundred Welsh immigrants enthusiastically followed Jones to America in 1849. Some settled in St Louis, to establish a Welsh-language staging post for those en route to Utah, the Mormons' promised land. There is much evidence of hardship. Evan Howell wrote from St Louis in 1851, 'Of the four hundred that came here about two hundred have died since we came here.' He was deeply disillusioned with the Mormons, claiming, 'People gave them money on promise of land', but many were 'left to die in the workhouses'.

WHAT TO BELIEVE AND CONCLUDE

Many Welsh prospered in the United States, or at the very least did rather better than they had done in Wales. There were also those who failed to thrive. In Alan Conway's fascinating *The Welsh in America: Letters from the Immigrants*, published in Minneapolis in 1961, there are letters revealing all sides. Some who sang the praises of America sought to justify their immigration, some had an economic interest in promoting their new home, and some liked to boast. In 1818, William Thomas of Utica wrote bemoaning lying compatriots who had exaggerated the potential of New York State. 'So many Welsh were disappointed from the letters of these men . . . I am thinking of coming home . . . Many of the Welsh are.' Some who complained had perhaps suffered bad luck or had had excessively high expectations. They miay simply have possessed a gloomy nature. One wonders whether, proportionately, Conway included too many letters of the discontented – or even of the contented, who are in the majority in his volume. There were also those who left no record of their experiences. The evidence requires careful weighing, but it still seems reasonable to conclude that for at least half of the Welsh emigrants, leaving Wales was a good choice.

Thousands of Welsh settled in Utah, many in coal-mining areas. In 1857, William Williams went to California and crossed 'Salt Lake Valley' en route. 'There are hundreds of Welsh there,' he told his mother. In 1855, a Welshman in California reported of his journey through Salt Lake City, 'I saw many Welsh there, many of them in very poor circumstances.'

A historian of Mormonism, Douglas Davies (1987), estimated that one-third of the 60,033 Welsh immigrants to America between 1847 and 1891 were Mormons, and that by 1887 there were 17,000 Welsh in Utah (15 per cent of the total Utah population). The official historian of the Mormon Church rejected Davies's figures as too low, contending that there were around 25,000 Welsh in Utah. Welsh immigrants John Parry and Evan Stephens were important in the development of the Mormon

Tabernacle Choir, a much-loved contribution to American cultural life. However, it could be argued that the Welsh immigrant who made the most significant contribution to the Utah community was Martha 'Mattie' Hughes (1857–1932).

Mattie was born in Llandudno to a family of Mormon converts. In 1860, they emigrated to Utah in order to escape hostility and live with other Latter-day Saints. The death of Mattie's baby sister on the hazardous journey across America influenced her subsequent desire to practise medicine.

Mattie responded to Mormon leader Brigham Young's requests that she become a typesetter and then a medical practitioner. Mattie typeset by day, attended night classes, then gained a chemistry degree from Utah's University of Deseret (1878). She washed dishes, made beds and did secretarial work to finance her study of medicine at the University of Michigan, where she and the other female students had to sit in a separate classroom so that the men could not see them. She graduated in 1880 and was then the sole female among the seventy-five students at the University of Pennsylvania's postgraduate medical school, from which she graduated in 1881.

The church appointed Mattie Hughes as the resident physician in Salt Lake City's Deseret Hospital, which focused on obstetrics. There she met Angus Cannon. When the US Congress made polygamy a felony in 1882, Mattie said, 'I believe in polygamy . . . I am a Mormon.' She said polygamy was 'a sacred duty' and in 1884 became the fourth wife of Angus, who had seventeen children and was old enough to be her father. Federal government officials called upon her to testify in their proceedings against plural marriages, because she was married to a significant figure in the Mormon Church and her practice of medicine had familiarised her with women in plural marriages who had given birth. While Angus was jailed, Mattie was protected by the Mormon 'underground'. She then fled to Europe because she was pregnant – conclusive proof that she had been cohabiting with Angus. Mattie wrote jealously to Angus from Europe that 'perhaps at this very moment you are basking in the smiles of your young Maria', whom he had married just as Mattie left Utah.

Although based in England while in exile, Mattie managed to visit relations in Wales. By 1887, the warrant for her arrest had expired and she returned to America. She opened Utah's first training school for nurses (1889), practised medicine and began to campaign for women's suffrage. Women had been voting in Utah territory since 1870, but the Edmunds-Tucker Act (1887) disfranchised them. Mattie campaigned with leading

American suffragists such as Susan B. Anthony, and testified before a congressional committee in Washington about the benefits of allowing women to vote. When the Utah state constitution of 1896 restored women's right to vote, Mattie ran as a Democrat for the Utah State Senate while Angus ran as a Republican. The *Salt Lake Herald* said both were praiseworthy, but Mattie 'is the better man of the two'. Both denied any disharmony when Mattie won election and Angus did not, but that there were tensions in the marriage is suggested by Mattie's warnings against marriage to any man 'who appreciate[s] you not and understands you less'.

In 1896, Mattie was the first woman to be elected to a state Senate in the United States. Her focus was public health. She promoted legislation to help the disabled, protect female employees, prevent food adulteration, establish a state board of health, ensure suitably qualified medical practitioners and control the spread of infectious disease. She was a staunch advocate of vaccination, but many Latter-day Saints' leaders declared it unsafe, and the result was a smallpox epidemic in Utah. She served on the state Board of Health (1898–1903), which helped to improve Salt Lake City's water supply and sewers. She also co-sponsored an act establishing a state-supported institute for the arts.

The national reputation that Mattie had gained was attested by an invitation to a reception at the McKinley White House and by talk of her as a potential candidate for the US Senate. However, she returned to notoriety when another pregnancy demonstrated her continued illegal cohabitation with Angus.

There were those who found Mattie Hughes Cannon's intellect and abilities frightening and even unwomanly. She noted how people said, 'the softer emotions of the human heart were unknown to me.' However, she was an exceptionally able and unusual woman who served Utah well in her commitment to improving the health of the community and contributed to the cause of gender equality through her medical career and her suffragist campaigning. She contended that women "have been slaves" and one of her defences of polygamy was that the wife was freer when the husband was preoccupied with his other wives. She argued that women could and should combine home and career: 'Somehow I know that women who stay home all the time have the most unpleasant homes there are. You give me a woman who thinks about something besides cook stoves and wash tubs and baby flannels, and I'll show you, nine times out of ten, a successful mother.' Although she said 'all men and women are created free and equal', she would also claim that 'women are better than men'. She certainly achieved far more than most men in an era when women had far fewer opportunities.

After her death, Mattie was all but forgotten for many decades, until the women's rights movement in the later twentieth century made her of interest once again.

LIFE IN THE WEST

Frontier life was challenging. The first Welsh in the Oneida area in heavily forested upstate New York had to leave directional markers on the trees in order to find their way back to their homes. The early Welsh pioneers in Ohio would build log cabins, then clear the forested land and plant crops such as corn, wheat, barley and potatoes. They constructed rail pens to protect their cattle, sheep and pigs from the deer, bears, wolves, wildcats and snakes of the surrounding forest, but they struggled to stop the squirrels and rats that availed themselves of stored grain. Some of the poorer Welsh who lived at the edge of the frontier near Racine, Wisconsin, lived at first in sod huts, which were holes dug in the ground and covered with logs topped with branches. Hugh Morris of Proscairon, Wisconsin, fondly recalled the 'raising' in which neighbours helped new residents to build their cabin, but he also remembered the poor communications, the 20–40-mile trips to buy flour and an 85-mile journey to Milwaukee's grain markets.

There were many potentially life-threatening hazards. In the early nineteenth century, the young son of Theophilus Rees took refuge from a pack of wolves in a tree in Welsh Hills, Ohio. The wolves nearly shredded the tree in their pursuit of him. In 1880, the Rev. William Davies Evans toured the Welsh settlements in America, and the descendants of Caernarvonshire-born John Owens told him of the problems with snakes when the family first settled in Proscairon, Wisconsin. 'Snakes would lurk under floorboards and other surfaces in houses such as Mr Owens'.' On one occasion, Mr Owens's daughter came running back into the house shouting, 'Mam, Mam! . . . There are snakes everywhere.'

> Mrs Owens grabbed a big stick and could not believe her eyes when she saw the assemblage of interweaving snakes so close to the house. She started to clobber them with her stick but in no time, Mr Owens arrived on the scene to help. As many as thirty-eight of the reptiles were killed that day, but the number that escaped was much higher. One does not come across snakes in such quantity these days.

Indians were another potential problem. In Waukesha County, Wisconsin, Methodist John H. Evans was preaching in his house in the early days, when 'several half-naked Red Indians with feathers in their hair entered the house begging for bread and meat. After Mrs Evans, the lady of the house, went to the cellar to fetch food for them, they left peacefully.'

Some Welsh people were among the hundreds of men, women and children killed by Sioux Indians in 1862, at which time many of the younger men were away with the Union army. The weather in the American interior was much harsher than that in Wales: two Welshmen froze to death in the Minnesota settlements in the winter of 1856–7. Staying fit was important: even in her sixties, Mary Evans from Cardiganshire regularly had to walk fifteen miles from her home to Gallipolis, Ohio, with a basket of eggs upon her head in order to sell them at market.

FARMERS VERSUS GOD'S CREATURES

According to a contemporary, David Jones Davis shocked other farmers in Minnesota: 'When the little gophers began to destroy the corn, and all had a plan of destroying them completely, he asserted that they had no right to do that, for they were the small creatures of the great Creator, and that it would be more reasonable to save them and feed them by scattering the corn along the surface of the land amply enough so that there would be no need for the little things to be forced to destroy the crop.'

Overall, though, Welsh settlers prospered. A contemporary wrote of 'many thousands of respected Welsh living' in Cambria, Wisconsin, which had been settled in 1845. 'These Welsh came here early enough that they got their land free or for low prices, and they have done well.'

Hiraeth

Many Welsh immigrants were sad to leave their homeland. In 1794, Morgan John Rhys described his feelings as his sailing ship passed the coast of Wales. 'With all my love to my native land, yet it is full time for me to lose sight of it . . . Oh! My friends in Wales, my spirit is with you.'

While Welsh immigrants found much to be happy about in America, some also suffered from homesickness. In 1880, the Rev. William

Davies Evans noted: 'In the early days, the Welsh in America felt *hiraeth* for their relatives and surroundings back in Wales.' Edward Peat of Llanbrynmair thought highly of Ohio, where he enjoyed attending chapel and eisteddfoddau, but confessed to someone back home, 'I am with you . . . in thought more often than you think, not because of homesickness for my old neighbourhood but [for my] relatives!!' John and Margred Owen recommended emigration to their relations in Wales, but they had some reservations about Americans and their attitude to land and religion. 'The natives are grasping, claiming the land before the Welsh,' they complained. 'Thousands in America despise [the gospel], but it is the only thing we have a longing for – that is our old friends with whom we worshipped.' In 1848, they were desperate for Welsh companions so as to be able to establish a church: 'We have as neighbours three Frenchmen, one Dutchman, four Irishmen, one Yankee, and from 15 to 30 Indians, so that we have had no religious meetings . . . but better times are coming. Two Welsh families are coming near us and we hope soon to have public worship.' For many, it was the church community back in Wales that they remembered most fondly. William Bebb wrote from Ohio to his uncle in the mid-nineteenth century about 'my mother . . . at times too she yearns for the religious meetings of Wales . . . Do not delay in giving us much news from there, good news from a far country is like cool water to a thirsty man.' In 1844, future minister John Evans told two other Welshmen, 'I am almost broken-hearted today; my thoughts, for hours, have been in the old Cefn-y-Waen Church [in Wales] . . . and I have come down here to this wilderness.'

The Church played a vital role in sustaining Welsh communities in America. It was commonly said amongst the Welsh in America, 'The first thing a Frenchman does in a new country is to build a trading post, an American builds a city, a German builds a beer hall, and a Welshman builds a church.' In 1872, the Rev. Robert D. Thomas estimated 83 Welsh-speaking churches with 3,695 members and 9,180 attenders in Wisconsin alone. Of those members, 2,300 were Calvinistic Methodists. It has been estimated that as many as six hundred Welsh Nonconformist chapels were built in the nineteenth-century United States.

There were many publications that maintained a sense of Welsh community in America. These were often written and organised by church ministers. *Y Drych* (*The Mirror*) was first published in New York City in 1851 and then upstate in Utica. It contained news of Wales and Welsh American settlements, and at one time its circulation hit twelve thousand. Major religious monthlies were published during the nineteenth century: the Calvinistic Methodist *Y Cyfaill* (*The Friend*) in 1838–1933, the Congregationalist *Y Cenhadwr* (*The Missionary*) from 1840 to 1901, and the Baptists' *Y Wawr* (*The Dawn*) 1876–96. Biographies of Welsh American ministers were frequently published in the nineteenth century, often printed by T. J. Griffiths in Utica. Welsh-language churches and publications survived into the early twentieth century.

ENEMIES TO EVERY OTHER DENOMINATION

Most of the Welsh in America belonged to any one of the Calvinistic Methodists, Congregationalists, Baptists, Wesleyan Methodists, Quakers and Anglicans. Some adopted the new Mormon religion.

There was often considerable intolerance amongst the Welsh church communities. Radnorshire-born Thomas Powell (1760–1848) settled in Welsh Hills, Ohio, in 1805. He disliked the way his fellow Welsh were building the Welsh Hills church and vowed he would never enter it. On every Sunday for the next four decades, regardless of wind, rain or snow, he sat on a tree stump outside the church, listening to the sermon and singing the hymns.

In 1856, H. and S. Roberts wrote from Ohio to their family back home in Wales. They did not think much of other religions. 'Calvinists are the most numerous in this neighbourhood, there are some thousands, transferred from . . . Cardiganshire. [They] are enemies to every other denomination . . . There are no Mormons in Ohio; they are of the same principles as Mohammed.' The Robertses declared that the Mormons were evicted from several places because they 'followed their occupation of stealing', then ended up in Salt Lake in Oregon Territory where 'they are now surrounded by Indians, whose land they usurp'. The Robertses reported with shock that the Mormon leader Brigham Young had sixty wives. 'Tell the fair wives of Wales that if they go to the Mormons they lose their legal rights and warn all to avoid following such a bestial sect.' Mr Roberts had also experienced 'the papal beast' while he worked on constructing a canal 'among 300 papist Irishmen; they rubbed their knives in our waistcoats almost every night before going to bed, saying, "Here is a knife that will rip the belly of an Englishman or a Welshman" . . . I was very near death many a time among them.'

Other religions and nations sometimes found Welsh piety irritating. English immigrants in Scioto County, Ohio, referred contemptuously to 'Those God Almighty Welsh'.

CONCLUSIONS

The ministers and committed churchgoers who braved both the dangerous transatlantic crossing from Wales to America and the hazards of frontier life, helped make the United States a nation that to this day remains
less secularised than other countries with a similar Christian heritage.
The Welsh religious, political and economic exiles worked hard in their
New World. They demonstrated in abundance the independent spirit
and work ethos that characterised and fortified the relatively unfettered
capitalist system that made America the world's wealthiest nation by the
twentieth century, and their frequent economic success contributed to
the growth and perpetuation of the belief in what became known as the
American Dream.

CHAPTER EIGHT

WELSH AMERICANS AND THE AMERICAN CIVIL WAR

T HE AMERICAN Civil War (1861–5) is one of the most important events in the making of the United States, because the union of the states was threatened, although ultimately preserved. Many Americans of Welsh descent participated in the war between the Northern states (the Union) and the Southern states (the Confederate States of America) and some have attributed the South's defeat to the poor leadership of the Confederacy by a man with Welsh ancestry, Jefferson Davis.

SOME SIGNIFICANT CIVIL WAR DATES

1860	November: Abraham Lincoln elected president (inaugurated March 1861)
1860–1	Winter: Alabama, Florida, Georgia, Louisiana, Mississippi, South Carolina and Texas seceded from the Union
1861	February: Confederate States of America established; Jefferson Davis chosen as president April: Confederate forces fired on Fort Sumter, President Lincoln issued a call to arms April–June: Arkansas, North Carolina, Tennessee and Virginia joined the Confederacy July: Confederate victory at First Manassas a.k.a. Bull Run
1862	April: Union victories at Shiloh and in New Orleans August: Confederate victory at Second Manassas/Bull Run September: Union victory at Antietam; Lincoln issued Emancipation Proclamation, effective in January 1863 December: Confederate victory at Fredericksburg
1863	July: Union victory at Gettysburg July: Union forces took Vicksburg
1864	May–June: Wilderness–Petersburg campaign, a war of attrition September: Union forces took Atlanta November: Lincoln re-elected
1865	April: Confederate General Robert E. Lee surrendered at Appomattox

JEFFERSON DAVIS (1808–89)

Jefferson Davis's great-grandfather Evan Davis emigrated from the Snowdonia area of north Wales in the early eighteenth century and settled in Philadelphia. Jefferson Davis's grandfather and father made frequent moves in search of a better life, so that Jefferson was born in Kentucky but grew up in the Mississippi Territory.

Figure 17. *The major battles of the American Civil War.*

Jefferson Davis attended West Point, where he was court-martialled for attending a tavern, and later involved in the famous West Point egg-nog riot of Christmas 1826. Davis had been instrumental in acquiring the alcohol but was not one of the drunken cadets who ran riot, so he somehow escaped punishment.

After a few years in the army, Davis was elected to the US House of Representatives and soon gained recognition for his impressive oratory. In 1846, he distinguished himself in combat in the Mexican War, in which the United States acquired vast Western territories. While a

US senator (1847–51), Davis supported the expansion of slavery to new territories, an issue that had become the most controversial in American politics.

Slavery and sectional tensions

The early American colonists imported African slaves, and each of the thirteen colonies contained slaves in the mid-eighteenth century. From late in the century, slavery slowly died out in the Northern states but remained central to life in the South. This was partly because the South's plantation agriculture necessitated plentiful and cheap labour, but also because nearly half the Southern population was black and even non-slave-holders valued slavery as a form of race control.

As the United States expanded, Northerners and Southerners were greatly exercised by the question of whether slavery should be allowed in new territories and states. Although many Northerners were as racist as Southerners, Northern criticisms of slavery and opposition to its expansion to the West made Southerners increasingly defensive.

Davis's views on slavery and black Americans

Jefferson Davis perceived slavery as a relatively benign system of labour relations. He admitted the system 'had defects' and was abused by 'the vicious, the ignorant and the wayward', but argued that it was obvious that sensible owners who valued their property would not mistreat their slave workforce. He treated his own slaves well by contemporary standards, allowing them to sell their garden produce and to learn to read and write. In a speech in New York City in 1858, he rejected abolitionist predictions of slave revolts. 'Our doors are unlocked at night . . . We lie down to sleep trusting to them for defence, and the bond between the master and the slave is as near as that which exists between capital and labor anywhere.' Davis was unusual in that he had a black overseer, the faithful James Pemberton, and gave his slaves weapons with which to oppose armed white trespassers on his land during the Civil War.

In 1864, when it was clear that the Confederacy was losing the war, Davis was willing to countenance slave soldiers. He was even ready to give up slavery in the cause of Southern independence. However, he argued that freed slaves would find themselves unprepared for 'responsibilities' and would not cope. He insisted that slavery was 'the most beneficient form of government' for 'those who are morally and intellectually unable to take care of themselves'. He claimed the South was bringing about an 'immense improvement' in slaves, elevating them 'from brutal savages into docile, intelligent and civilised agricultural labourers', and supplying them 'not only with bodily comforts, but with careful religious instruction, under the supervision of a superior race'. He claimed that the free black population of the Northern states was 'miserable, impoverished, loathsome from the deformity and disease which follows after penury and vice' and was 'filling the penitentiaries' of the North. His views on race remained constant throughout his life. After the Civil War, the Republican Congress gave black Americans voting rights, and Davis accused them of making the black male population 'more idle and ungovernable than before'.

Jefferson Davis shared the characteristic white supremacist views of the vast majority of his contemporaries in both North and South. He had grown up in a society where slavery was the norm and central to the continuing prosperity of plantation owners such as the Davis family. As he told fellow Mississippians in 1849, Northern anti-slavery sentiment 'strikes at our prosperity, our property, and domestic security'. Southerners had fought for and won new Western territories in the Mexican War, and Davis was incensed that Northerners did not want Southern slave-owners to take their human property to those new territories. He told the Senate that the South needed Northerners to halt their hostility against 'an institution so interwoven with its interests, its domestic peace, and all its social relations, that it cannot be disturbed without causing their overthrow'. He believed that Northern attitudes threatened the American Constitution.

Davis, states' rights and secession

Jefferson Davis was named in honour of Thomas Jefferson and shared his views on the importance of maintaining the balance of power between the state and federal governments. From 1857, Davis was the leading spokesman for states' rights in the US Senate. He declared it unconstitutional to deny the equality of states and argued that each state had the right of equal access to the new territories.

In the 1860 presidential election, the Republican presidential candidate, Abraham Lincoln, reaffirmed his opposition to the expansion of slavery into new states, but also assured Southerners that he had no intention of abolishing slavery in states where it currently existed. That failed to reassure Alabama, Florida, Georgia, Louisiana, Mississippi,

South Carolina and Texas. They seceded from the Union and set up a new nation, the Confederate States of America.

Davis had spoken out against secession in 1858. While he believed that each state had a sovereign right to secede, he feared the North would not let the South go, and recognised that the South lacked the military and naval resources to defeat the North. By 1861, however, he felt the South had little choice, and when Mississippi seceded, Davis resigned from the US Senate. In his final Senate speech, on what he described as 'the saddest day of my life', he reminded his colleagues of the nation's history. He said that the United States was born on the principle of the right to withdraw from a government that threatened people's rights. He argued that each state had entered the Union voluntarily and therefore had the right to leave it when it chose. 'We but tread in the path of our Fathers when we proclaim our independence.'

Here lay two competing visions: Southerners such as Jefferson Davis wanted to continue making America in the image of the Founding Fathers, many of whom were slave-owners and all of whom had conceded the continuation of slavery; Northerners such as the Republican Abraham Lincoln wanted a remaking of America in which slavery would at the very least be excluded from any new territories.

President Davis

History is usually written by the victors, so it is not surprising that Jefferson Davis has been much criticised. He led a nation that was not only defeated but also supported the evil of slavery.

Davis claimed that he did not want to be President of the Confederate States of America: 'I have no confidence in my capacity to meet its requirements. I think I could perform the functions of general.' His wife Varina recalled how in spring 1861 he told her that he had been chosen as president 'as a man might speak of a sentence of death'. When a Mississippi official asked Davis what the future held, the new president answered that 'there would be war, long and bloody'. It concerned him greatly that the seven Southern states that had seceded from the Union contained only 10 per cent of the US population and 5 per cent of its industrial capacity. In the hope of avoiding war, Davis offered to pay the South's share of the national debt and to purchase federal property in the South, but while in 1776 Lincoln's ancestors had thought it their right to declare their independence from a government they disliked, Lincoln considered the Confederacy illegitimate and refused to negotiate in 1861.

Davis and the first shots of the American Civil War

Fort Sumter, an offshore federal fortification in Charleston, South Carolina, became a test of both Northern and Southern credibility: Lincoln had said he would hold federal property in the South, while Southerners believed no sovereign nation could accept a foreign fort in one of its major harbours. President Lincoln warned the South that he would resupply Fort Sumter, but President Davis and his cabinet unanimously agreed that that must not happen. When Lincoln attempted the resupply, Davis's Confederacy fired the first shots of the Civil War. As Davis and his Cabinet had hoped, this brought the slave-holding upper South states of Virginia, Arkansas, North Carolina and Tennessee into the Confederacy. Virginia was particularly welcome, because its industrial capacity was as great as that of the seven original Confederate states combined.

Did Davis lose the war for the South?

Like most leaders, Jefferson Davis has divided opinion. His vice president Alexander Stephens declared him 'weak, timid, petulant, peevish, obstinate', and responsible for the South's defeat. Historian David Potter (1968) considered Davis the most important reason why the Confederacy lost, and claimed that it would have won had it been led by Lincoln. On the other hand, the best-loved hero of the Confederacy, General Robert E. Lee, said he could not think of anyone who would have been better. A *New York Times* reporter said Davis was 'all that kept the Confederacy going'. Amongst modern historians, David Donald, Jean Baker and Michael Holt (2001) argued that much of the criticism of him did not take into account the 'insuperable difficulties' he faced, and that no other Southern political leader 'even approached Davis in stature', while Steven Channing (1987) said he 'gave the Confederacy a sense of identity and purpose'. However, a majority of historians are highly critical of Davis's leadership.

Many point out that Davis struggled to establish a good working relationship with several colleagues, both civilian and military. He had an excellent relationship with the Confederacy's most revered and able general, Robert E. Lee, but some of his chosen generals were poor – his friend Leonidas Polk is a good example. Lincoln also made both good and bad military appointments, but was better able to work with others.

It is generally acknowledged that Davis struggled to delegate. He became involved in detailed decision-making in the War Department.

The war effort was essential to the survival of Davis's country, and considerable involvement on his part was probably sensible: he had had successful military experience in the Mexican War and had been an impressive Secretary of War (1853–7). However, his preoccupation with the shortage of soap for the soldiers in August 1864 is but one example of his unwise micromanagement.

Some contemporaries accused Davis of being a despot, but many historians have criticised him for not using his powers enough. David Donald said the Confederacy was so concerned with individual liberties that it 'died of democracy', but others argue that Jefferson Davis got the balance right. He could be tough when necessary, despite contemporary concerns about states' rights and individual liberty. For example, he promoted the Conscription Act (1862), imposed martial law in threatened areas and supported the impressment of supplies.

Davis has been accused of having made poor decisions and being indecisive. His economic understanding was certainly limited, and he was slow to focus upon financing the war. The Confederate Congress was equally guilty. When Congress proved reluctant to vote taxation, the Confederate war effort was usually financed by inflationary printing of money. Prices rose by a factor of 5,000 between 1861 and 1865.

Davis has been criticised for not having been inspirational, but he made frequent and dangerous frontline visits that served to encourage Confederate soldiers, and he made three tours of the South to try to raise morale. In late 1862, he visited Tennessee, Mississippi, Alabama, Georgia and North Carolina, travelling 3,000 miles in twenty-seven days and making countless public appearances and speeches for 'the noble cause'. On a thirty-two-day tour in 1863, he travelled through Mississippi, Georgia, South Carolina, North Carolina and Alabama, and once again was greeted everywhere with great enthusiasm. However, by the time of his September 1864 trip west to try to maintain troop morale after the fall of Atlanta, the troops saluted but no longer cheered him. Confederate morale was poor by this time, and he admitted in his speeches that over half the men of the army were absent without leave. Many had deserted in order to protect their families as the Northern armies closed in.

Clearly, there are good arguments both for and against the leadership of Jefferson Davis. What everyone is agreed on is his dedication and hard work, and what many rightly emphasise is that the Union victory was probably inevitable. Jefferson Davis was surely correct when he told the Mississippi legislature in December 1862: 'The wonder is not that we have done little, but that we have done so much.'

Was the South's defeat inevitable?

Davis believed the Union's victory was inevitable, and many historians have agreed with him. In his March 1862 message to the first Congress, Davis acknowledged the 'serious disasters' the Confederacy had suffered and said it was because the government had tried to defend all its territories while lacking 'the means for the prosecution of the war on so gigantic scale'. The North had three times as many men of fighting age as the South. Only 5.5 million of the South's 9 million population were white, and many slaves did not want to aid the South and slowly slipped away. The South possessed only 10 per cent of the industrial capacity of the North, which had more industrial and agricultural productivity, ships, railways and gold reserves. The Confederacy struggled to finance the war because it had limited gold reserves, exports were restricted by the Union naval blockade and the states often borrowed or printed money rather than raise taxes. Jefferson Davis had to create a new nation from scratch, and it was a nation with far weaker economic foundations and far less manpower than its rival. His was surely an impossible task.

Jefferson Davis was captured by Union soldiers within weeks of General Lee's surrender in April 1865. The victorious Northerners made much of the fact that he had borrowed an item of his wife's clothing while trying to escape. He was jailed for two years, but never brought to trial. Some of his former slaves petitioned the Governor of Mississippi for his release, saying, 'Some of us well know of many kindness[es] he [had] shown his slaves on his plantation.' After his release, he urged reconciliation and acceptance of the Union and wrote a defence of himself and the South.

While many consider the South and Davis indefensible, he argued in his memoirs that while secession had been 'impracticable . . . this did not prove it to be wrong'. He was surely in the right in constitutional terms, but in contrast to Thomas Jefferson, Jefferson Davis seems to have been genuinely blind to the immorality of slavery. He was not alone in that. He was very much a Southerner of his time, and that he had earned the respect and affection of millions of white Southerners was demonstrated by the warmth of the reception he received whenever he travelled in the South in his declining years and by the mourning at his death.

JEFFERSON DAVIS'S VISIT TO WALES

After his release from prison, Davis participated in business ventures that involved a first trip to Britain in 1868. The Davis family landed at Liverpool and stayed in the house of a prosperous former Confederate who also owned a summer residence in north Wales. Jefferson Davis stayed in that holiday home for a few days, and his visits included slate quarries, coal mines and Caernarvon Castle. One wonders whether he was on a pilgrimage to connect with his Welsh ancestry, although subsequent visits to Britain suggested that it was Scotland rather than Wales that had captured his heart. His mother was Scots-Irish and he made prolonged visits to Scotland, writing enthusiastically of historical and literary landmarks that he saw there. It seems likely that Davis had never been interested in his Welsh ancestry – he sometimes confused his Welsh immigrant great-grandfather Evan Davis with his grandfather Evan Davis Jr.

VARINA HOWELL DAVIES,
FIRST LADY OF THE CONFEDERACY

In 1845, the widower Jefferson Davis married Varina Howell. Her Howell ancestors emigrated from Wales in the early eighteenth century, settled first in Delaware, then moved to New Jersey, where Varina's grandfather Richard Howell was born. He was elected to four terms as Governor of New Jersey. It is difficult to ascertain if Varina ever reflected on her Welsh ancestry, whether on the Davises' visit to Llandudno in north Wales in 1868, or when the preparation of Welsh rarebit in a fireplace was one of the several recipes she contributed to a cookbook in 1885. Contemporaries were certainly aware of it: while she was First Lady of the Confederacy, there were snide comments about her dark skin, which some attributed to her ancestry.

Varina was an exceptionally well-read woman whose decided views led to several periods of conflict with her conservative husband, who was less cosmopolitan and intellectually flexible. Significantly, she much preferred her years as a senator's wife in Washington to her years as First Lady of the Confederacy in Richmond, Virginia. She did her best as First Lady, but it was not a role she relished. Although born in the South, she had strong ties to Northern relations and friends and kept up friendly communications with them throughout the Civil War. Had it not been for her husband, she might well have sided with the Union.

WELSH AMERICAN CONTRIBUTIONS TO THE UNION VICTORY

The Civil War ended slavery. This was an early and essential step on the road to the remaking of the nation into a more equal society. Welsh Americans played a part in the growth of the Northern anti-slavery sentiment that led to the outbreak of the war, and also in the military operations.

Northern Welsh American attitudes to slavery and black Americans

In the late eighteenth century, slavery was criticised by enlightened Welsh ministers such as Richard Price and Morgan John Rhys. During the mid-nineteenth century, influential Welsh American ministers such as the Rev. Benjamin Chidlaw of Ohio, and Welsh American publications such as *Y Drych*, became increasingly militant in their abolitionism. One of the most influential of preachers, writers and publishers was Robert Everett, a Congregational minister who had emigrated from Flintshire in 1823 and settled in Utica, in Oneida County, upstate New York. In the late 1830s and early 1840s, Everett's congregation pelted him with eggs for preaching abolitionism, but Northern attitudes to slavery and the South hardened during the controversies over the expansion of slavery to the Western territories. Everett campaigned incessantly against slavery, in Welsh-language publications that obviously had a market and presumably an influence. His publications earned him praise from the leading black abolitionist, Frederick Douglass, who expressed regret that he could not understand Welsh and noted that anti-slavery meetings in Oneida County contained 'a considerable number of Welsh, who are to a man, go-ahead Abolitionists'. Amongst Everett's publications was a Welsh-language edition of Harriet Beecher Stowe's highly influential abolitionist novel, *Uncle Tom's Cabin*.

In 1851, Welsh anti-slavery sentiment caused a clash over the insertion of a Welsh memorial slab in the Washington Monument in the nation's capital. Committees were established in several Welsh settlements to raise the required $400. The Pottsville Welsh told *Y Drych* 'That we, although foreigners through birth, are Americans and Republicans in sentiment; and have made Washington's country our adopted land; and appreciate the Freedom and Conveniences that we are allowed to enjoy'. However, not all Welsh Americans agreed. The Welsh in Bradford, Pennsylvania told *Y Drych*, 'That it is not consistent with our principles to build a memorial to the first slave-holding president in our country'.

Ministers such as Chidlaw and Everett no doubt played a part in promoting the enthusiastic Welsh American support of the new, anti-slavery Republican Party. Such ministers assured their congregations that it was their Christian duty to vote Republican. Everett wrote: 'We the Welsh are one of the many peoples which constitute America's citizens: and although we are but a small nation by comparison . . . the whole thing might turn upon a small majority, and we can make up that majority.' Welsh American votes may have helped the Republican presidential candidate John Frémont win states such as New York, Wisconsin and Ohio in the presidential election of 1856, but he failed to win the election. In 1860, the Republican Abraham Lincoln stood for President. He seems to have been expecting tens of thousands of votes from Welsh-speakers, because he had 100,000 election pamphlets published in Welsh. David C. Davis of Utica, New York, was similarly convinced of Welsh interest: he printed a Welsh-language campaign biography of Abraham Lincoln. In 1864, some Welsh Americans were so keen to see Lincoln re-elected that Welsh American Republican soldiers clashed with Irish Democrats in the Union army on election eve.

Despite the strong pacifist tradition among Welsh Americans, many responded to Lincoln's call to arms in 1861. The impact of anti-slavery preachers in Welsh-language chapels can be traced in the language in Welsh American correspondence, such as the letters of Humphrey and Sarah Roberts, who emigrated from the Brymbo area in north-east Wales and settled in Madison in Jackson County, Ohio, in the 1850s. In June 1861, they wrote to relations in Wales: 'A very dark cloud hangs over our land at present . . . the cause of the tumult . . . the sum of it is the self-seeking and hellish lust of the slave dealers to spread slavery throughout the land and to govern and oppress black and white under foot.' Their sons Benjamin and William Roberts were early volunteers in the 18th and 22nd Ohio Regiments respectively.

Welsh American soldiers often demonstrated enlightened attitudes during the Civil War, as when John G. Jones wrote from the Union camp in Louisiana in November 1863, 'I liked the colored troops just as well as the white ones.' John B. Morgan from Newport, Ohio, served on the *USS Vermont* and his letter in *Y Drych* described the four hundred or so 'black lads' who constituted half the crew as 'of wondrous use' and invaluable. He spent 'so much of time amongst them' and was teaching some to read. Erasmus Jones, a Congregationalist from Oneida County, New York, described the Welsh as 'instinctively'

'THE ONLY WELSH NEGRO IN HISTORY'

The Welsh settlement in Picatonica in south-western Iowa County, Wisconsin, was established in 1846 by emigrants from Pennsylvania. At a prayer meeting in 1865, $22.75 was collected 'to help the Free Negroes, who in their thousands are crossing the line from slavery to freedom'. A former slave called James D. Williams lived with the John H. Williams family, attended a Welsh church, sang hymns in Welsh, and jokingly declared himself 'the only Welsh Negro in history'. Like many in the settlement, he both farmed and mined lead. When Williams died in 1903, the *Dodgeville Chronicle* pointed out that 'although "Jim", as he was known by his friends, was one of the colored race, he was very highly esteemed by his acquaintances'. The qualification of 'although', along with the facts that he was remembered as 'Nigger Jim' by second-generation residents, and that the lead diggings on his land were known as the 'Nigger Mine', led Robert Humphries (2012) to wonder whether Welsh Americans had grown more similar to other white Americans in their views on race by the late nineteenth century.

anti-slavery, and he specifically requested that he serve with black troops when he volunteered. In 1864, he became chaplain of the 21st United States Colored Infantry. He reported pointedly that during the attack on James Island, 'the black soldiers displayed more heroism and determination . . . than the white'.

Welsh American soldiers frequently wrote that it was slavery that had inspired them to fight. John B. Morgan wrote in a letter published in *Y Drych*: 'I was remarkably in favour of freeing the slaves before leaving Newport [Ohio]; in truth, that was what was foremost on my mind driving me to take up arms against the rebels ... I desire their freedom even more today.' A letter from John W. Hughes published in *Y Drych* said, 'Well, perhaps you are thinking that I regret coming to such a place. Not at all. Listening to the Negroes talk about the treatment they receive is enough to make everybody become soldiers.' When Welsh American soldiers talked of their motivation, some said they were fighting for the Union, some for abolitionism, and some conflated the two. When Thomas H. Jones of Ohio saw a 'nearly white' slave girl sold in Kentucky in April 1863, he said this practice 'will be our destruction of the country'. Welsh American volunteers in the 22nd Wisconsin Infantry aided fugitive slaves in Kentucky, a slave state that remained within the Union during the Civil War. The small Welsh American population in Covington, Kentucky, feared 'a coat of tar and feathers' for their anti-slavery beliefs.

After Lincoln's Emancipation Proclamation, Welsh American publications progressed from their anti-slavery stance and began urging Welsh Americans to go to the South to help the freed slaves as missionaries and teachers. For example, *The Cambrian* proudly recorded that the Carmarthenshire-born Rev. Daniel W. Phillips, a Baptist minister in Boston, arrived in the South in 1864 and founded the Nashville Normal and Theological Institute in 1866. The Institute trained freed slaves to be teachers and ministers, and subsequently became Roger Williams University. The Welsh American clergy continued to be out of step with many white contemporaries. When the Rev. William Davies Evans visited Missouri in 1880, a Mr Thomas Francis informed him that the local Welsh ministers defied Missouri customs and declared it 'a supreme honour' to baptise black Americans.

WELSH RACISM

The strength of Welsh anti-slavery sentiment did not mean that all Welsh Americans advocated racial equality. Merthyr-born Charles Evans mined coal in Ohio. In 1868, he wrote that he would not be voting for the Republican presidential candidate in the forthcoming election: 'Almost all the Welshmen are on the radical [Republican] ticket and I would be so except for the nigger equality which does not agree with my views that the Creator never intended them to be equal to the white man.'

In 1888, an *Y Drych* article warned of 'the perils of immigration' and desired that America be kept free of Asians, Africans and Southern and Eastern Europeans. An 1893 article in *Y Drych* said it would be inappropriate for Welsh blood 'to mix with the black Negro and the red Indian, or the bloody Dago'.

Southern Welsh American attitudes to slavery and black Americans

There were many of Welsh descent in the Confederacy and it was natural that most should see slavery and black Americans differently from those of Welsh descent in the North. Considerable numbers of second-generation Welsh Americans had migrated from Pennsylvania to North Carolina in the 1720s and to the Pee Dee River area in South Carolina in the 1730s. When forty-eight Welsh Americans from the Welsh Tract in Delaware moved to Welsh Neck in South Carolina in 1736, they took seventeen slaves with them. The first US census, taken in 1790, listed the Welsh as 8.8 per cent of the population of South Carolina and 11.6 per cent of that of North Carolina, and most of those of Welsh ancestry would no doubt have been assimilated into Southern society by the time of the Civil War. They had grown up in a slave society, many were slave-owners and most were willing to support and/or fight for the Confederacy. When Benjamin and William Roberts of Ohio were with the Union army in Memphis, Tennessee, they told their family they had 'encamped for a time on the farm of an old Welshman, who was a hotheaded rebel; he had been there 50 years.' Perhaps he was the 'old Welshman by the name of Davis, originally from Carmarthenshire' whom Union soldier William S. Jones met.

BALTIMORE AND SLAVERY

The state of Maryland fought for the Union in the Civil War, but it was a border state and had Southern characteristics. Considerable numbers of Welshmen were employed in the copper works in Baltimore, which was Maryland's largest city. Metal worker Henry Davies wrote to his father in Wales after the clash at Fort Sumter that Baltimore's Welsh population was anti-slavery and pro-Union: 'If somebody says one word against slavery here, it is a strange thing if that man does not receive a bullet or two in his stomach; as a result, we Welsh have to be quiet on that matter.'

The 1860 US census recorded nearly 46,000 Welsh immigrants, only 950 of whom lived in what became the Confederacy. These more recent Welsh immigrants to the South were more ambivalent about the Confederacy. William Pierce of New Canton, Virginia rejected demands that he and his sons fight for the Confederacy, and was jailed for his beliefs. In 1866, he wrote from Charlottesville, Virginia: 'There were many Welshmen here in the first two years of the war but they left one by one as they got the chance.'

'SOME OF OUR NATION ARE LIVING HERE'

D. M. Williams of the 18th Wisconsin Infantry found a few Welsh-speakers in northern Louisiana ('some of our nation are living here'), a graveyard there that contained 'many a Welshman', and a Mr Griffith who claimed to be a keen reader of Welsh anti-slavery publications.

Welshman Benjamin T. Jones was an enthusiastic abolitionist living and working as a missionary in Marion, Arkansas, when the Civil War started. He was attacked by '12 wicked men on horseback', who stopped him preaching in the chapel and 'wanted to take my life, because I was, they said, an Abolitionist'. He managed to escape to the Welsh settlement of Gomer in Allen County, Ohio, having got through Tennessee with the help of Samuel Roberts of the Brynffynon settlement in eastern Tennessee. Back in 1856, the Rev. Benjamin Chidlaw had warned Roberts against settling in a slave state, but to no avail. When Tennessee became a major Civil War battleground, the anti-slavery but pacifist Roberts wrote with feeling of the depredations of both Union and Confederate soldiers. Brynffynon was in a strongly pro-Union part of Tennessee, and Roberts's failure to give open support to the North made him deeply unpopular, both amongst his neighbours and in the North. Humphrey and Sarah Roberts of Ohio wrote to relations in Wales that the 'American Welsh have worshipped Samuel Roberts, but he would get a coat of tar and feathers which he deserves' if he ever preached in the North.

SAMUEL ROBERTS AND THE AMERICAN SENSE OF DESTINY

Samuel Roberts alienated many with his pacifism, and no doubt when he expressed his view that, 'There is reason to fear that the United States . . . thinks that there is no one like the United States on the face of the earth; that we are wiser than everyone and that we can conquer everyone'. It is not surprising that he returned to Wales in 1866.

Samuel Roberts's Brynffynon associate William Bebb was vociferously anti-slavery, and as Governor of Ohio (1846–8) had tried, but failed, to get Ohio to abolish laws that discriminated against black Americans. He wrote a letter from Illinois in 1861, in which he begged President Abraham Lincoln for a post in his administration, reminding Lincoln that he had campaigned for his election: 'You know I thereby lost my home . . . in Tennessee.' He was given a humble clerkship in the Pension Office in Washington, DC.

It is difficult to assess the impact of attitudes, but it may be that the common Welsh American dislike of slavery and frequent acceptance of black Americans influenced the attitudes of others. The attitudes certainly inspired some Welsh Americans to fight for the Union in order to make America more worthy to be called 'the land of the free'.

The number of Welsh Americans in the Union army

According to an anonymous piece in *Y Drych* in April 1863, there had been 'scarcely an important battle . . . in which our fellow countrymen have not been present'. Welsh American publications such as *Y Drych* printed soldiers' letters, biographies and obituaries, so it is possible to get a rough idea of the number of Welsh-speakers who fought on Lincoln's side.

The Welsh American Baptist journal *Y Seren Orllewinol*, printed in Pottsville, Pennsylvania, recorded in June 1861 that

> 2000 soldiers left Schuylkill County – some hundreds of them Welsh, about 50 from Minersville alone . . . similarly they were departing from the regions of Scranton, Danville, Pittsburgh, etc. . . . We were assured by a friend who visited 'Camp Curtin' in Harrisburg at the start of last month that one could hear Welsh being spoken at just about every part of the camp. In New York, Ohio, and other states, a number of Welsh have enlisted, although it is difficult to provide a tally of a number.

The Rev. Benjamin Chidlaw claimed that by summer 1862, 'There are thousands of Welsh[-speakers] from New York, Pennsylvania, Ohio and Wisconsin in the field'. While it is possible to name over three thousand Welsh-speaking soldiers, there were no doubt more – some have suggested that it may have been as many as ten thousand. Only a few hundred of them served in Welsh or mostly Welsh companies.

The Welsh Americans had volunteered enthusiastically in 1861, and William Rowlands of Welsh Prairie, Wisconsin, noted that while in 1863 'many places failed to meet the demand and the result was drafting', the Welsh were once again quick to volunteer. In June 1861, *Y Seren Orllewinol* proudly claimed: 'Of all the nations in the country, nobody has come out more heartily at the President's call to defend the government than the Welsh.' However, the writer regretted that it was hard to put an accurate number on the Welsh volunteers, as 'hundreds of Welshmen are being lost amongst other nations'. He pointed out that while enterprising individuals of other national origins were forming companies of which they were then officers, the Welsh had 'hardly any' such officers and 'only common soldiers', so Welsh companies were not formed. The Rev. John M. Thomas, chaplain to several new Pennsylvania regiments, echoed that lament: 'It is a pity that the Welsh did not awaken in time and enlist under officers of their own and offer their service as Welsh regiments.' The Irish and Germans did so, but not the Welsh. This was because most of the

Welsh American population was spread out in rural areas and because Welsh Americans were outnumbered by other national groups. The 1860 US census recorded 1.6 million Irish- born, 1.3 million German-born, but only 45,763 Welsh-born (29,868 in the 1850 census). In August 1863, the *Seren*'s editor was still lamenting that the Welsh soldiers in the Union army were 'swallowed from sight by the majority' and consequently 'are not receiving much public honour from other nations for their heroism'. John E. Roberts clearly felt 'swallowed' when he told *Y Drych* that he was one of only two Welshmen in the 5th Pennsylvania Cavalry. However, by the time of that second *Seren* lament, there were several Welsh or majority-Welsh companies, such as the two in the 56th Ohio Volunteer Infantry, the one from Scranton in the 77th Pennsylvania, and the one from Oneida County in the 97th New York.

There is ample evidence of the Welsh American desire for Welsh American enlistment and bravery to be known. Contemporary ethnic groups for whom English was not their first language were clearly vying to prove themselves to be good Americans. Evan Griffiths of Iowa wrote to the Welsh American Congregationalist monthly *Y Cenhadwr Americanaidd* that he wanted to memorialise Welsh soldiers: 'I cannot believe that they have been slower to take up arms against the rebellion in our country than other nations.' He then listed fourteen of his Welsh neighbours who had joined the 22nd Iowa Infantry, including his son Griffith Griffiths.

While a considerable amount is known about some Welsh-speaking Union soldiers, there would have been others of whom we know less or nothing – tens or even hundreds of thousands who were either Welsh-speaking, or of Welsh descent, or fully assimilated. Although Carmarthen-born Joshua T. Owen served with Pennsylvanian regiments and was promoted to brigadier, he did not write to Welsh-language publications and they wrote nothing of him.

Enlisting together

Given the closeness of chapel-centred Welsh communities, it is not surprising that so many Welsh-speaking Americans enlisted together. For example, fifty-seven members of Horeb Chapel in Oak Hill in Jackson County, Ohio, enlisted, while the small Welsh community of Radnor, Ohio, contributed 161 soldiers to the Union army.

There are many examples of how many Welsh American families contributed more than one soldier to the Union army. David Morris emigrated from what the Crawford County, Ohio, history described as 'Cumbach' in

Wales in 1840. A mine superintendent in Ohio, Morris had twenty children, five of whom fought in the Civil War. One was the mining engineer who blew up Fort Hill, Vicksburg, and died from wounds received in the operation. Welsh-born Humphrey and Sarah Roberts of Ohio were wholehearted supporters of the Union. They wrote home that after Fort Sumter, 'The free states rose like one man, with men and money, to assist the Union . . . Benjamin was working in Portsmouth . . . he went with a company from Fronton, there were many Welshmen with him.' In 1863, the Robertses explained that when their sons Benjamin and William were in Portsmouth, Ohio, 'There was a Welshman recruiting a company and the two assisted him in raising the men'. Many Welsh Americans from Ohio were in the same company or regiment. William S. Jones wrote in *Y Drych* that there were 150 Welsh-speakers in the 56th Ohio Volunteer Infantry, while D. M. Hughes reported '110 of the heroic boys of the Welsh of Putnam, Gomer and Vanwert' in one company in the 118th Ohio when it mustered in Cincinnati in September 1862. In spring 1863, twenty-three Welshmen from Gomer, Ohio, volunteered together, and there were 'large numbers' of Welsh in the 50th, 76th and 115th Ohio, according to historian D. B. Mahin (2002). There were similar group enlistments in other states with large Welsh American populations. Company G of Pennsylvania's 77th Regiment consisted of Welsh miners from Scranton.

A member of Company F of the 22nd Wisconsin Infantry said most of his company were Welsh and known as the 'Cambrian Guards'. Company F was captained by Owen Griffith. Assisted by the Rev. W. J. Hopkins, Griffith had recruited the company's soldiers in Racine County, Wisconsin, in August 1862. Their recruitment meeting sent a resolution to the government from 'the Welsh citizens of Racine', swearing their loyalty and deriding cowards who fled to Canada. Lincoln had not yet issued the Emancipation Proclamation, and the Racine resolution urged the government that slaves 'should be hereafter and for ever declared free'. The 22nd Wisconsin Infantry must have made its anti-slavery sentiments widely known, because it gained fame as 'the abolitionist regiment'. According to Mahin, there were also 'large numbers' of Welsh in the 23rd Wisconsin, the 9th Minnesota, and the 117th and the 146th New York.

WELSH AMERICAN MUSICIANS IN THE ARMY

Daniel P. Davies, known as 'the big bass', played tuba in the 24th Wisconsin Infantry regimental band. Elias J. Prichard, a musician with the 22nd Wisconsin Infantry, wrote of his wish to see the rebellious secessionists defeated.

Sergeant Daniel T. Jones of Company H, 126th Illinois Infantry, wrote to *Y Drych* saying the majority of his company was Welsh and that after 'we left our home in Coal Valley . . . Illinois . . . off we went with deep enthusiasm and an indescribable feeling for democracy, freedom, and the rights of humanity'.

There was a small group of Welsh soldiers in the 14th Vermont Infantry. All were immigrants from north Walian slate-mining communities who worked in the slate quarries in Fairhaven, Vermont. There were four other Welsh quarrymen in the 4th Vermont, who 'went from the Quarry in cold blood, they said, and they enlisted without being drunk'.

Dying together

Many Welsh-speaking Americans enlisted together and many died together. In summer 1862, Dr J. M. Jones in Ebensburg, Pennsylvania, was recruiting what became Company F of the 133rd Pennsylvania Volunteer Infantry. Their losses were particularly heavy at the Battle of Fredericksburg, when fifteen Welsh Americans of Company F died on the same day. All came from Ebensburg. There was a Welsh population of 800 in Oshkosh, Wisconsin, 52 of whom went to fight for the Union, and 19 of whom died. From the Winnebago, Wisconsin, settlement alone, 52 Welshmen served and 10 of them died in the notorious Confederate prison at Andersonville in Georgia. Out of 21 known Welsh-speaking soldiers of the 9th Minnesota Infantry, 7 were captured and sent to Andersonville; 1 escaped, one survived, and 5 died there. John S. Davis was imprisoned there for six months: 'He was turned into a fleshless skeleton, like thousands of others, before being set free. He reached the house of his father, with his flesh having blackened from starvation, three days before his death.' He was nineteen years of age. Another who died at Andersonville was Joseph Griffiths of the 5th Iowa Cavalry. Sometimes several from the same family died. In late 1864, Jane Jones lost her two sons, Josiah and Jonadab Jones of the 94th Illinois Infantry.

Published obituaries tell a great deal of the losses of the Welsh American community of Minersville, Pennsylvania. One obituary told of a woman who 'received her son's kit and the amount due to him at the time of death'. The obituary of John Jones told of how he was born in Monmouthshire but 'came to this country about 18 years ago' and settled in Minersville. He 'felt it to be his duty to defend his country' and signed up for a three-year term and then re-enlisted for another three. He was involved 'in many skirmishes' in South Carolina and Virginia, died in 1864 at the age of twenty-five and was buried in the Welsh

Congregational Cemetery. The obituary of Lewis Lewis declared that he was born in south Wales, came to Pennsylvania in 1851 and served in Virginia under General Ulysses S. Grant. Lewis died after a leg amputation in 1864. He was twenty-one years old and he too was buried in the Welsh Congregational church in Minersville, as was Corporal John Powell. Powell was born in south Wales and had come to the United States aged thirteen years. He enlisted for three years, then re-enlisted for another three, but died in 1864 from a war wound received fighting in the Battle of the Wilderness in Virginia. Lieutenant William Williams was also born in Wales. He was brought to America when he was very young and his family lived in Tremont, near Minersville. He died in 1864 from a war wound, aged thirty-seven.

Private John Griffith Jones

Sometimes the whole army career of an individual can be traced in his letters. Private John G. Jones wrote frequently to 'my dear father and mother' in Wisconsin. He enlisted with eleven Welsh-speaking friends in Company G of the 23rd Wisconsin Infantry. In August 1862, he wrote telling his parents of his training at Camp Randall, in Madison, Wisconsin: 'We have been very busy drilling . . . I have been talking to 18 Welshmen, strangers, six from Sauk County, three from Lake Cross, two from Prairie du Chien, seven from Spring Glenn.' In December 1862, he wrote from Memphis, Tennessee: 'I do not know where all the letters you write go to, they must go somewhere . . . I am in strong hope that I may be allowed to come home before very long. It is nearly 4 months since we are bearing arms.' In March 1863, he wrote from Milliken's Bend encampment in Louisiana: 'We have found Welsh boys in the 22 Iowa and the 25 Iowa and the 108 Illinois, there seems to be very many Welsh boys in the army.' He clearly enjoyed it when Company G of the 23rd Wisconsin Infantry was put in the same camp as the 22nd Wisconsin and the 118th Ohio, which had a Welsh company. The result was that 'there is a lot of singing here with all of the Welsh'. In 1863, he wrote giving his brothers advice:

> We hear that there is a great deal of commotion in the old state of Wisconsin over the draft. A word to Richard and Owen, my brothers: you are both too young for the draft, do not enlist while you can stay home. Do as I tell you, do not do as I did. Although I do not regret coming. I have a strong feeling that I shall come home again, but when I do not know.

In July 1863, he wrote from 'Vicksburg Camp', thanking his parents for sending him *Y Drych*:

> I do not know when I shall get home . . . You were saying that you thought I would have learned to speak English by now. I now prefer to speak English to Welsh, it is easier as we are continually with the English . . . I hear that John T. Edwards is going to enlist again, I would advise him to stay home. I should think he has suffered enough.

Although promoted to corporal, John had become increasingly down-hearted, telling his mother that 'there is nobody left [bar two] out of the Welsh boys . . . I never thought that I would be left all by myself when we were in Kentucky and there were 12 of us together.' Soon after, in an October 1864 skirmish at Sandy Bayou, Louisiana, Corporal Jones died.

'Feeling very well' – or not?

Jones was of course not the only Welsh American to find war a sobering experience. Some had doubts immediately after enlistment. Welsh-speaker David Davies of Oneida County enlisted in January 1862 and recorded an honest account of it in his diary. Before he left, he attended chapel twice on what 'may be my last sabbath among friends'. He hoped to take advantage of those who admired him for enlisting: 'Leila Hughes turned to me to say farewell, to whom I gave a "Farewell Kiss"; I got a slap for repayment!' He 'broke down while conducting family prayers' on the Monday, and there was 'a spell of crying after breakfast'. However, things improved at the railway station, where he was treated by admirers: 'Got plenty enough to drink there for free.' That left him 'feeling very well' as he boarded the train.

Some referred to the horrors of battle. A Welsh immigrant in the 7th Iowa, Benjamin Thomas, wrote that after several hours of the 'bloody battle' at Corinth, 'I was almost on the point of collapse'. After his first battle at Shiloh, Robert J. Thomas of the 14th Wisconsin Infantry wrote telling his brother in Oneida County, New York, 'I never want to see the battlefield again.' Vermont quarryman John Rowlands wrote in his diary after the battle of Gettysburg that 'this is the most terrible day that has ever been upon me and I do not wish to see another of its sort again.' Others were more positive. Evan Davis of Minersville so hated the slave-owning Confederacy that he wrote gleefully in 1862 of 'discharging our guns . . . The work appeared pleasant, and looking at the body kicking as it bade farewell to the soul was sweet.'

A HERO OF GETTYSBURG

Winfield Scott Hancock (1824–86) was a career soldier with Welsh, Scots and English ancestry, who was considered one of the great heroes of the Battle of Gettysburg (1863).

'Our nation in the army'

Although still steeped in Welsh culture, Welsh-speaking Americans were patriotic Americans. Pontypool-born William H. Powell, manager of the Lawrence rolling mill in Ironton, Ohio, recruited and then captained a company of cavalry, although not all recruits were Welsh. He was repeatedly promoted, and by May 1863, Colonel Powell commanded the 2nd West Virginia Cavalry, which contained the Ohio company he had originally recruited. By the end of the war, he was a brigadier general. Ohio cavalryman Howell Hopkins described Powell as both a fellow Welshman and an American patriot, illustrating the common contemporary perception that one could be both a Welshman and an American. The Welsh soldiers of the 22nd Wisconsin described themselves as 'sons of Wales . . . defending the [US] government'. Benjamin F. Thomas's family had emigrated from Llangeitho in south-west Wales to Gallia County, Ohio, when he was two. In his letters to his mother, he made it clear that he believed that his duty to the US government was on a par with his duty to God. Father of six Dafydd Roach of Iowa County, Wisconsin, was conscripted in 1864. His wife Ann visited him at his camp in Madison and brought him donations designed to enable him to hire a substitute. However, it was recorded in *Y Cenhadwr Americanaidd* in July 1865 that he refused this opportunity to hire a substitute because 'he felt it was his duty to his God and his country to go himself'. He was shot in the stomach at Hatcher's Run in Virginia and buried on the battlefield.

Many correspondents clung to and declared their longing for Welsh-language publications. They were particularly keen to have a Welsh bible or a Welsh-speaking preacher. Like many Welsh Americans, Benjamin F. Thomas carried his Welsh bible with him throughout the war. Howell Hopkins said he would like 'to see *Y Drych*, a Bible and a preacher before dying'. There were several Welsh American chaplains with the Ohio men, including Benjamin Chidlaw, chaplain of the 39th Ohio Volunteer Infantry. The diarist David Davis was one of many Welsh Americans who wished he could hear sermons in Welsh while in the army. Perhaps he was one of those with whom the Rev. J. D. Jones was concerned when he wrote asking Robert Everett for 'about a dozen Welsh testaments for the use of the Welsh . . . in the 4th Oneida of which I am chaplain'. Amongst the other Welsh American chaplains with New York contingents were Baptist Robert Littler with the 74th New York Infantry and Franklin Jones with the 1st New York Volunteers. Many from New York and other states took great solace in religion and in each other's company: a group of eleven Welsh Americans in the 154th New York Infantry, all from the same chapel in Freedom, Cattaraugus County, had a 'Christmas dinner on the banks of the Rappahannock', according to a Gwilym ab Ioan letter published in *Y Drych*. For some, their Welsh culture was more important than anything else: John E. Roberts belonged to the 5th Pennsylvania Cavalry, which had a visit from President Lincoln, but Roberts said that receiving *Y Drych* was 'more pleasing to me'.

There were of course many of Welsh descent who, as William S. Jones wrote in *Y Drych*, were content to be in English-speaking regiments and thereby 'denying the language of their mothers'. Some simply found themselves amongst and outnumbered by other ethnic groups. John Davies wrote to his mother in Wales from Washington, 'I am . . . content . . . without but one Welshman near me.' When future Brigadier General Joshua T. Owen was a colonel of the 69th Pennsylvanian, it consisted mainly of Irishmen. No doubt there were many Union soldiers of Welsh descent for whom English was their first language. In Nashville in 1865, Welsh writer John Griffith met 'General [George] Thomas, Welsh by descent, and though unable to speak Welsh, he holds a strong attachment to the old nation. He was born in the state of Virginia, his grandfather having emigrated from Wales, and settled in some part of Pennsylvania.' Thomas was known as the 'Rock of Chickamauga', on account of one of his many impressive military performances in Tennessee.

Sometimes correspondents were painfully aware of the distance from Wales. While in West Virginia, Theophilus Davies said he was thinking of 'my dear mother who is on the other side of the sea' as he mentally prepared himself to meet his maker. Others found reminders of the Old Country. D. M. Williams of the 18th Wisconsin Infantry found the landscape of the Lake Providence area in northern Louisiana like the 'top of the hills of Cwm Nedd, in Glamorgan . . . around 15 years ago . . . [in] the time of childhood . . . And to make the place even more dear to me, there are some of our nation living here.' John W. Jones of the 23rd Wisconsin Volunteer Infantry found in Kentucky 'roads cobbled like the Old Country'.

Whether they were homesick or Welsh-speaking or not, all offered their lives to maintain the Union and contributed to the remaking of America as a nation without slavery.

DESERTERS, DISSENTERS AND SUBSTITUTES

Not all Welsh Americans wanted to serve the Union cause. James Thomas served in the 3rd Pennsylvania Heavy Artillery, but in his letter in *Y Drych*, he told of a brother who had gone to dig for gold in Pikes Peak, Colorado. In 1862, David Williams, a soldier from Waukesha, Wisconsin, took to *Y Drych* to denounce some local residents who were avoiding the draft. He claimed 'scores' of them asked to be excused on medical grounds, and some 'escape away to Canada or the Old Country'. He was answered in *Y Drych* by Thomas D. Jones, who said Williams 'accuses them falsely' and insisted that some were rightly excused military service. *Y Drych* named and shamed some deserters. A letter from the 22nd Wisconsin Infantry in January 1863 reported that 'several have fled from the regiment . . . and I am sorry to say that three of these men are Welsh'. They were Evan G. Roberts from Nelson Flats, New York and then Cambria, Wisconsin; Thomas Hall, who had worked in Racine, Wisconsin; and Samuel Thomas from Berlin, Green Lake County, Wisconsin.

There were also some Dissenting pacifists, some of whose writings were published by Welsh American religious journals during the war, and those who paid for others to fight for them. James Davis emigrated from Swansea in 1841, made his fortune in transporting coal in Coshocton County, Ohio and proudly boasted that he paid $1,200 for a substitute to fight for three years in his place.

Non-combatants

Many Welsh Americans contributed to the Union cause through efforts other than soldiering. Amongst them were the Welsh American chaplains who have been noted. The most famous was the Rev. Benjamin Chidlaw (1811–92), born in Bala in north Wales. He did missionary work with Union volunteers in the southern Ohio military camps before becoming chaplain of the 39th Ohio Volunteer Infantry. Isaac Cheshire from Wisconsin worked in the Department of the Interior in Washington as a bookkeeper. As the North became increasingly desperate for labour during the Civil War, Welsh immigration increased and many of these new Welsh immigrants worked in the coal mines, which made an important economic contribution to the Union.

Some Welsh-speakers did voluntary work. The Welsh of New York City contributed to the United States Sanitary Commission's great national fair in Washington. That Commission was one of the major national organisations established to help maintain the health of Union troops. The Welsh women of Remsen in Oneida County, New York, established a Society for Aiding the Soldiers, the Sick and the Injured. A subgroup containing ten- to fifteen-year-old girls sent a package to Washington that included twenty-three pairs of woollen mittens for the soldiers. The Second Congregationalist church of Utica sent clothing direct to the 26th New York Infantry, because the regiment contained Welsh soldiers from the area. John H. Williams recorded that 'the young women of West Brattleboro' in Vermont sent a box to the Welsh soldiers in the 14th Vermont Infantry containing 'butter, cheese, wine, pies, tea, sugar, cakes, herrings . . . It was good to get a bit of Vermont's tasty food in warlike Virginia.'

FIGHTING FOR THE CONFEDERACY

While there is evidence of several thousand Union soldiers having been Welsh-born or American-born Welsh-speakers, it is hard to identify more than a handful who fought for the Confederacy. There are several explanations for the disparity. Although considerable numbers in the South had Welsh-sounding names, their ancestors had emigrated long before, so that subsequent generations were no longer Welsh speaking and were by now well assimilated into Southern society. The North had a far greater population than the South, and the vast majority of nine-teenth-century Welsh immigrants had settled in the North. Roughly 90 percent of those recorded in the censuses of 1850 and 1860 lived in four Northern states, New York, Pennsylvania, Ohio and Wisconsin, and most of the rest lived in other Northern states. Welsh-speaking Americans read strongly anti-slavery Welsh-language materials printed in Wales and America, and those materials frequently emphasised the similarities between Southern slave-owners and the aristocrats who had oppressed the Welsh in Britain. Finally, Britain was sympathetic to the Confederacy rather than the Union, which helped revive some anti-British sentiment among the Welsh.

Henry Morton Stanley, famous for finding Dr Livingstone, was one of the ten or so Welshmen known to have fought for the Confederacy. He wrote in his 1893 autobiography of having 'a secret scorn for people who could kill one another for the sake of African slaves. There were no blackies in Wales, and why a sooty-faced nigger from a distant land should be an element of disturbance between white brothers was a puzzle to me.' He arrived in New Orleans in 1859 and enlisted with the 6th Arkansas Infantry when the Civil War broke out, but subsequently became a Union soldier rather than remain captive.

Jefferson Davis was no doubt one of thousands with Welsh ancestry who served the Confederacy. We know of a Welsh-born volunteer in the 6th Louisiana and of a Captain Edward Thomas of Savannah, Georgia. The latter was descended from John Thomas, who was thought to have captained the first ship to bring colonists to Georgia. Although Kentucky fought on the side of the Union, it was a slave state, and one Kentuckian who enlisted in the Confederate army was Colonel Jacob Wark Griffith, who believed himself descended from Welsh warrior kings. His ancestors had settled in Maryland in the early eighteenth century. His son was the movie-making pioneer D. W. Griffith, who was told by his mother that his name David meant 'dearly beloved' in Welsh.

Confederate General Sterling Price had Welsh ancestry, while James Evans, whose family had emigrated to Charleston, served on the Confederate warship *Alabama*. The *Alabama* captured some Union ships and persuaded four Welshmen on board them to switch allegiance. The *Alabama* doctor was a Dr David Herbert Llewellyn of Pembrokeshire, and its chief engineer was Miles J. Freeman, a Welsh immigrant in New Orleans. Catesby ap Roger Jones was a commander in the Confederate Navy. His adoption of the 'ap' (Welsh for 'son of') suggests either a pride in his Welsh ancestry, or more likely in the members of the illustrious Jones family who had served the US Navy with distinction in the Revolutionary War, the War of 1812 against Britain, and the Mexican–American War. From 1863, he was in charge of the Ordnance Works in Selma, Alabama, which produced vital weaponry for the Confederacy.

There were some Democrats in the North who sympathised with the Confederacy. They incurred the wrath of the Welsh American press. Y *Drych* named and shamed some of them: 'You have three at least in Utica.' The Rev. Jenkin Jenkins's son David had worked on a Missouri riverboat before the war and joined the Confederate army with a few friends. 'He went to the land of the enemy; that was completely repugnant,' lamented his father. 'Yet despite that we now often cry for him.'

THE WELSH CONTRIBUTION TO A CIVIL WAR THAT HELPED MAKE AMERICA

The American Civil War ended slavery, if not racial inequality and racism, in the United States. It also ensured that the Southern states would remain within the Union. Welsh American churches, publications and soldiers contributed to a Union victory that the vast majority of Americans see as vital in the making of America. Proportionately, their efforts and losses were as great, if not greater than those from other ethnic groups – if less well known.

CLAIMING THE LINCOLNS

'Nearly all the soldiers are in favour of Lincoln,' wrote Private John P. Jones of the 23rd Wisconsin. Such was the Welsh admiration for Lincoln that several contemporary Welsh American writers tried to claim that the President had a Welsh connection. Some reported the false rumour that Mrs Lincoln was 'a Welsh woman . . . a native of Newport, Monmouthshire'. The attempts to emphasise a link continue. Many believe that Abraham Lincoln's mother was of Welsh descent, and the owner of a derelict farmhouse in Ysbyty Ifan in the Conwy Valley contends that it belonged to one of her ancestors, a view shared by the American tourists it attracts.

THE PERILS OF ETHNIC HISTORY

In recent decades, there have been studies of European ethnic groups in the American Civil War by William L. Burton (1998) and Dean Mahin (2002). Burton in particular discusses and illustrates the problems facing writers who focus on the role and contribution of ethnic minorities in the Civil War and, one might add, in any period of American history.

One problem is to what extent a foreign-born immigrant is more or less of an 'ethnic' than an individual born to two immigrant parents. The 1860 US census recorded a population of 34.5 million Americans, of whom 4.1 million (over 12 per cent of the total population) were foreign-born. The largest group of foreign-born was the 1.6 million Irish, followed by 1.3 million Germans, and then 587,775 British. The British-born immigrants comprised 433,494 English, 108,518 Scots, and 45,736 Welsh. It is difficult to say whether and to what extent the 45,736 Welsh-born, some of whom fought for the Union, were so much more 'Welsh' than those American-born Union soldiers who wrote letters in Welsh to their immigrant parents in states such as Wisconsin and Ohio.

The difficulty in deciding who exactly constitutes an 'ethnic' makes it hard to assert with any certainty just how many of a particular ethnic group fought in the Civil War, especially as estimates can be exaggerated and available statistics can be inaccurate and vulnerable to selective usage for ethnic point-scoring. Still, Mahin wrote that the evidence suggests that the German immigrants volunteered for the Union army at a higher rate than the general population, but the Irish and British immigrants at a lower rate. Another difficulty there is that the Welsh immigrants are incorporated under the 'British' umbrella and the Welsh may conceivably have enlisted at a higher – or lower – rate than the English and/or Scots.

Burton was infuriated by contemporaries and ethnic historians who were keen to emphasise and/or exaggerate the contribution of fellow countrymen. He rightly emphasised the importance of those of English ancestry in the making of America, and he had little patience with the nationalism of ethnics, particularly the Irish. That may explain why, for Burton, the Welsh barely merited a mention, except as a part of 'the British' and as a nation of poets who sometimes wrote bad poetry.

So, where does this leave the historian of the Welsh contribution to the American Civil War (and indeed, to the making of America)? Proportionately the numbers of Welsh who fought for the Union were perhaps no more and no less than other ethnic groups, but while historians generally agree that few Union soldiers fought to free black Americans, the carefully documented research of Jerry Hunter (2007) persuaded Mahin at least that Welsh-speaking soldiers were more likely to be motivated by the desire to abolish slavery than any other group. There, perhaps, a Welsh historian is entitled to boast of the Welsh contribution to the American Civil War.

JAMES GARFIELD, CIVIL WAR AND THE AMERICAN DREAM

From log cabin . . .

James Garfield (1831–81) was born in a log cabin in Orange, Ohio. According to Emma Elizabeth Brown's 1881 biography, the young Garfield enjoyed hearing his mother's stories about distant Welsh ancestors, including a knight at Caerphilly Castle. Although 'I was born to poverty' (his father died when he was two), Garfield worked hard and eventually acquired a good education. He was an enlightened young man who became an enthusiastic abolitionist while attending Williams College, Massachusetts, and considered women 'wronged socially and intellectually by the usages of society'. In 1859, he left teaching for the Ohio Senate.

. . . to the Ohio legislature (1859–61) and the battlefield

When the Civil War broke out, Garfield was without any military experience but wanted to fight, which the Democrat *Weekly Portage Sentinel* attributed to political ambition. After Garfield was made a Colonel in the 42nd Ohio Infantry, he recruited soldiers from amongst his former students for the Regiment. Garfield's performance at the Union victory at the Battle of Middle Creek (1862) was rewarded with promotion to brigadier general. His service at Shiloh (1862) and Chickamauga (1863) led to his elevation to major general.

... to the US House of Representatives (1863–80)

Garfield told a friend the post-war settlement would be 'of even more vital importance than the ending of the war'. He played a part in that settlement while serving in the US House of Representatives. From 1863 to 1868, he joined other Radical Republicans in pressing Presidents Lincoln and Andrew Johnson to be tougher on the South.

Garfield wanted freed black Americans enfranchised. 'Let us not commit ourselves to the absurd and senseless dogma that the color of the skin shall be the basis of suffrage,' he said, while nevertheless worrying that 'the great mass of ignorant and degraded blacks' would be voting without having been educated. He admitted that the thought of black political equality aroused 'a strong feeling of repugnance' in him. Perhaps it was racism, perhaps the passage of time that made Garfield, like many other Northerners, more conciliatory towards Southern whites by the 1870s.

Overall, Garfield gained considerable respect in Washington politics for his fiscal sense, hard work and effective leadership in the House. As a result, when the Republicans reached deadlock over the choice of their presidential candidate in 1880, Garfield was chosen as the compromise candidate. Some claimed that was what Garfield and his supporters had intended from the first. After a Republican campaign that emphasised Democrat blame for the Civil War, Garfield narrowly defeated the Democrat candidate in the popular vote.

... to the White House (1881)

James Garfield is often considered one of the weak 'forgettable' presidents of the later nineteenth century, but there were promising signs during his presidency. He combated partisan senatorial influence on federal appointments, and corruption in Post Office Department contracts and civil service appointments. He continued to advocate black civil rights, declaring in his inaugural address:

> The elevation of the Negro race from slavery to full rights of citizenship, is the most important political change we have known since the adoption of the Constitution of 1776. So far as my authority can lawfully extend, they shall enjoy full and equal protection of the Constitution and laws.

He saw 'the saving influence of [free] universal education' as essential for preventing black Americans becoming a permanent underclass and for enabling them to exercise the franchise, but Congress and Northern whites rejected his suggestion of federal funding for education. He made several significant black appointments, including Frederick Douglass as recorder of deeds in Washington, DC. Garfield and his Secretary of State

James G. Blaine anticipated America's rise to economic and political greatness with their promotion of free trade, commercial treaties with Latin America, expansion and modernisation of the Navy, and interest in Hawaii.

Assassination, lunatics and medicine

After a mere six months as President, Garfield was shot at a railway station by a disgruntled office seeker, Charles Julius Guiteau. One shot scraped Garfield's arm, but the other went through his back, shattered a rib and stuck in his abdomen. Several doctors probed his wound with unwashed fingers, as was customary amongst older physicians sceptical about Pasteur and Lister's work on germs and infection.

Garfield's medical care was dominated by Doctor Willard Bliss (Doctor was his name), who had dealt with gunshot wounds during the Civil War. Within one week of the shooting, Garfield's wound began discharging what Bliss considered 'healthy looking pus'. The belief in 'praiseworthy pus' dated from the ancient Greeks but had lost credibility amongst younger physicians. Further and daily probing for the bullet with unsterilised fingers and instruments pushed the pus back down deep into the wound. Doctors debated the whereabouts of the bullet, Alexander Graham Bell tried but failed to locate the bullet with a primitive metal detector and the general public offered helpful tips. One gentleman recommended hanging President Garfield by his toes so that the bullet would fall out and a Maryland man wrote telling the *Washington Evening Star* that the bullet had appeared in his Maryland house. A Kansas country doctor begged Bliss to soak the wound with Lister's carbolic acid and to stop probing, but he was ignored. Meanwhile, Bliss gave the president food that was difficult to digest, such as meat. As pus pockets developed all over his body, Garfield was starving to death and rotting from the inside. From August, he could not keep his food down, so he was 'fed' nutritional enemas of beef stock, egg yolks, milk and whiskey, which served mostly to give him flatulence. He succumbed to infection more than two months after having been shot.

The lunatic Guiteau insisted that he was not guilty of murder: he pointed out that the doctors had said that Garfield would recover and that it was obviously their fault that he had not. The lunatic got it right: Garfield's doctors had ensured his death.

The significance of James Garfield

Garfield illustrates the affection for and belief in military heroes that is characteristic of American voters. As the Rev. William Davies Evans noted in 1880, he epitomised the American Dream in his rise from log cabin to White House: 'This President is looked upon as an example of a notable man who succeeded to the position he came to hold by his own exertions alone.' While many historians have simply grouped him with the 'weak' presidents of the later nineteenth century, the 70,000 citizens who passed by his coffin as his body lay in state in the Capitol building, and the 150,000 who paid their respects in Cleveland, suggest that he was respected by those in Washington and his home state, and there are historians who consider Garfield a promising president.

CHAPTER NINE

The Welsh and the Industrialisation of America

THE EARLY development of the US economy is reflected in the life and career of the little-known Welsh American inventor, Oliver Evans.

OLIVER EVANS (1755–1819)

Oliver Evans was born in 1755 to Welsh settlers in Newport in Delaware's Welsh Tract. Oliver's father was a shoemaker, one of the many Welsh and Welsh American artisans of the colonial period. Colonial America's economy was primarily agricultural, and Oliver's upwardly mobile father purchased a large farm.

Evans's automated flour mills

Oliver and two of his brothers bought part of their father's Delaware farm in 1782 and opened a mill there in 1785. At this time, grain was ground into flour through a slow, labour-intensive and dirty process. Evans mechanised the process, making it faster and cleaner: propelled by gravity, friction and waterwheels, the grain passed through the stages of milling and refining via multiple conveyors and chutes and emerged as finished flour. The only manual labour required was the single individual who set the automatic production line in motion. Oliver Evans had introduced the concept of manufacturing as a continuous, integrated and fully automated process. The production line idea that he pioneered would prove a crucial factor in America's twentieth-century industrial pre-eminence.

Although other mill owners were initially sceptical about Evans's process, his automated mills had been copied all along the eastern seaboard by the 1790s. George Washington and Thomas Jefferson were enthusiastic supporters of Evans's ideas and of his *The Young Mill-wright and Miller's Guide* (1795). This manual for millers was a best-seller for over half a century, with fifteen editions printed between 1795 and 1860.

As Evans's revolutionary mechanisation had made milling a much more profitable business, the number of American mills rocketed, flour prices fell, and the quality of the flour and the bread improved dramatically. Oliver Evans had helped feed the multitudes whose labour was making America.

Evans's steam engines

The US economy remained primarily agricultural, but Evans's inventions illustrate how the demands of agriculture often stimulated industry.

In Philadelphia in 1801, Evans built a stationary engine that crushed the limestone used in farming. A few years later, he produced an engine to sow grain.

Steam engines were used as a power source in America from the late eighteenth century. Evans's contemporaries believed only heavy, low-pressure steam engines were practical, but Evans invented smaller and more efficient high-pressure steam engines that had many more uses, such as powering locomotives and steamboats.

Manufacturing steam engines was a slow, inefficient process. Evans knew an ironworks and specialist tools were essential if engines were to be built on a large scale, so he established the Mars Iron Works in Philadelphia in 1807. With this, he laid the foundations for Philadelphia to become a leading centre for the production of heavy machinery. The Mars Iron Works would produce over one hundred steam engines by the time Evans died, along with milling and farming machines and the cannons commissioned by the federal government for the US Navy during the War of 1812 against the British. His engines were used in the processing of cotton, a contribution to a textile industry that was America's premier industry in the first half of the nineteenth century.

OLIVER EVANS ON THE ADVANTAGES OF STEAM

Evans pointed out the two greatest disadvantages of waterpower: the number of suitable water sites was limited and there were problems with freezing in the winter. He noted that animals were 'tedious' and 'subject to innumerable accidents'. In contrast, 'Steam at once presents us with a faithful servant, as commanding all places, in all seasons.'

The large potential market for Evans's steam engines in western Pennsylvania, Kentucky and Ohio encouraged him to co-found the Pittsburgh Steam Engine Company in 1811. The company produced steam engines and boilers for use in mills, factories, the iron industry's rolling mills, and steamboats. The early nineteenth-century United States underwent a transportation revolution of which steamboats, along with roads, canals and railroads, were an important part. Pittsburgh was situated on a major tributary of the Mississippi River and the availability and accessibility of high-pressure steam engines from Evans's Pittsburgh company led to their widespread use on steamboats on the Mississippi River system. As so often, Evans's career typified the trajectory of the industrialisation of America: the manufacture of heavy machinery would be America's most important industry by the late nineteenth century.

OLIVER EVANS'S DESIGNS

Evans thought up ideas for a refrigerator, a solar-powered boiler, a machine gun, a rudimentary breadmaking machine, a hot-air central heating system and gas lighting for towns and cities. His visionary ideas and designs were invariably far beyond what most contemporary engineers could understand. Others frequently hesitated to accept his ideas or were slow to praise him. Former President Thomas Jefferson was one of the few who recognised his genius, and of the even fewer who sympathised with Evans's struggles to have his patents respected when others freely stole his engine designs and his milling process.

Overall, Oliver Evans was a significant figure who had contributed to the food, textile, iron, manufacturing and transportation industries, all essential elements in the industrialisation of the United States.

INDUSTRIALISATION

The USA developed an industrialised economy during the nineteenth century. In 1860, the textile industry was the biggest industrial employer. It was concentrated in the north-east, and its factory workers were mostly women and children. Although many Welsh men and women worked in the textile mills of Oneida County, New York, the Welsh and Welsh Americans did not make a significant impact on the textile industry. However, they played a crucial role in other major industries.

By the last thirty years of the nineteenth century, the manufacture of machinery was America's most important industry, followed by the coal-fuelled production of iron and steel. Industrialisation in Wales had a half-century head start over industrialisation in the United States, and as a result, Welsh expertise in puddling iron and cutting coal was in great demand in America. Welsh coal miners and iron mill men were pioneers in the American coal and iron and steel industries, so that by the 1850s there were thriving Welsh industrial communities in the coal and iron regions of Pennsylvania and Ohio. Historian Ronald L. Lewis's Welsh ancestry does not make his 2008 contention any the less persuasive:

> The United States built its industrial empire on coal and steel, and, despite their comparatively small numbers, no immigrant group played a more strategic role per capita in advancing basic industry in America than the Welsh. The American industrial revolution can

be read as a story of Welsh technical skills being transferred to Pennsylvania and from there dispersed to other regions . . . with the Welsh mine and mill managers in the vanguard.

THE CHANGING NATURE OF WELSH IMMIGRATION

Before the mid-nineteenth century, Welsh immigrants to America generally originated from rural Wales. After that time, most were industrial workers – miners, iron and steel workers and tinplate workers from south Wales, and slate quarrymen from north Wales. In 1870, the Rev. R. D. Thomas noted the changing nature of Welsh immigration to Ohio: while earlier Welsh immigrants to Ohio were farmers, the number employed in industry grew dramatically in the second half of the nineteenth century. R. D. Thomas counted 24,810 Welsh residents in Ohio, of whom 45 per cent lived in farming communities and 55 per cent in the coal and iron area.

Letters suggest better wages were the main 'pull' factor. There was also an element of 'America fever', spread through the 'chain migration' that operated through letters, family links and recruitment by US companies.

IRON AND STEEL

Virginia produced most of the iron that made the American colonies the world's third largest producer of iron by 1776. From the early nineteenth century, Welsh ironworks were considered world leaders and Welsh expertise was important in the further development of America's iron industry. In 1832, the Rev. John J. Vinton wrote from Pittsburgh: 'Pittsburgh is a great place for ironworks; it is called Iron City and I met hundreds of Welsh men and women.'

American ironworks were keen to recruit skilled Welshmen such as Rhys Davies and David Thomas. The story of Rhys Davies, recounted most recently by Nathan Vernon Madison (2015), suggests that he might be but one among many unsung Welsh heroes who contributed to the making of industrial America.

The Tredegar ironworks and the rediscovery of Rhys Davies

In 1957, a teacher living in Tredegar in the south Wales valleys wrote asking the Tredegar Company in Richmond, Virginia, whether Richmond's Tredegar Iron Works were in any way connected with the south Wales iron town of Tredegar. A representative of the Richmond company replied that the early works had employed Welsh immigrant ironworkers, but that was all. Then, in 1997, someone spotted an obituary in the *Hereford Times* of 24 November 1838: 'Rhys Davies. Died in Richmond Virginia early Sunday morning in consequence of having been stabbed a fortnight ago.' From there, the story was pieced together.

Rhys Davies was born in the late 1790s in Llangynidr, Breconshire, thirty miles north of the Tredegar ironworks in which he worked from the age of eleven years. In 1836, he was asked to contribute Welsh expertise to the creation of a foundry and ironworks in Richmond, Virginia.

Davies, along with his father and several other workmen from the Tredegar area, masterminded the construction of the first mill for rolling iron for the Virginia Foundry Company's ironworks in Richmond. He was the mill's first superintendent. When the president of the works wrote to the Mayor of Tredegar asking if he could name the Richmond works in honour of the iron town in Wales, it may have been to honour Rhys Davies, but it was more likely in order to exploit the name and fame of the Welsh works. The mayor agreed, and in 1837 Tredegar Forge and Rolling Mill began operation in Richmond. A Richmond newspaper said the 'works are admirably constructed under a most skilful engineer, Mr Reese [*sic*] Davies . . . The iron is of excellent quality, and is in demand in different markets in the United States.'

Rhys Davies came to an unfortunate end. He was stabbed to death by a worker within weeks of beginning work on a new rolling mill for the Belle Isle Manufacturing Company, near Richmond. According to the *Richmond Compiler* newspaper, 'He gave way to his passion and fell its victim.' The killer was 'examined and discharged', which suggests that Rhys Davies was considered culpable.

The significance of Richmond's Tredegar works

The *Hereford Times* christened Rhys Davies a 'mechanical genius'. He had left an important industrial legacy, aided by the other Welshmen who had emigrated with him. After his death, they remained in the Tredegar Iron Works, which was the largest producer of iron in the United States by 1840. It was producing rails, spikes, railway chairs, car wheels, boxcars, flat cars, freight cars, passenger cars and engines by 1860. That constituted a particularly important contribution to the burgeoning railway system that was revolutionising American settlement, communications and industry. The Tredegar Iron Works proved essential to the Confederacy in the war, supplying guns, ammunition and the plates for its ironclad warships such as the *CSS Virginia*.

RAILWAY CONSTRUCTION AND OPERATION

Several Welsh engineers were of significance in the construction of America's railways. Daniel Howell (1824–95) emigrated from Llanbrynmair, Montgomeryshire and was chief engineer for the construction of several routes out of Milwaukee. In 1866, Morgan Jones (1839–1926) emigrated from Tregynon, Montgomeryshire and built railways across Texas. Aberystwyth-born L. W. Lewis was a bridge and railway engineer whose Kansas company employed 200 workers, and the Rev. William Davies Evans noted approvingly that he was 'an employer who make[s] sure he hires the Welsh when they arrive in the district he is engaged in.'

Working on nineteenth-century trains was hazardous: in 1874, Welsh immigrants William Hutchins and his father died in a boiler explosion en route to Columbus, Ohio.

David Thomas, 'the father of the anthracite industry'

Prior to 1840, many American blast furnaces still used charcoal to smelt iron, although Richmond's ironworks used the bituminous coal deposits around the city. When the mid-1830s saw increased demand for iron ships and iron rails for America's mushrooming railway network, American ironworks struggled to meet the demand. The early American railways relied on expensive imports of 'Dowlais Rail', produced in south Wales by the Dowlais Ironworks near Merthyr Tydfil. America needed a revolution in its iron industry, and this was where David Thomas was important.

David Thomas was born in 1794 on the family farm in the Neath Valley in south Wales. The family was Welsh-speaking, but David learned English at school. A series of poor harvests prompted the family to finance his apprenticeship at Neath Abbey Iron Works. After five years there, Thomas became superintendent of the furnaces and iron ore and coal mines of George Crane's Ynyscedwyn Iron Works at Ystradgynlais, thirteen miles up the Swansea Valley. Thomas worked there for twenty years. The local anthracite coal was considered unsuitable for iron smelting, but David Thomas's son recalled his father deciding that God had put anthracite coal alongside iron ore for a reason. Thomas discovered that the application of a hot blast in the furnace made it possible to smelt iron with anthracite coal. This revolutionary process made excellent-quality iron at far less cost. There is no consensus as to whether the process was discovered by Thomas or Crane or both, or even by someone in Scotland, but Crane patented it.

From the Neath Valley to Pennsylvania

The revolutionary process used at Ynyscedwyn came to the attention of an associate of eastern Pennsylvania's Lehigh Coal and Navigation Company who made frequent visits to the Dowlais Ironworks in Wales. On his return to eastern Pennsylvania, which was rich in both anthracite coal and iron ore, he suggested that David Thomas be offered well-paid employment 'for a period of five years to manage the setting up of a furnace on or near the River Lehigh to smelt iron with anthracite'. Whether or not Thomas was the sole and/or first inventor of the anthracite process, it was he who successfully introduced it to the United States.

In 1839, Thomas and his family journeyed from Swansea to Liverpool and on to New York. The Pennsylvania company provided them with three comfortable staterooms on the sailing ship *Roscius*, one for Mr and Mrs Thomas and two for their children. During the twenty-three-day voyage, the family discussions illustrated the extent to which the Welsh American experience had permeated the consciousness of the Welsh nation. Thomas's teachers had told him of Madoc and the Mandan Indians, and he told his family how John Evans had found the Mandans. He told them of how John Miles had settled Swanzey in Massachusetts. He explained that William Penn's Welsh secretary had doubts about the name 'New Wales' and how Penn, while not keen to have his colony named after him, was satisfied with the name Pennsylvania because 'Pen' meant high or chief in Welsh and 'Sylvania' signified woods. The family talked of how the American Declaration of Independence was primarily the product of Welsh settlers, and the children recounted what they had learned in school about Richard Price. David Thomas assured his family that Welsh was spoken in the streets of Philadelphia and pointed out that Thomas Wynn from Caerwys, Flintshire had helped William Penn design the street layout there.

David Thomas and the Pennsylvania iron industry

The Thomas family travelled from New York to Philadelphia and then on to Allentown. Thomas's first Allentown furnace was built at Catasauqua in the Lehigh Valley in 1839–40. Two new Welsh immigrants, William Phillips and Evan Jones, took charge of its operation. George Crane wrote congratulating Thomas, saying, 'I agree with you that one day you will see America the most important iron working country.' Starting in late 1842, Thomas constructed four more furnaces for the Lehigh Crane Company, each with greater productive capacity than the last.

The first Thomas furnace was quickly copied by other Pennsylvania ironmasters such as William Henry. It took yet another Welsh immigrant ironworker, John Davis, to get Henry's anthracite furnace in the Lackawanna Valley, near Scranton, operating successfully in 1842, but it was Thomas whom contemporaries knew as 'Father of the American Anthracite Iron Industry'.

In 1854, David Thomas established his own Thomas Iron Company at Hokendauqua on the Lehigh River. For decades, his company would be America's largest anthracite iron producer. Thomas became a director of many ironworks, coal mines and railways, and was a very wealthy man when he retired in 1868. Two of his sons, John and Samuel, became influential and innovative leaders of the American iron industry.

David Thomas's contribution to American industrialisation

David Thomas contributed to American industrialisation in several ways. He introduced a revolutionary and far more productive iron-making process that reduced the American dependence on imports, and he did so in the face of considerable initial scepticism. Upon his arrival in Allentown, one charcoal master had said to him, 'I will eat all the iron you make with anthracite.' Thomas's process helped in the development of America's transportation system: his Lehigh Valley furnaces played an important part in the American shipbuilding industry and were also vital to the production of the rails that were covering and opening up the North American continent. By 1870, the United States produced far more pig iron than Wales, and over half of that American iron came from Pennsylvania. Thomas had contributed some of Wales's best iron manufacturing ideas and men to the industrialisation of America.

In his book on David Thomas, Peter N. Williams argued:

> There is every reason to agree with those nineteenth century writers who called David Thomas the Father of the American anthracite iron industry, and to concur with those writing much more recently, who argue that David Thomas should be recognised as one of the most influential men in the growth of American industry in the nineteenth century.

William R. Jones (1839–89)

'Bill' Jones was the son of an ironworker and nonconformist minister who emigrated from Wales to Pennsylvania in 1832. At the age of ten,

David Thomas and Contacts with Wales

Once in America, Thomas received several letters from Welshmen bemoaning the poor harvests and lack of employment in Wales and telling of hundreds of families leaving in hope of a better life in America. One of Thomas's cousins, William John, wrote that he was employed in the Victoria Iron Works in Monmouthshire, where wages were low and food 'very dear'. William said he was determined to do better for his family and would leave Wales without regret to those 'who have no heart to quit it'. He would seek work as an ironworker in Pennsylvania, and their mutual friend 'Lewis Caarfilly' would also come if Thomas could get him a job. That suggests Thomas was known to help fellow Welshmen gain employment.

Thomas recognised the importance of Welsh links and culture to his workers. The Welsh settlement at Catasauqua centred around the ironworks, and Thomas speedily established a Welsh chapel and Sunday school there in late 1840. Thomas retained his own ties to Wales for a long time. His mother remained there and he supported her (she wrote to him in 1840 that she needed some money from him 'rightaway'). After his retirement, however, he told his niece Jane back in Wales that he had sufficient 'cause at home' for donations to churches, so that 'it is a little far to give money to churches so far away' in Wales. 'You will admit I know that charity begins at home.' America had become 'home'.

Jones worked at the Lehigh Crane Iron Works under David Thomas, who had known his father when both were still in Wales. When Jones worked at the Cambria Iron Works in Johnstown, Pennsylvania, he so impressed the managers that they sent him to construct a new furnace at Chattanooga, Tennessee. There he met and married Harriet Lloyd, whose Presbyterian family shared his abolitionist views.

In July 1862, Jones enlisted for nine months in the Union army. His enlistment period proved difficult for his family, because he did not receive any pay until February 1863. After the nine months were up, Jones returned to the Cambria Iron Works. The government discouraged ironworkers from volunteering to fight because iron was needed for the weaponry and rails that armed and moved the Union troops, but when President Lincoln called for 500,000 volunteers in July 1864, Jones immediately enlisted again and was promoted to captain. He fought in two of the bloodiest of the Civil War battles, Fredericksburg and Chancellorsville, but the man who would play such an important part in Jones's subsequent life paid another to fight in his place. That man was Andrew Carnegie.

A few years after the end of the war, Jones began working for Carnegie and became general superintendent of Carnegie's steelworks in Braddock in the Pittsburgh area. Jones was unusual in his insistence on good pay and an eight-hour workday for his mill workers. 'Flesh and blood cannot stand twelve hours of continuous work,' he said. In 1888 however, Carnegie reverted to the twelve-hour workday used by all other steelmakers. Jones contributed greatly to Carnegie's wealth: he ran a productive steelworks and he invented improvements in steelmaking processes such as the Jones Hot Metal Mixer. Jones explained to his family that he did not take up Andrew Carnegie's offers of partnership because, as he said, 'I do not trust the man.' Jones once referred to him as 'an oatmeal-eating son of a bitching Scotsman.'

HOW 'WELSH' WAS BILL JONES?

Although he toasted 'Our Fatherland'on St David's Day, Jones was not enamoured of Welsh workers. In 1877, he recommended that Carnegie's company 'steer clear . . . of Englishmen', and instead seek out 'Germans and Irish, Swedes and . . . young American country boys', because they were 'the most effective and tractable' of workers. He seems to have had reservations about employing the Welsh – 'Welsh can be used in limited numbers.' Despite those reservations, Bill Jones spoke some Welsh and belonged to Pittsburgh's St David's Society, a charitable organisation. In December 1883, Jones wrote to Carnegie suggesting that he should join Jones in donating to and supporting the local eisteddfod:

> I felt that the efforts of this class to improve themselves morally and mentally needed encouragement and assistance. I felt it my duty as the son of a Welshman to encourage [them] . . . In appealing to you to help me in this matter, I can only say that [you would help] had you witnessed the efforts of these, I may say rather crude citizens, to elevate themselves . . . Do not forget that the Welsh as a class are poor, but always remember that 99% of them always vote right, and like the Scots are always supporters of good government.

In 1889, Jones organised relief efforts after a burst dam caused the Johnstown flood, in which it was estimated that Johnstown's Welsh community had lost around $1 million worth of assets. Many family friends of Jones were affected. The dam had been weakened by the construction of the South Fork Fishing and Hunting Club, amongst whose members were Henry Clay Frick, Andrew Mellon and Andrew Carnegie. The press kept quiet about who exactly belonged to the club, which contributed to Jones's increasing disdain for Andrew Carnegie.

The achievements of Bill Jones

Bill Jones helped America become the world's leading steel producer. In 1908, the leading Austrian iron manufacturer Karl Wittgenstein wrote that 'the Jones-Mixer represents only a very small part of what Capt Jones has done for the iron-industry . . . he has shown new ways to the iron industry of America.' The Jones Hot Metal Mixer, which Jones patented in 1888, converted hot iron ore into steel. It saved time, fuel and labour and produced the steel of a greater consistency that was important in the construction of the bridges and skyscrapers which proliferated in late nineteenth-century America. Unlike the Bessemer process, the Jones Mixer remains in use today.

There is no doubting the regard in which the ordinary people of the Pittsburgh region held Jones, for when he died after an industrial accident, 10,000 people joined his funeral procession.

PITTSBURGH – 'THOUSANDS OF WELSHMEN'

In 1882, H. J. Thomas complained to a newspaper editor, 'I rarely see in your paper anything about the thousands of Welshmen who live around and about the Birmingham of America [Pittsburgh].'

Skulduggery?

Jones had been planning to form his own steelmaking business in Ohio, in partnership with Joseph Green Butler, who came from a family of iron manufacturers and had taught himself Welsh. Two days after Jones's death, a representative of Carnegie Brothers secured all of his patents from his heartbroken, confused and bedridden widow, who had multiple sclerosis and relied heavily upon laudanum for her pain. The Carnegie company paid a paltry $35,000, but the Jones Mixer earned Carnegie millions.

Jones's descendants believed the patents had been unfairly and cheaply acquired. Furthermore, there were three things that made them suspicious. First, the family found it hard to believe that the meticulous Jones had not left an updated will. Second, although a great deal of correspondence between Jones and Carnegie survives, there was nothing for the last four years of Jones's life, which has puzzled Carnegie's biographers. Third, while the local doctors who first treated Jones were sure he would survive, it was when Carnegie sent his own medical practitioners that Jones died – suddenly and unexpectedly. Had Jones lived and set up his own company, and had Carnegie thereby lost control of the Jones Mixer, it would have cost Carnegie millions.

'The country was building, and I gave it iron to build with'

Rhys Davies, David Thomas and William R. Jones were exceptional pioneering individuals in the growth of the American iron industry. There were also tens of thousands of ordinary Welsh ironworkers. Their contribution to the industrialisation of America was best articulated in James J. Davis's memoirs.

James J. Davis (1873–1947)

As a small child in Tredegar in south Wales, James Davis worked the night shift in the iron mill. The family emigrated to Pennsylvania in 1881, and at the age of eleven, he took his first full-time job in America in a nail factory. He began work in a rolling mill at twelve, and was a master puddler in Pittsburgh by the age of eighteen. During the economic depression of the early 1890s, he spent some time working in a rolling mill in Birmingham, Alabama.

Davis was typical of many of the Welsh in America in his dedication to self-improvement. He studied at night with a reading light that so infuriated his three Birmingham roommates that he had to find alternative accommodation. The economic depression convinced him that he needed to learn other skills, so he worked in the tinplate trade in Elwood, Indiana. Davis became a union man and was then elected as city clerk. This paid lower wages than the tin mill, but he hoped it would 'lead to something better' – and it did. After four years as city clerk, he was elected county recorder. He invested in businesses run by trusted acquaintances and eventually became a prosperous banker. Although he moved beyond manual labour, its significance was recognised in his inimitable memoir, *The Iron Puddler*.

> The country was building, and I gave it iron to build with. Railroads were still pushing out their mighty arms and stringing their iron rails across the western wheat lands. Bridges were crossing the Mississippi and spanning the chasms in the Rocky Mountains. Chicago and New York were rising in new growth with iron in their bones to hold them high. My youth was spent in giving to this growing land the element its body needed . . . My days were spent at forge and puddling furnace. The iron that I made is civilization's tools . . . I hear the bridges rumble underneath the wheels, and they are a part of me. I see tall cities looking down from out the sky and know that I have given a rib to make those giants. I am a

> part of all I see, and life takes on an epic grandeur. I have done the
> best I could to build America ... the tin and iron I wrought with my
> hands have helped make America the richest country in the world.

Davis subsequently became Secretary of Labor under three Republican presidents, Warren G. Harding, Calvin Coolidge and Herbert Hoover. Immigration was a Labor Department responsibility at that time, and as Secretary of Labor from 1921 to 1930, Davis focused upon it. He established the United States Border Patrol and advocated greater restrictions upon immigration. He responded to the pleas of the iron and steel workers' union, and in combination with Harding persuaded U.S. Steel to cut their twelve-hour workday. He also promoted labour–management cooperation. He represented Pennsylvania in the US Senate from 1930 to 1945, co-sponsoring the Davis–Bacon Act of 1931, which aimed to establish fair wages for labourers working on public works projects.

Harding's biographer John W. Dean (2004) declared Davis 'an outstanding labor secretary', although in 1943, Isaiah Berlin of the Senate Foreign Relations Committee described Senator Davis to the British Foreign Office as

> violently hated by organised labor, since he is regarded as having prostituted his labor connexion only in order to betray his fellow-workers over and over again. He is a pure opportunist, put into the Senate by the powerful Sun Oil interest in Pennsylvania, declares that he is not an Isolationist [opposed to international entanglements and alliances]. This is true only in so far as he appears to have no convictions of any kind, and will vote in whatever direction is required by the interest which is running him at any given moment.

When he failed to get re-elected to the US Senate, Davis continued to work for the Loyal Order of Moose, a fraternal order that he had invigorated while serving as its director-general prior to joining Harding's Cabinet.

Welsh ironworkers elsewhere

The Ohio iron industry well illustrates the importance of Welsh ironworkers. Some were important in establishing the iron industry in Ohio's great industrial area around Youngstown. The first iron furnace in the area was constructed on Governor Tod's farm by the Welshman William Philpot and managed by Welshman William Richards, while in 1872

Welshmen and Americans invested in the new coal-fired technology in that area. Some grew wealthy from the iron industry in Ohio. In 1869, Edward Jenkins wrote from near Cleveland: 'The first works built here were by two Welshmen, D. and J. Jones, brothers . . . from Tredegar, Monmouthshire. They did not have much wealth when they came here . . . Today they are acknowledged to be [the] greatest ironmasters in the United States.' In her 1997 study of Welsh immigrants on Ohio's industrial frontier, Anne Kelly Knowles noted Welsh prosperity (see table below) in Jefferson township in Jackson County, Ohio, in 1870, and attributed it to Welsh farmers who had invested in the Jefferson Furnace from the 1850s. The iron produced at that furnace made a big contribution to the contemporary railroad construction boom.

Ethnicity of heads of households in Jefferson, Ohio	Number of heads of household	Mean net worth
Welsh	171	$4,703
American	323	$910
German	28	$667
Irish	25	$180

There were of course those who did not grow wealthy or introduce the industry to particular areas, but their labour was vital to the industrialisation of Ohio and the nation. By the late nineteenth century, there were several thousand Welsh industrial workers in the Youngstown region, and several hundred in other Ohio ironworks such as those in Cleveland, where 400 Welsh people lived in 1872, and in Columbus. Columbus attracted Welsh ironworkers in the 1870s. The Steel Rail Company of Columbus was run by a Welshman called Lewis, who had been followed to Columbus by many others who had worked with him in south Wales. At least two-thirds of the employees at Lewis's mill were Welsh. In 1913, the Rev. Daniel Jenkins Williams was a little embarrassed to recall: 'In the days of the steel rail mill there were many indulgent Welshmen in Columbus . . . Some of them could be classed as low and given to very excessive drinking.' However, he optimistically maintained, 'The number of those who drink intoxicants is becoming smaller year by year.'

Welsh ironworkers also played an exceptionally significant role in Tennessee. After the Civil War, the brothers Joseph and David Richards recruited Welsh ironworkers to work in the Knoxville ironworks they co-owned with John H. Jones. Over a hundred Welsh immigrant families

'THE PRESTIGE OF AMERICAN COMMERCE HAS
BEEN MATERIALLY ADVANCED'

In 1903, Professor Ewing Summers edited a collection of biographies of eminent eastern Ohioans. Several of his subjects were Welsh or Welsh Americans. In his biography of Tredegar-born John W. Rogers, he struggles to share fairly the credit for this eminent citizen:

> The picturesque and prosperous county of Monmouth, South Wales, is a portion of Great Britain which has long held high relative precedence in connection with the great iron industry, and from its confines, after receiving excellent discipline in the various details involved in the mining and manufacturing of this great natural product, have come to America many men who have here found ample opportunity for the practical and successful exercise of their abilities along the same line of industrial enterprise, while the prestige of American commerce has been materially advanced through the able and discerning efforts of such representatives of the British isle [sic]. Rogers, who is now incumbent of the office of secretary and treasurer of the Youngstown Steel Casting Company at Youngstown, Mahoning county [sic], has the distinction of being a native son of Monmouthshire, though his parents emigrated thence to the United States when he was a mere child, so that his training is purely American, and he is imbued with that progressive spirit which is so characteristic of our great Republic.

In his 2006 study of Britons in Ohio, William E. Van Vugt declared, 'Ohio's heavy industries would not have developed spectacularly as they did without the Welsh . . . Welsh immigrants made disproportionately great contributions to Ohio's [iron] industry.'

moved from the Welsh Barony in Pennsylvania to East Tennessee, settling in what is now Mechanicsville, Tennessee, and in part of Knoxville. In 1871, the Rev. Thomas Thomas boasted of the contribution of Welshmen to post-war Knoxville in *Y Cenhadwr Americanaidd*:

> The city and its surroundings at that time was nothing but a pitiful skeleton of refuse left after the war . . . The coming of the Welsh to this city gave it a new lease of life; and it is with pride that I note here that the character of the Welsh is held in high esteem in this place. And some of the residents believe that all the Welsh as a nation are religious. (O that their opinion was only true.) And

in reality it is the Knoxville Iron Company, and the [affiliated] Machine shop which belongs to the Railways, that is the life of the city.

Writers in Welsh American periodicals were always keen to praise the contribution of their countrymen to the making of America, but Thomas Thomas's honest confession of the irreligious nature of many Welsh suggests that his claims about the Welsh contribution to the revival of Knoxville may be true. By 1900, the Knoxville Iron Company employed around 850 workers, mostly Welsh immigrants and black Americans. Another Tennessee iron centre was the city of Chattanooga, where Welshmen held key positions in the various ironworks – twenty of them in the Roane Iron Company alone.

The manufacture of machinery

Welshmen with knowledge and expertise in the iron industry often became successful manufacturers. Amongst them were Thomas Rees Morgan and Henry Clay Evans. Thomas Rees Morgan (1834–97) was born in Penydarren, Merthyr Tydfil. He worked down the mines from the age of six, and at the age of ten lost his leg below the knee when he was run over by a coal wagon. At fourteen, he became an apprentice in the machine shop at the Penydarren Ironworks. He emigrated to Pennsylvania in 1865 and became a foreman at the Allegheny Valley Railroad in Pittsburgh. He then set up his own business in Pittsburgh, manufacturing machinery for iron and steel works. Wisconsin-born Henry Clay Evans was a Welsh-speaker who had served in the 41st Regiment, Wisconsin Volunteer Infantry, in the Civil War and then settled in Chattanooga. He was employed by the Roane Iron Company from 1874 to 1884 and worked his way up from secretary to general manager. He was elected mayor of Chattanooga in 1881, and by 1887 he held the biggest share of the Chattanooga Car and Foundry Company, which specialised in building freight cars. He was a single-term congressman.

As the nineteenth century wore on, ever more machinery was manufactured and many Welsh worked in manufacturing companies. For example, the Rev. Daniel Jenkins Williams noted that one-third of those of Welsh blood in Columbus, Ohio, were engaged in manufacturing (many in the John Demming Threshing Machines Company) and mechanical industries, and that some of them were skilled. Overall, he proudly said, 'relatively few are labourers.' Another one-third were white-collar workers, with about 10 per cent who were professionals.

COAL

Wood constituted 90 per cent of the fuel consumed in America in 1850 but only 5 per cent by 1890. Coal replaced wood, and America had ample coal reserves in the Appalachian Mountains from Pennsylvania to Kentucky. From the third decade of the nineteenth century, American capitalists eagerly recruited Welsh miners to help develop the American coal industry, and mass Welsh immigration to the coalfields of western and north-eastern Pennsylvania and Ohio helped ensure that the Welsh dominated the emerging industry. Marcus Lee Hansen's 1940 history of the Atlantic migration described this as 'the Welsh era in the history of American mining'.

FAREWELL TO WALES

The railway station platforms at Merthyr and Aberdare in the south Wales valleys were commonly full of relatives and friends seeing off coal miners about to emigrate to America. By the late nineteenth century, there was scarcely a family in industrial or rural Wales that did not have a relative in the United States.

The Welsh and eastern Pennsylvania

US census statistics help illustrate the importance of the Welsh miners experienced in mining anthracite who flocked to eastern Pennsylvania's anthracite fields in the later nineteenth century, although the statistical evidence is not precise and there may well have been twice the recorded number of Welsh.

US CENSUS STATISTICS OF WELSH-BORN IN THE UNITED STATES

1850 nearly 30,000, of whom 89 per cent resided in New York, Ohio, Pennsylvania and Wisconsin

1860 nearly 46,000, only 500 of whom lived in the Southern states

1870 nearly 75,000

1880 just over 83,000

1890 over 100,000

1900 over 93,000, 38 per cent of whom were in Pennsylvania, where over half of them lived in three counties centred on the iron and coal areas of Scranton, Wilkes-Barre and Pittsburgh. Of the others, 20 per cent lived in New York and Ohio, with 18 per cent in Illinois, Indiana, Iowa, Kansas, Wisconsin and Utah

1950 30,000

In 1830, the Delaware and Hudson Railroad sought the latest mining tech-
niques and therefore recruited seventy Welsh miners, who settled with
their families in Carbondale in north-eastern Pennsylvania's Lackawanna
Valley. By 1833, there were three Welsh churches in Carbondale. There was
some disillusionment. According to David Davies, writing to his mother in
1834, many were disappointed – 'everyone here want[s] to return home.'

Carbondale was the largest Welsh settlement in the Lackawanna
Valley until overtaken by Scranton in the 1850s. By the later nineteenth
century, Scranton had the largest concentration of Welsh people in the
United States and outside Wales itself. Welsh historian William Jones has
written an excellent case study of the Welsh in Scranton.

The Welsh and Scranton

Scranton's industrial expansion was triggered by a Welshman. The settlement's leading family, the Scrantons, sought someone experienced
in using anthracite to smelt iron in their unproductive iron furnaces.
Tredegar-born John F. Davis arrived and began work at the ironworks
in January 1842. He was soon joined by mine foreman Evan Williams.
Scranton's population was 1,169 at this time, but Davis and Williams
quickly attracted more Welshmen. By the 1850s, the mining of coal
had become even more important than the iron industry and Scranton
became known as the 'Anthracite Capital of the World'.

Year	Population of Scranton
1850	7,000 (roughly 400 Welsh)
1870	35,000 (4,177 Welsh-born, constituting 12 per cent of the city's total population and 25 per cent of its foreign-born)
1890	90,000 (roughly 5,000 Welsh-born, along with many whose parents were Welsh-born)
1900	Over 100,000

Late nineteenth-century Scranton was predominantly a city of immigrants. The Irish constituted the largest immigrant group. Most of them
were unskilled labourers. There were also Germans, Scots, English and
Welsh. The Welsh were Scranton's second largest immigrant group until
the 1890s and they remained a significant proportion of the population
in much of the first half of the twentieth century. Most of Scranton's
Welsh immigrants lived in the Hyde Park district, which a leading citizen
of Scranton, Judge H. M. Edwards, described in 1909 as 'another Wales'.

WELSH OCCUPATIONS IN SCRANTON

In 1870, *Webb's Scranton Directory* listed a great range of Welsh-run shops and services. Richard J. Hughes owned a tinware shop, and Henry D. Jones a grocery store with a sideline in assisting Welsh immigrants with money and tickets. Thomas Jones was a barber, Mrs John P. Williams a milliner and Lewis C. Davis advertised himself as a 'fashionable Merchant Tailor'. E. M. Thomas boasted that he sold 'Everything from a Light Fancy Boot or Shoe to a Heavy Miner's Boot'. Several Welsh men and one Welsh woman, Mary E. Evans, ran saloons, while Mrs William M. Thomas ran the 'Welsh Boarding House'. William Price ran a funeral parlour, Henry Jones a restaurant. Sarah J. Jones offered elocution lessons, while J. D. Williams made and sold ice cream. There were four Welsh music teachers in Hyde Park, and Benjamin W. Phillips sold sheet music and other musical goods. B. G. Morgan and John Davies had drugstores. From 1873 to 1883, the postmaster was Thomas D. Thomas, a native of Blaina, Monmouthshire, who had been crippled in a Pennsylvania mining disaster in 1867. There were Welsh policemen, including police captain R. J. Edwards, and Welsh educationalists, including three Welsh superintendents of schools. Unfortunately, the *Scranton Republican* reported several complaints against Principal J. T. Jones in 1893. It was said he inflicted excessively severe corporal punishments. There were Welsh doctors such as the Rev. E. B. Evans and Welsh lawyers such as William T. Lewis. The West Side Bank, set up in 1874, had mostly Welsh managers and three Welshmen set up three new banks in the early twentieth century.

In 1913, a writer in *Druid* said that in the Pennsylvania bituminous coalfield, 'Sons of Welshmen never work in the mines, unless it is a case of failure everywhere else . . . a healthy state of affairs compared to the days when almost every Welshman sought work in the mines'.

Down the Pennsylvania coal mines

In the early 1870s, most Scranton Welshmen were miners. Nearly 45 per cent of heads of Welsh households in Scranton were still miners in 1880, but by the end of the nineteenth century, many Welsh were in service industries and white-collar workers. Of those still working in the coal industry, a disproportionate number were in supervisory and managerial positions. For example, Colonel Reese A. Phillips had risen from mine door boy to superintendent in the central office by 1900. According to those of other nationalities, Welshmen favoured other Welshmen. One high-ranking American reported that the Welsh 'are clannish and the best places at their disposal are given to their friends'.

BENJAMIN HUGHES (1824–1900)

Benjamin Hughes was born in Brynmawr, Breconshire. His father was a foreman at the Nantyglo Ironworks. Benjamin emigrated to Pennsylvania in 1848. He worked as a miner in Pottsville until 1855 and was then appointed superintendent of a D.L.&W. Mine in Hyde Park, Scranton. When he became general inside superintendent of that company in 1865, he was responsible for 7,000 workers and was considered north-eastern Pennsylvania's greatest mining expert. He actively recruited Welsh miners and helped to train them for key positions. He wrote to them in Welsh if there was an issue with their work, saying that he would endeavour to keep it quiet so long as they remedied it.

Welsh foremen were frequently accused of bullying, mostly by Irish workers. Two Welsh foremen were murdered by aggrieved Irishmen, and many other Welsh officials were beaten up. Criticism of Welsh managers from within the Welsh community was evident in *Y Drych* in the 1870s and 1880s: an anonymous 1874 article described Hyde Park as a 'Slave Athens in Free America', although some other correspondents disagreed. Whatever the truth about Welsh managers, the heating and industrialisation of America owed much to their expertise, and to the labour and lives of Welsh miners.

In September 1869, most of the 110 who died at the Avondale mine near Wilkes-Barre were Welsh. The dead miners found underground appeared as if they had simply fallen asleep. William R. Evans held a son in each arm, while a third son's head rested on his father's chest. Inside manager Evan Hughes seemed to have died praying, his head bent forward, his hands clasped before him. Considerable numbers were hurt or killed in the frequent roof falls in other mines. Charles Laramy, one of the three Welsh funeral directors in late nineteenth-century Hyde Park, published an advertisement in *Y Drych* in the early 1870s in which he thanked his fellow Welsh for their great support for his coffin-making business.

Welsh miners helped bring a greater awareness of mine safety to America. Before mine inspections were established in Pennsylvania in 1870, the death rate in Pennsylvania coal mines was three times higher than that in Britain, where safety measures had already been adopted. Welsh contributors to the Welsh-edited *Pottsville Miners' Journal* emphasised just how far ahead the British were in safety measures. Primarily as a result of Welsh agitation, the Schuylkill County Ventilation Act was passed in 1869. Within months, Luzerne County experienced the

Avondale mining disaster and as a result, an 1870 act applied the safety rules throughout Pennsylvania and introduced inspectors, a majority of whom would be Welsh. In 1887, Cardiganshire-born James E. Roderick, in his capacity as mine inspector, persuaded the Pennsylvania legislature to build a state miners' hospital at Hazelton. In 1899, he was appointed chief inspector of mines and promoted further beneficial legislation.

WELSH MINE INSPECTORS EVERYWHERE

When inspectors were introduced in the Ohio and Illinois coalfields, the Welsh were involved again, and it was a Welsh inspector who persuaded the Utah legislature to make safety improvements in 1901.

John E. Williams was born to a Merthyr Tydfil minister in 1853. The family immigrated to Illinois in 1864. John worked as a miner from the age of thirteen to twenty-eight. He led a miners' self-improvement society that spent a whole winter working through John Stuart Mill's *Political Economy*. After an underground fire killed 250 miners in Cherry, Illinois, he was credited with the Illinois legislation that safeguarded the widows and orphans left after such disasters. His union involvement led him to national fame as an industrial mediator.

Mine safety was not the only problem. There was also suffering during periods of economic dislocation and depressions. In 1865, L. and Mary Roberts wrote from Scranton to their parents in Wales: 'Many have emigrated this year to the coal districts and most of them are bitterly disappointed . . . Dozens of Welsh families have had this experience in America this year.' Such was the great slump in the sales of anthracite in the late 1860s and the 1870s that a Welsh American publication reported in February 1875 that some Hyde Park families containing over seven people had no bread in the house.

There was considerable ethnic antagonism and rivalry in and over the mines. Skilled workers down the mines were paid three times as much as their labourers and worked fewer hours. The labourers were usually Irish and resentful of the Welsh skilled workers:

When I worked in Hyde Park, I was not only obliged to do my own work but the greater part of that miner that hired me . . . when there was enough coal cut, no matter how hard or how long the labourer had to work, Mr Welshman put on his coat and went home to enjoy himself in the bosom of his family, cultivate his mind if he felt so disposed or engage in any other amusement.

And we get a nominal one-third of the sum total, whilst we performed nine-tenths of the sum total of work.

The Welsh–Irish antagonism was such that after the Avondale disaster, it
was rumoured amongst the Welsh that antagonistic Irishmen had started
the fire. The 1890s saw an influx of southern and eastern Europeans into
the eastern Pennsylvania coalfields, so that in 1895 assistant foreman
John R. Williams wrote to his old mentor in Aberdare that the place
was 'swarming with foreigners – Poles, Hungarians, Slavish, Swedes,
and Italians, etc – who are fast driving the English, Welsh, and Scotch
miners out of competition'. Reflecting the management perspective, Williams thought that the Welsh had only 'their foolhardy and unreasonable
impositions in pretty well everything' to blame, because they 'at length
became perfectly unmanageable' and drove the operators to send for
the foreigners.

GOOD CITIZENS?

The Welsh were always keen to present themselves as good citizens. Many
Welsh American chapel-goers were committed to temperance. According to
Phoebe Gibbons's article 'The Miners in Scranton' in *Harper's New Monthly
Magazine* (1877), the Welshman 'does not drink as much here as at home,
for he has bidden his native land farewell with the intention of making
money'. However, there is also a great deal of evidence concerning Welsh
drunks and drinkers. In 1870, a writer in *Y Drych* lamented the similarity
between his home town of Scranton and Sodom and Gomorrah. He blamed
recent arrivals from the Welsh valleys, 'the scum of the works of Wales':

> On Main Street there are Welshmen . . . keeping a bar nearly
> every other house. If you want . . . Welsh grogshops, whisky
> holes, gin mills, rum cellars, go to Lackawanna Avenue, Main
> Street and Hyde Park. There you will see sons and daughters,
> husbands and wives, half-drunk all the time, playing silly games,
> hanging about and singing in Welsh such as that they bring
> shame to even the half-civilised Irish. If you want lack of respect
> on the Sabbath, if you want to hear the language of hell . . . from
> Welsh mouths, go for half an hour along the streets and into the
> Welsh saloons in Hyde Park.

His disgust was echoed by another correspondent from Iowa, who cited
the thirty Welsh saloons in Scranton. When the Rev. Mr Edwards of
Edwardsville near Wilkes-Barre led a campaign against saloon licences,
his church was dynamited.

The Welsh were guilty not only of an affection for alcohol. In 1876, the *Scranton Times* told of small boys carrying revolvers in Hyde Park, and there were suggestions of gang warfare there. In the Mahonoy City area, there were Welsh anti-Irish gangs such as the Modocs and the Chain Gang. There were also famous individual Welsh sinners. In the 1870s, William M. Thomas was so often involved in robbery and violence that he was known as Bully Bill. He worked in the southern coalfield and frequently clashed with the Irish. After the young Rhymney-born preacher John Hindes tried and failed to have sex with Mary Ellen Davis in 1883, he almost succeeded in killing himself when he drank a bottle of laudanum. He was expelled from his church and was rumoured to be attempting to join the Mormons.

Welsh miners in Ohio

Welsh coal miners and ironworkers were important in establishing the great industrial area around Youngstown in Mahoning County, Ohio. Ohio Governor David Tod invited John Davis to develop the coal on his farm, and Davis recruited Welsh miners. The first commercial mine in neighbouring Trumbull County, the Cambria, was opened and operated by Welshmen. The second half of the nineteenth century saw mass Welsh migration to Trumbull and Mahoning Counties: well over half of the identifiable mine managers there were Welsh-born, and Ohio had the second greatest population of Welsh miners in America from the 1860s to the 1880s. Most were in the Mahoning Valley near Youngstown, the Tuscarawas Valley near Canton and Massilla, and the Hocking and Ohio River towns in south-eastern Ohio.

An 1892 county history said that the 622 population of Thomastown, Ohio, was 'composed largely of coal miners, mostly Welsh', and there were other such 'Welsh towns' in the Ohio coalfields. Many of the Ohio miners and their descendants were upwardly mobile. William H. Davis, who originated from the south Wales valleys, employed 3,000 coal miners in Ohio. Dowlais-born miner Anthony Howells emigrated to the United States in 1850, continued to work as a miner in Youngstown and by 1870 was recruiting Welsh workers and managers for his own coal company. He became a state senator and US consul to Cardiff in the years 1893–7. In 1901, he sold his mining companies and built the luxury Courtland Hotel in Canton, Ohio.

WELSH MINERS DOWN SOUTH

Welsh miners in Tennessee and Kentucky

Soon after the Civil War, several mining towns sprang up in Tennessee and adjacent Kentucky. These coal towns were frequently established by enterprising Welshmen such as the brothers Joseph and David Richards, the owners of the Knoxville Iron Company. They bought a coal mine in Coal Creek in 1869. 'This coal is regarded as being the best within the States [and] it is the Welsh who have the reins in their hands,' according to *Y Cenhadwr Americanaidd*. Another Welsh mining company eventually employed 500 miners at Soddy and supplied the iron manufacturers of Chattanooga. A group of Welshmen opened what proved to be the profitable East Tennessee Coal Company in Jellico, Kentucky. The coal mine that opened in 1892 in the nearby settlement of Proctor employed around 250 miners and was dominated by the Welsh. Nearby Williamsburg's seven mines employed around 700 miners. Many of them lived in Mountain Ash, which was named after the town in south Wales.

However, as a writer in the *Knoxville Journal* recalled in 1891, Welsh miners soon ceased to be a dominant force in Tennessee. The writer recalled the 'desperate look to be seen on the faces of the thrifty Welsh miners whose places in the mines were being filled by the scum of the earth . . . convicts'. A Mr Llewellyn wrote in 1882 that he had spent seven years in Coal Creek 'superintending the works of the Knoxville Iron Company until forced away by the introduction into the mines of that great curse – convict labor'. The *Cambrian* recorded in 1885 that, 'The mines were owned and operated at first, almost exclusively, by the Welsh people,' but that under the new owners 'the Welsh miners and all free labour has been almost entirely displaced by . . . the convict labour system'. In 1891, miners at the Tennessee Coal Company's Briceville mine repeatedly freed the convicts and put them on the train from Knoxville. Once they simply freed them and the *New York Times* banner headline read NEARLY FIVE HUNDRED CRIMINALS LOOSE IN TENNESSEE AND KENTUCKY. The forced use of convicts in coal mines was made illegal in 1895, but many Welsh miners had already left after the 'Coal Creek War'.

A Welsh mine manager in Birmingham, Alabama

Llewellyn W. Johns (1844–1912) described himself as born 'atop of a coal mine' in Pontypridd. He worked down the Welsh mines, then emigrated to Pennsylvania in 1863. He went West and tried gold prospecting, lumber-jacking and Indian-fighting. He was working in mines near Scranton in 1868 when he became acquainted with the family of David Thomas. During the depression of 1873, Johns tried silver mining in Nevada, but then went to the South and worked for one of David Thomas's grandsons. He became the leading mine manager in the Birmingham, Alabama, coal and iron district. Although his ties to Wales remained strong ('If wages were the same here as in Wales, I would have stayed in my native land'), he was like other Welsh managers and owners in the South in that he preferred to employ cheaper and more pliable black American miners.

Welsh miners and the mineral frontier

When the so-called 'mineral frontier' moved westward beyond Pennsylvania, Welsh miners followed it to the bituminous coalfields of Indiana, Illinois, Iowa, Missouri, Kansas, Colorado, Utah, Idaho, Wyoming and Washington state. When new coal mines were opened, experienced Welsh mine managers were employed and many Welsh miners followed them. Iowa illustrates this. Between 1860 and 1930, Welsh mining communities developed on the southern Iowa coalfields. Welsh expertise was valued and many who came to Iowa had worked in the Welsh and/or Pennsylvania coalfields. While early settlers in Iowa had been farmers, half of Iowa's over three thousand Welsh-born were in mining communities by the 1880s, although they were soon replaced by immigrants from southern and eastern Europe. There were many individual tales of Welsh upward mobility in Iowa. For example, John W. Bowen was born in Wales in 1844, grew up in a Pennsylvania coalfield, fought with the 15th Iowa Infantry Volunteers during the Civil War, went down the Iowa mines, became a postmaster and then bought farmland in Nebraska.

Sometimes, the names of coal towns have disappeared from modern maps, but the small town of 'Wales' can still be seen on maps of Utah. The story of that 'Wales' began in the midst of a depression in the south Wales iron industry in 1840. The *Cambrian* recorded the arrival of 'Mormonite' missionaries from America during that depression and told of how 'swindlers of this knavish sect' enticed Welsh people 'to a strange country'. A few months later, The *Cambrian* recorded that seventy 'ignorant fanatics' from Wales had emigrated after their conversion. Thousands went to Utah with the Welsh missionary captain Dan Jones in 1849 and 1853, so that as late as 1990 the US census recorded a higher percentage of people with Welsh ancestry living in Utah than in any other state. Brigham Young asked his Welsh Mormon settlers to help establish coal and iron industries in Utah, and two of his Welsh followers led several Welsh families in mining coal that was transported north-east to Salt Lake City by wagon. They named their mining community 'Wales'. When the Rev. William Davies Evans visited in 1880, he was pleased with the role of Welsh women there:

> In Utah there is a colony of Welsh people called 'Wales' where the wives have refused to allow their husbands to practise polygamy. When one man tried his luck by taking on another wife some years ago, all of the neighbourhood's wives got together and placed this woman on a wooden horse and after carrying her to a distant meadow, left her to find her way home the best she could. From then on, the men gave up this loathsome practice.

Welsh miners had a good reputation across the nation. The Garrett family from Wales made their way to the Black Diamond mine in Washington state in search of work, and it seems likely that they had been told beforehand that the supervisory and managerial positions in the mine were held by Welshmen. When the superintendent's son told Mr Garrett, 'We have all the men we need,' his Welsh father came out of his office saying, 'You hire that boy. He's a Welsh coal miner.' When Edgar White and Henry Taylor wrote their *General History of Macon County, Missouri* in 1910, they noted that

> One of the leading industries of Bevier township in this county, as everybody in this part of the state knows, is coal mining ... The discovery of the coal and the continuous and successful development of the industry have been largely due to persons of Welsh nativity or ancestry, who have themselves been connected with the same line of work in Wales, or their parents have, and who have been, therefore, well-qualified for the skillful and profitable operation of the mines.

WELSH COWBOYS AND INDIANS

When the Garrett family crossed America to get to the Black Diamond mine in Washington State, they were surprised to meet a Welsh-speaking cowboy en route. There were other Welsh cowboys. Robert Kenrick, who came from near Cardiff, worked on a Wyoming ranch and in the late 1880s and early 1890s became acquainted with Buffalo Bill and Butch Cassidy. Arthur Owen Vaughan wrote to his family in Wales in 1880 that he loved the 'bully life, riding all day' in Colorado. He said it was 'fun' having to 'defend the herd and our scalps' from Indians. When he was older he wrote accounts of cowboy life for magazines.

Some Welshmen became ranch owners. Buffalo Bill and Wild Bill Hickok were frequent visitors to the ranch of Rhayadr-born rancher Morris Price in the foothills of the Black Hills of Dakota. Ranching became more profitable thanks to the Radnor family from Presteigne, who were the first to import Hereford cattle to the United States. Other ranchers soon replaced longhorns with Herefords because the latter produced more meat. Sheep farmer William Davis of Bedwas, Monmouthshire, worked his way up to ownership of 3,000 acres in Texas.

The life of ranchers and cowboys could be dangerous: Robert Owen Pugh of Dolgellau found himself in a cabin surrounded by Indians in Wyoming. He put a rifle in each window and ran around firing each gun, all the while shouting in a variety of voices. The Indians failed to realise that he was alone and gave up. Pugh subsequently married the daughter of an Indian chief.

Some Welshmen served in the US army and fought against Indians. Gregory Mahoney of Pontypool was awarded the Congressional Medal of Honour for bravery in action against the Comanche. Solomon Rees, whose parents had emigrated from Wales, married a girl who was part Welsh and part Indian, and lived with her on a reservation in Kansas, but went on to work for the army and scalped a dead Indian in Kansas. Sergeant William Bowen James, who was born near Haverfordwest, died along with General Custer at the Battle of the Little Bighorn in 1876. John Davies was born in south Wales in 1868, raised in Ohio, and joined the US army in 1887. He won the Indian Medal for his performances in fighting the Indians, but was court-martialled for refusing to eat pork that he insisted was not properly cooked, and encouraging others to do likewise. He then changed his name and joined the Marines.

Some Welshmen engaged in law enforcement. Sheriff John T. Morris of Collins County, Texas, rid the West of James Reed, husband of Belle Starr, Queen of the Outlaws. Sheriff (later Marshal) Jesse Prichard, whose Welsh parents had emigrated to Gomer, Ohio, kept the peace in several Colorado mining towns. Lawmen such as Wyatt Earp and Bat Masterson lodged at the boarding house of Dollgellau-born Annie Ellis in Wichita, Kansas, and then Dodge City.

All those Welsh and Welsh Americans who worked on ranches or served in the US army or helped in the maintenance of law and order, contributed to the conquest, the opening up, the profitability and the 'civilising' of the Wild West.

A striking Welsh woman in Ludlow, Colorado

Mary Hannah Williams (1887–c.1975) was born in the Ogmore Valley. She married Tom Thomas, a heavy drinker and great womaniser whose parents had sent him from Pennsylvania to Wales. Thomas returned to Pennsylvania and promised to send for Mary and their two daughters, but she heard nothing from or about him for three years until she learned that he was in Colorado. When Mary arrived with the girls in Colorado in 1913, she forced an unwilling Tom to support them.

Within weeks of her arrival in Colorado, there was a strike at the Ludlow mine. Mary was regarded as a troublemaker because she led the singing of union songs and the heckling of guards. She was assaulted by a militiaman, and when she responded, she was arrested and locked in a rat-ridden cell for eleven days without charges or trial. The authorities had her on record as 'a vociferous, belligerent, and abusive leader of the mob' who used 'unwomanly language', attacked the troops with fists, feet and umbrella, and planned to threaten a newspaper editor with a pistol for writing that her husband had knocked down a woman. Much of that information was probably fabricated to discredit her. The militia attacked and destroyed the miners' temporary tents at Ludlow, and two women and eleven children were killed in what became known as the Ludlow Massacre. Mary and her two children were put in jail for three weeks, after which she was one of those taken to Washington, DC, to describe their experiences of the Ludlow Massacre. She recorded that during a visit to the capital, 'I met many influential people of Welsh parentage, and at that time Wales meant a lot to me'. She and a group then went on to address sympathetic crowds in several great cities, including New York. She met the famous novelist Upton Sinclair, who told her he was writing a novel about the strike called *King Coal* – and 'you, Mary, are its heroine.'

Mary had received no income during the speaking tour, but within a few months she had ascended from destitution to ownership of a dance hall and restaurant in Lockwood, Nevada. When Prohibition was enacted, she purchased bootleg whiskey for her premises. In the early 1920s, she moved to Hollywood, married a man with whom she had fallen in love on that first transatlantic crossing back in 1913, and opened a profitable ladies' sportswear shop on Hollywood Boulevard. In 1950, she attended a celebration of half a century of unionism, but recorded that the obvious wealth of the union leaders made her feel like screaming.

The Welsh and labour unions

In his study of the British role in the development of Ohio, Van Vugt recorded the contribution of Britons to the development of labour unions, noting that 'though the United States was ahead of Britain in political democracy, Britain was miles ahead in industrial democracy'. Welsh miners, ironworkers and labour leaders had a significant impact upon the development of American unions, and particularly miners' unions. This was not always to their advantage. It was the opinion of Dewi Emlyn Davies that the Welsh miners in Ohio brought about their own ruin. He wrote from Portage County in 1880: 'There are strikes nearly every week ... The complaint is that the Welsh are foremost in these and many of the masters, because of this, are prejudiced against them and choose other nationalities.' People disagreed about the merits and wisdom of the exercise of worker power. In 1895, John R. Williams wrote from Algoma, West Virginia, of the 'foolhardy and unreasonable impositions on pretty well everything' that caused the operators to rid themselves of the 'unmanageable' Welsh and to bring in foreigners. Welsh union militancy was not confined to the coal mines. In 1881, T. Puntan wrote from Newport, Kentucky, that there had been no work for six months because of a strike in the iron mill. 'It seems that the chief purpose of the masters is to break the unions ... as did the masters of the Welsh works years ago. There is the same tyrannical, oppressive and overbearing spirit in masters on this side of the Atlantic as on the other.'

Welsh-born ironworker David Morgan immigrated to Ohio with his family in 1869. He and his son John Morgan worked in the Morton Tin Plate Company from 1890. After election to the Ohio Senate in 1895, John focused on working conditions. In 1901, the governor of Ohio appointed him chief inspector of workshops and factories, and as such Morgan obtained regulations that protected workers (especially women and children) and supported labour unions.

Unsurprisingly, many of the Welsh coal miners rose up the union ranks. Swansea-born David R. Jones emigrated to Wilkes-Barre and became a coal miner, but then attended college and became a teacher. Miners in the Pittsburgh area entrusted him with the leadership of the Miners' Association, and he worked hard to create a national miners' organisation. He began practising law in 1882, and in 1888 was elected to the Pennsylvania legislature, where he sponsored pro-union legislation.

Thomas and Mary Lewis emigrated from Dowlais to Pennsylvania in 1866. Thomas began working down the mines in Ohio in 1879. Their sons William and Thomas prospered through their self-improvement and labour activism. William went down the mines aged six, and when older worked hard to promote a single national miners' union. His brother Thomas began work at the coal mine aged seven. Thomas grasped every opportunity for an education, including attending night school while working down the mines. His work as a career union officer elevated him to the middle class. He was president of the UMWA (United Mine Workers of America) from 1909 to 1912. During his presidency there was much conflict because of his belief that a national organisation was preferable to districts doing their own negotiations. Most miners agreed with his position, but it would take the most famous Welsh American miners' union leader, John L. Lewis, to win that battle.

INDUSTRY AND BUSINESS

The Rev. Robert D. Thomas wrote that he had visited Cambria, Wisconsin, in 1857 and 1870, during which time 'it had grown very little' because the Welsh focused on their farming and 'neglect to pay proper attention to the need to build towns and to establish businesses in them in order for their settlements to succeed'. However, he found many success stories in other Welsh American settlements. For example, in 1869 he found 'several Welsh craftsmen and rich businessmen' in Emporia, Kansas.

> ### AN EXCEEDINGLY INDUSTRIOUS AND ALSO A RELIGIOUS PEOPLE
>
> Robert Llewellyn Tyler's study of the extent of Welsh economic advancement in the Missouri coal town of Bevier, the Vermont slate town of Poultney, the Pennsylvania steel town of Sharon and the town of Emporia, Kansas, found some who did not attain the American Dream. While there was considerable economic advancement in the Welsh community in Bevier, it was not universal. There was some upward mobility in Sharon, but a 'large proportion' of the Welsh workers remained blue-collar. In Poultney, most remained tied to the quarry. The Welsh were most successful in Emporia. In 1868, *The Emporia News* noted: 'The Welsh in this vicinity are both an exceedingly industrious and also a religious people, bringing their principles with them from the mountains and mines of the fatherland, and constitute a very valuable element in our community'.

Some Welsh immigrants were pioneers in certain industries. Richard Griffith from Anglesey established the first of the many breweries in Milwaukee, Wisconsin, in 1840. By the late nineteenth century, oil was emerging as a potential rival to coal as a source of fuel, and one early oil entrepreneur was Samuel Milton Jones (1846–1904), who was born in Beddgelert, Caernarvonshire. His family emigrated in 1850, and in his early twenties he bought oil leases in western Pennsylvania. He drilled Ohio's first large oil well at Lima. He sold his interest in the Ohio Oil Company to Standard Oil in 1889, then began manufacturing oil drilling equipment in Ironville, East Toledo, Ohio. He invented several processes to improve oil extraction, then became preoccupied with social programmes for the working class. He was repeatedly elected mayor of Toledo (1897–1904). As mayor, he introduced holiday pay and an eight-hour working day for urban workers, along with municipal playgrounds, kindergartens and golf courses. He considered the Toledo police use of billy clubs too brutal and ordered them replaced by light canes. He was nicknamed 'Golden Rule Jones' because of his exemplary care for his employees.

Amongst the other Welshmen who made a fortune in oil was Montgomeryshire-born John Roberts, who immigrated to Ohio in 1889. He recognised that great profits were to be made from the internal combustion engine, and in 1902 joined other Welsh immigrants in forming the Cambrian Oil Company, near Venedocia. He then invested in the automobile industry.

Welsh businessmen did especially well in Knoxville, Tennessee. The Price brothers founded the Knoxville Furniture Company, while John D. Evans opened the area's first marble mill and R. W. Owens sold slate roofing. Stonemason Evan J. Davies, born near Carmarthen, emigrated to Ohio in 1870, then moved to Knoxville, where he spent three years slate-roofing a government building. He progressed from his construction company to the presidency of the East Tennessee Coal Company, which had its headquarters in Knoxville, and he owned mines in Dowlais, Kentucky.

Welsh miners and ironworkers often progressed to ownership. William Johns (1805–65) was born in Pembrokeshire, immigrated to Pennsylvania in 1832 and after a time working down the mines bought a colliery at St Clair in 1846. He was worth $2 million at his death. Glamorgan-born Abraham Lloyd emigrated aged eighteen in 1863. He worked his way up to co-ownership of the Soddy Coal Company, then opened another three mines in Arkansas during 1895–91. It was the traditional Welsh mining expertise that led to Griffith J. Griffith's great wealth.

Griffith J. Griffith (1850–1919)

Born in Bettws, Glamorgan, Griffith emigrated to Pennsylvania in 1865 and settled in San Francisco in 1873. In 1878, he became a mining correspondent for a San Francisco newspaper and amassed a fortune from companies keen to exploit his knowledge of the West Coast mining industry. He moved to Los Angeles in 1882 and in 1896 gifted 3,015 acres to the city of Los Angeles as 'a Christmas present'. The city named it Griffith Park in his honour. Griffith said:

> It must be made a place of rest and relaxation for the masses, a resort for the rank-and-file, the plain people. I consider it my obligation to make Los Angeles a happy, cleaner, and finer city. I wish to pay my debt of duty in this way to the community in which I prospered.

In 1903, Griffith shot his wife while staying in the Arcadia Hotel in Santa Monica. His trial was headline news, a story told by Robert Peterson in his *The Hidden History of Los Angeles* podcast. Tina Griffith survived but was greatly disfigured and lost an eye. Wearing a veil, she testified at her husband's trial that, contrary to the general opinion, Griffith was not a teetotaller but a secret drunk who downed two quarts of whiskey daily and suffered paranoid delusions. For example, he was a Protestant and she was a Catholic, and he was convinced that she was plotting with the Pope to poison him and steal his fortune. She said that just as he pulled the trigger she had jerked her head to one side and thereby saved her life. She then jumped out of the window. The hotel owners pulled her to safety and then called the sheriff.

Griffith's defence attorney argued that this was assault rather than murder because Griffith suffered 'alcoholic insanity'. Griffith was sentenced to two years in San Quentin, and the judge ordered that he be given 'medical aid for his condition of alcoholic insanity'. After his release from prison in 1906, Griffith frequently lectured on prison reform. In 1912, he offered Los Angeles a second 'Christmas present'. Not all Angelenos were keen to accept anything from him, but when he died in 1919, most of his $1.5 million estate went to the city and funded the Greek Theatre (1929) and Griffith Observatory (1935).

QUARRYING AND THE STONE INDUSTRY

Welshmen experienced in quarrying and stone masonry worked in several states, such as Ohio, where according to Van Vugt, they 'made very significant contributions to the industry'. They were particularly active and important in the slate industry.

THE WELSH ROOFED AND HEATED AMERICA

It was sometimes claimed that Wales roofed and heated America. Most of the slate roofing in America before 1785 was imported from Wales, and Welsh immigrants were important in the development of the American slate industry. In a similar pattern, Welsh coal was imported for heating and Welsh coal miners were important in the development of the American coal industry.

Slate had been quarried in America since colonial times. In the nineteenth century, an influx of immigrants from the north Wales slate-quarrying communities into the slate mines of Granville, New York, and Fair Haven, Vermont, contributed to a boom in American slate production. Welsh quarry workers also congregated on the Pennsylvania–Maryland border in America's other great slate-producing area. There they lived in the five towns constructed for them between 1850 and 1942. It took two Welshmen to recognise that there was valuable slate in what became the community of Slatington, Pennsylvania, where a quarry was opened in 1845 and a factory producing slate roofing was built in 1847. In 1880, the Slatington Slate Trade report noted that quarries in the town of Slatington alone had produced 81,402 squares of roofing slates, 40,486 cases of school slates and 243 cases of blackboards.

The Slate King of America

Hugh W. Hughes was born in 1836 in Llanllyfni, Caernarvonshire. He arrived in the United States aged twenty-one and worked, like many other Welshmen, in the lead mines of Dodgeville, Wisconsin. When he learned of an expanding Welsh settlement adjoining the slate quarries of Vermont, he went east and found employment there in 1859. He also worked on the New York side of what became known as Slate Valley, at Hampton. He saved hard and opened his first quarry in Fair Haven, Vermont, then further quarries at Pawlet in Vermont, and Hampton and Granville in New York. He manufactured so much slate that he became known as the Slate King of America. He had never attended school and was illiterate, but he left an estate worth $140,000. It was perhaps *hiraeth* that led him to import paintings and antiques from Wales to his Granville mansion.

PENRYN GRANITE WORKS

The Penryn Granite Works were established near California's Sierra Nevada mountains by Welsh immigrant Griffith Griffith (1823–89), who named the works after the Penrhyn Slate Quarry in north Wales, where he had worked in his youth. Part of the California State Capitol building in Sacramento, which was built between 1861 and 1874, was constructed from the granite from the Penryn Granite Works. This high-quality granite was also used in the construction of many buildings in San Francisco.

COPPER AND TINPLATE

Swansea's reputation as 'Copperopolis' helps explain the presence of Welsh miners in America's copper mines. William Edwards and Thomas Merchant emigrated from the Swansea area in the mid-nineteenth century and set up one of the early copper works in Ducktown, Tennessee. In the 1880s, Welsh copper miners flocked to copper mines in Butte, Montana, Jerome, Arizona, and southern Tennessee. At one time, Baltimore's copper works were almost totally manned by workers from Swansea and Llanelli.

The American tinplate industry was slow to take off. In 1844, a contemporary noted that tinplate works had been opened in America near Pittsburgh and 'most of the owners are thorough Welshmen'. Before 1890, Wales was the world's greatest producer of tinplate, and the United States its biggest customer: Wales provided over 70 per cent of US tinplate requirements. When the McKinley tariff of 1890 cut Welsh tinplate imports, Welsh expertise in rolling tinplate was in great demand in America. As a result, thousands of Welsh tinplate workers emigrated to the Pittsburgh area in particular, but also to Philadelphia and Ohio. The centre of the American tinplate industry was situated in the triangle between Pittsburgh (Pennsylvania), Wheeling (West Virginia) and Youngstown (Ohio). One Llanelli native described Youngstown, where there were already thousands of Welsh iron and coal workers, as 'the Welsh metropolis of America'. Welsh businessmen ran several tinplate companies, and amongst them was the millionaire J. C. Williams in West Virginia.

Welsh tin workers went to Alaska in the late nineteenth century, which helps explain why there is a settlement called Wales on Cape Prince of Wales on the westernmost tip of Alaska.

CONCLUSIONS

The eminent Welsh historian Glanmor Williams argued in 1979 that the years 1815–1914 constituted a 'unique chapter in Welsh American relationships, the like of which can never be repeated. Wales gave America a host of her sons and daughters; America offered them a haven, opportunity and a future.'

The combination of their Calvinistic emphasis on hard work and industrial expertise ensured that Welsh immigrants made a considerable contribution to the development of American industrial capitalism. The historian Ronald L. Lewis wrote that his study of the Welsh in the American coalfields made him realise that

> the Welsh, and other British immigrants, were instrumental in establishing the American coal industry and in shaping it into the engine of the American industrial revolution. I also became keenly aware of the extent to which the Welsh were/are invisible in American historiography . . . [Their] importance to industrialising America was far greater than their comparatively modest numbers would suggest.

America's gain was Wales's loss. From the late 1860s, newspapers in south Wales lamented the loss of ironworkers and coal miners. In 1869, the *Merthyr Telegraph* lamented how 'we lose our best workmen and our competitors gain their services and while we suffer they are advantaged'.

CHAPTER TEN

ASSIMILATION AND THE VANISHING WELSH

IN 1880, the Rev. William Davies Evans visited Philadelphia, Pennsylvania. He noted that while the 'Welsh influence was very strong here at one time', the descendants of the early Welsh settlers 'are 100 per cent American by now'. This Americanisation process occurred in all areas with Welsh populations. The Welsh arrived in Ohio long after they had settled in Philadelphia, but the pattern was the same. In 1913, the Rev. Daniel Jenkins Williams published *The Welsh of Columbus, Ohio: A Study in Adaptation and Assimilation*. In a chapter that he entitled 'The Vanishing Welsh', he noted:

> Each of these [Ohio] Welsh settlements has reached its summit as a flourishing   community of the Welsh type, and is now descending the hill on the other side. The communities are rapidly becoming assimilated into the great American people . . . The time is not far distant when complete assimilation into the great American people will take place . . . The Welshman has lived in America too long and he has become Americanized . . . [Those of Welsh descent] have been influenced by American life and institutions . . . Many . . . are of the third and fourth generation . . . The process of Americanization will prevail over the efforts of any foreign group to the contrary. And under the influence of American institutions an American type of man will ultimately be evolved . . . ultimately all must be melted into a uniform American people . . . But while . . . the Welsh in America . . . thus lose their life, they also find it, for in losing their identity they make their permanent contribution to the American race.

The pace of assimilation seems to have varied. In 1911, William Allen White wrote in his venerable *Emporia Gazette*: 'The Welsh people of this [Kansas] community have lived here for over a generation . . . They have Americanized.'

HOW AND WHY THE WELSH 'AMERICANIZED'

The Welsh often proved adaptable and exceptionally keen to assimilate. An 1872 article on Welsh immigrants in *Y Drych* noted that 'nearly all of them . . . rush to study the institutions and form of government in America'. This was recognised by some who were not Welsh. In 1903, Professor Ewing Summers wrote biographies of eminent East Ohioans. In his biography of Sheriff James M. Thomas, born in south Wales in 1867, Professor Summers claimed,

No class of foreign-born citizens surpasses the Welsh in quick and appreciative adaptability to American institutions. They imme-diately enter upon the duties of citizenship with a keen, almost juvenile enthusiasm, insisting on their children having the best education that can be obtained, and rearing them to respect their adopted country and participate in its functions.

Similarly, an article originally printed in Iowa and reprinted in the *Cambrian* in 1891, said that the Welsh were keen 'to digest the true genius of our government'.

In 1909, Judge Henry M. Edwards who had emigrated from Ebbw Vale to Pennsylvania aged twenty in 1864, explained the Welsh adaptability to 'the American spirit' in the *Druid*:

No race ever comes to America that gets into the American spirit more quickly than a Welshman . . . There is no essential element or principle loved by the American people [that has not been] part of the blood and principle of the Welsh people for the past 1000 years . . . I was an American citizen 1000 years before I was born.

Edwards's belief that the Welsh shared with Americans a love of liberty and democracy had a long tradition amongst Welsh immigrants. There were other cultural similarities between the Welsh and many Americans, including exceptionally enthusiastic Protestantism and a strong work ethic. The Welsh also related with ease to the similar legal traditions of America. The author of the *Cambrian* article drew a sharp contrast between the Welsh and 'certain classes of foreigners' who were guilty of 'displaying native prejudices and foreign practices'.

A writer in the *Druid* in 1920 felt that the Welsh had Americanised so speedily because 'the general tendency of the Welsh people has been to join and affiliate with other social and fraternal organisations, thus losing their national distinction'. While many might feel nostalgic about Wales and the friends and relations who lived there, they had come to America to get on, and it was sensible to try to fit in. As a Pittsburgh minister wrote in 1840, 'The advantages on a personal level beckon every Welshman to make himself a citizen without delay.' In 1900, the percentage of immigrants who had not yet applied for citizenship was only 7 per cent among Welsh immigrants, compared to 13 per cent among English and Scottish immigrants. That Welsh rate of application was one of the highest amongst all immigrant groups. American citizenship required the renunciation of allegiance to the British

Crown, and Welsh resentment of English domination perhaps made this a relatively easy choice for the Welsh. The Welsh immigrants were also exceptionally likely to remain in America. Historians have estimated that the percentages of Britons who returned to their native land between 1908 and 1923 were extremely low when compared with eastern and southern Europeans: 13 per cent of the Welsh and Scottish and 21 per cent of the English.

The dilution of Welsh communities in America

It was difficult to sustain community cohesion. The desire to get on and fit in, along with geographical factors, served to dilute Welsh communities in America. In his *Hanes Cymry America* (1872), the Rev. R. D. Thomas emphasised the importance of how spaced out the Welsh settlements were. He counted over two hundred, scattered over twenty-three states, 'and the majority of the states are 10 times the size of the whole Principality of Wales'. A comparatively small Welsh population, constituting only 1/332rd of the total American population, was scattered all over a vast expanse. This made it more difficult to maintain any Welsh identity, as did the several factors that contributed to dispersal within each small community. In 1913, Daniel Jenkins Williams recorded that the Welsh in Columbus were no longer living in close proximity to each other: aided by improved transportation and cheaper housing, the Welsh 'are rapidly abandoning the old stamping ground' into which others such as Italians were moving. Upward mobility often necessitated moving away from the Welsh immigrant community. It also reduced the need for mutual support and cooperation. Assimilation was further hastened by the decline in the use of the Welsh language.

Immigrants whose first language was Welsh no doubt took a little longer to assimilate than the more anglicised immigrants from the industrial areas of south Wales. When writing of Columbus, Daniel Jenkins Williams noted: 'the average period of the persistence of the Welsh language and Welsh communities is about three generations or about 80 years . . . When a Welshman loses his native tongue, it is difficult to distinguish him from any other normal American citizen.' That was also noted by Judge Edwards. He wrote in the *Druid* in 1909 that although Scranton 'was undoubtedly the greatest Welsh center in the United States . . . In the last 15 or 20 years, there has been a great change. The use of the Welsh language is less and less every year and it is safe to say that 15 years hence there will be very little Welsh spoken.'

While children in rural areas might go months without meeting an English-speaker, Welsh immigrants in the industrial areas found it more convenient to converse with the multitudes in English. It made sense to blend in. As the Rev. R. D. Thomas said, 'ENGLISH *is the language of the country*, and it is necessary for us and for our children to learn to understand it, to speak it, to read it, and to write it before we are able to feel happy and successful and gain influence and respect here.' The Rev. W. R. Evans wrote to *Y Drych* in 1909:

> to perpetuate the many languages in this country would be folly beyond imagination. The peace and civil and religious success of this country demands that one language should swallow all the others, and it will come to this despite every lament and effort to the contrary. The effort to perpetuate the Welsh language in this country is as useless as trying to stem the tide with a broom. It would be far better for those who wish to keep it to go back to Wales.

As John Howell Williams said in *Y Drych* in 1923, 'We came here not to keep the language alive, but to keep ourselves alive.'

The decline in the use of the Welsh language was closely related to the Welsh-speaking churches around which both rural and urban Welsh communities so often clustered. In 1871, a contemporary noted part of the congregation of the First Welsh Baptist Church in Hyde Park, Scranton, broke away because of 'the young people of the church who did not enjoy the Welsh language'. This was a common occurrence in many Welsh-speaking churches. In 1952, Emrys Jones studied the assimilation of the Welsh community in Utica, New York, and found that the American-born children of Welsh immigrants rebelled against the Welsh language and religion.

'We are not exiles. We are Americans.'

It was of course only polite to advertise one's desire to assimilate and be loyal to the country in which one lived. As a Pittsburgh minister wrote in *Y Cenhadwr Americanaidd* in 1840, 'The friendliness of the Americans towards us as a nation calls on us to show that we are their friends too.'

Jenkin Jones was born in Glyn Neath and emigrated to Scranton in 1863. In 1877, he opened a coal mine in West Virginia, and by 1930 his son James was employing 4,000 workers at nine coal-mining operations. Jenkin Jones belonged to several Welsh American societies and dreamed of sponsoring an eisteddfod in the South, but found 'it was an

WELSH AMERICAN PUBLICATIONS
AND THE LANGUAGE ISSUE

Y Drych contained news of Wales and Welsh Americans settlements. An *Y Drych* editorial of 1893 asserted, 'When a Welshman loses his Welsh, he is no longer in the eyes of his nation a Welshman ... The Welsh will surely lose themselves in and melt into the American nation when the language is lost.' Although *Y Drych* published solely in Welsh until the 1930s, it was predominantly English-language by 1950, and while 34 per cent of its news coverage originated in Wales in 1856, it was only 2 per cent by 1958.

From 1880 to 1886, *The Cambrian* was published twice monthly in Cincinnati, Ohio under the auspices of the Rev. Daniel Jones. Jones found ever-decreasing use of Welsh in the settlements he visited in many states, and feared that Welsh Americans might forget their past. Jones attributed the success of *The Cambrian* to 'the simple fact that it is published in the English language'. *The Cambrian* had subscribers in Ohio, Pennsylvania, New York, California, Washington state, Colorado, West Virginia, Missouri and Illinois. From 1886 to 1896, the Rev. Edward Evans of Remsen, New York, took charge of publication, and *The Cambrian* was printed at Utica, New York, by T. J. Griffiths, who also printed *Y Drych* and hundreds of Welsh American books. In 1896, Griffiths became the owner of *The Cambrian*. It ceased publication in 1919 because it was losing money. The flood of Welsh immigrants had dried up and previous generations and their children were assimilated by now.

impossibility as they scarcely know what a Welshman is down there'. The Welsh American newspaper *Druid* described him as 'one of the most aggressive, energetic and successful Welshmen in this country. He came to America, like many of us, poor; but, unlike many of us, he is today a millionaire.' He told one group at a Welsh gathering that 'love for his native land clings around the Welshman's heart like lichen to the rock', but speedily added: 'I yield to no man in my fealty to the United States.'

There was frequent consideration of the issue whether immigrants and their offspring were Welsh or American. Writing in *Y Drych* in 1896, R. C. Roberts of Utica said he was 'proud to be a native of Merioneth, but prouder still to be a citizen of the United States', while Dr G. W. Prees of Cambria, Wisconsin said that he had left Wales to better himself materially and to escape the 'sickness' that resulted from centuries of 'English oppression'. He declared that America was clearly a far better environment. In 1933, *Y Drych* columnist Sam Ellis of Utica wrote that those like himself who were 'more Welsh people than Americans' should understand 'that the United States is as dear to our children as Wales is to us'.

In 1954, the Welsh scholar Emrys Jones told of attending a Welsh prayer meeting in which an old Welshman who had lived for forty years in Utica, New York, thanked God he was a Welshman. However, after the meeting, a second-generation Welshman approached Jones, and his 'indignation knew no bounds after reading a Welsh newspaper's reference to *Welsh exiles in the United States*. He was insistent, 'We are not exiles. We are Americans.'

The Welsh were invariably keen to present themselves as good Americans. In 1910, the *Druid* declared that Scranton's Welsh Day, first held in 1907 and attended by 23,000, 'is truly an American gathering where a continual note of loyalty is sounded to America'.

THE ACCEPTANCE OF THE WELSH – A MYTH?

Despite the assertions of both contemporaries and historians (most frequently those with Welsh ancestry) that the Welsh were easily and fully accepted into American society, some immigrants recorded evidence of prejudice. When in 1898 future senator James Davis stood for election as city clerk in Elwood, Indiana, he recorded that would-be voters had 'read that Mr Davis is an ignorant foreigner unfitted for the duties of city clerk':

> When . . . I ran for city clerk, they [the Republicans] passed around the rumor that I was a wild Welshman from a land where the tribes lived in caves and wore leather skirts and wooden shoes, and that I had my first introduction to pants-wearing people when I came to America. They said that I had not yet learned to speak English, could not spell my own name, and was unable to count above ten.

Davis responded by demonstrating his arithmetical and spelling skills during meetings with would-be voters. When Mary Hannah Williams arrived in Colorado in 1913, she felt she was regarded as one of 'those damn foreigners' and looked down upon.

There was great anti-Welsh feeling during the unsuccessful Welsh-dominated miners' strike in the north-eastern Pennsylvania coalfield in 1871. Other ethnic groups and native Americans resented being unable to work, and Welsh strikers and Irish strikebreakers came to blows. The Welsh were traditionally loyal Republicans, but even the *Scranton Republican* turned against the 'these chosen people of God', these 'Taffys', and lamented how it was 'strange that the little dependency of Wales should have a patent for the exclusive manufacture of mining bosses'. The newspaper told somewhat scathingly of 'a crowd of frenzied Welsh females' who attacked strikebreakers and of 'Welsh women giving full vent to the force of their lungs in the most terrific howls' when two Welsh miners were shot during the violent clashes. Their deaths broke the spirit of the Welsh strikers, and the *Scranton Republican* gloated that the Welsh 'cheese-eaters', 'barbarians' and 'nation of strikers' had been taught a severe lesson. During the strike, it was frequently claimed that the Welsh were un-American. Scranton's *Daily Democrat* asserted that 'of all the people that touch these shores, the Welsh are the hardest to Americanise'.

A letter written in *Y Drych* said the antagonism during the 1871 strike owed much to native American prejudice against all immigrant groups, whom they considered 'white niggers'. The letter said such prejudices surfaced most strongly during crises such as the strike:

> We are regarded as good 'citizens' while we work quietly, without interfering in matters that are our concern just as much as they are the concern of those who were born here. Oh, everything is all-right as long as we accept American roguery quietly at all times, and then during elections we will receive their earnest recommendations to remember to vote this or that ticket. They wish us to believe we are so respectable; yet lift the veil, and it can be seen that most Americans' benevolence is a Judas Kiss.

WELSH, WELSH AMERICAN OR AMERICAN?

The question of the stage at which a member of an immigrant group and his descendants became an American was explored by the Rev. E. C. Evans, who wrote frequently for the *Cambrian*. He noted that there were Welsh-born, American-born Welsh who spoke Welsh, American-born Welsh and their descendants who self-identified as Welsh but did not speak the language, and descendants of the Welsh in America who had lost their identity. John L. Lewis and Frank Lloyd Wright were two of the most famous Americans of the twentieth century and both had Welsh immigrant parents. Lewis showed little interest in that Welsh background but was nevertheless greatly influenced by it, while Wright was interested and, some thought, greatly influenced. Both help illustrate the process of assimilation, and John L. Lewis was significant in attempts to remake America.

THE TWENTIETH CENTURY AND THE MAKING OF AN ECONOMIC AND MILITARY SUPERPOWER

Late nineteenth century	• 'Old Americans' were uneasy about 'new' immigrants from southern and eastern Europe • Workers attempted to organise unions • An increasingly expansionist America acquired overseas possessions, such as the Philippines and Puerto Rico from Spain • Many Americans were uneasy about 'robber barons' and monopoly capitalists • American industrial productivity increasingly rivalled that of European powers such as Britain and Germany
1901–9	Republican President Theodore Roosevelt pursued an aggressive foreign policy, along with domestic reforms such as the increased regulation of big business
1913–21	Democrat President Woodrow Wilson encouraged progressive domestic reforms that were pro-labour and anti-big business. He took the United States into the First World War (1914–18) in 1917, primarily because America's economic relationship with Britain and France caused German attacks on US shipping
1921–33	• Republican Presidents Harding, Coolidge and then Hoover were opposed to the increased federal government interventionism of the Wilson years • The creation of the world's first communist state in Russia aroused American fears of socialism and communism – and of immigrants with those beliefs • After a post-war recession, the 1920s were a period of economic boom, especially in consumer goods
1929– c.1939	The Wall Street crash helped trigger the Great Depression, when 25 per cent of the American workforce was unemployed
1933–45	• During his twelve-year presidency, the Democrat Franklin Roosevelt introduced unprecedented federal government intervention in the economy and society, with a New Deal that aimed to alleviate unemployment and poverty • With the rise of aggressive fascist powers, Roosevelt focused increasingly upon foreign policy, and his aid for opponents/ victims of fascism led the United States into the Second World War in 1941
1945	• The United States emerged from the Second World War as by far the richest and most powerful nation in the world • The Soviet Union was the world's second most powerful nation, which inevitably caused fear of and tension with the United States. The fear and tension were exacerbated by their opposing political and economic beliefs and combined to lead to half a century of Cold War rivalry

JOHN L. LEWIS (1880–1969) AND THE AMERICAN DREAM

Miners' leader John Llewellyn Lewis was one of the most influential of Welsh Americans and probably the most unpopular. Naughty children were told, 'You had better be good, or John L. Lewis will get you.'

Welsh family background

Welsh immigrants John Watkins and Tom Lewis were coal miners in Lucas, Iowa, in the last quarter of the nineteenth century. It was said that Tom had two loves, his labour union and John Watkins's daughter Louisa. Tom and Louisa married and John L. Lewis was one of their children. Both John Watkins and Tom Lewis suffered because of their union activities. When Tom was blacklisted by employers, he and his young family had to move from coal camp to coal camp in order for him to find work.

John L. Lewis does not appear to have been greatly interested in his Welsh heritage, although he and his wife searched for antiques in Cardiff and Swansea during a long vacation in Europe in 1923, and while working in London in the mid-1950s he acceded to someone else's suggestion that he spend a free weekend catching up with relations and family history in the Cardiff/Swansea area. He interviewed many Welsh miners during that latter visit and concluded, 'I think our problems are the same.'

Despite his relative lack of interest in his family's Welsh origins, John L. Lewis was shaped by his Welsh background.

Achievement – personal

As with many Welsh immigrants and Welsh Americans, John L. Lewis rose far above his humble beginnings. After an early restlessness, when he mined for gold, silver, lead and copper out West, he returned to Lucas, Iowa, and worked down the coal mines. In 1907, he married Myrta Bell, who came from a socially eminent Lucas family. Their families did not attend the wedding, perhaps because John's Mormon parents felt discomfited that Myrta was not of their religion, perhaps because her parents felt she was marrying beneath her. It might have been consciousness of perceived social inferiority that encouraged Lewis to engage in a business venture and to stand for mayor of Lucas in 1907. He failed in both attempts and in 1908 decided on a career in labour unions.

The hard-working Lewis proved adept at winning the favour of powerful men, manoeuvring his way through union politics and gaining and retaining power in the United Mine Workers of America (UMWA). The UMWA had 400,000 members in 1920 and was America's biggest and probably most militant labour union. Leadership of the UMWA was one of the most influential positions in the American labour movement, and Lewis held that post from 1920 until he decided to retire in 1960. It brought him wealth and influence. He provided well for his family and gave several of them union posts. He always travelled first class and stayed in top hotels such as New York's Waldorf Astoria. His cars were Cadillacs and Lincolns, and his wife wore mink. In 1929, a miner might average $30 weekly, but Myrta Lewis spent $35 on a nineteenth-century English sterling silver soup ladle. John Lewis had upper-class friends, several country club memberships and, later in life, a Florida vacation home. He always enjoyed a standard of living far higher than that of the rank-and-file members of his UMWA. It could be argued that he was engaging in a necessary display of the union's power and resources that helped make those with whom he had to negotiate take him more seriously. Similarly, Lewis was frequently portrayed in the press as thuggish and even animal-like (it was quite common to depict miners thus), so it could be argued that what some considered to be social pretentiousness on his part was a way of countering the frequent dehumanising of miners. On the other hand, it could be argued that his lifestyle was materialistic and hypocritical.

Achievements – the miners

Assessments of Lewis's professional achievements vary. He constructed a solid miners' union machine over which he created dictatorial powers. He used less than admirable methods to maintain control of the UMWA. One colleague said he 'has actually relied a considerable number of times on the use of direct violence in achieving his end'. For example, his sympathisers beat up one of his critics in his hotel room during the 1927 UMWA convention. 'He was the kind of guy would commit murder,' another union official declared, although there is no proof that Lewis ever contemplated or did this. Sometimes he was simply dishonest: during a 1932 referendum on striking in the troublesome Illinois coalfields, a Lewis man stole the ballots and Lewis promptly declared a state of emergency because of the theft. The strike was then called off, as Lewis had always wanted.

Despite all of the above, many miners worshipped Lewis. After any mining disaster, Lewis would be there, appearing visibly moved. After

Figure 18. *John L. Lewis at the West Frankfort mining disaster, 1951*

the 1951 explosion in the West Frankfort mine in Illinois, he accompanied the rescue teams down the mine each day, while insisting that his younger associates stay above ground for safety. Lewis had his critics within the UMWA and he sometimes miscalculated, as in two strikes in the 1920s, but he served most of the UMWA members well for the most part and for most of the time. Whereas some unions and occupations were hamstrung by internal divisions, Lewis's UMWA dictatorship made contract talks easier and he was a canny negotiator. Journalist C. L. Sulzberger described how Lewis would speak with mine operators:

> Gentlemen, I speak to you for the miners' families . . . The little
> children are gathered around a bare table without anything to eat.
> They are not asking for a $100,000 yacht like yours Mr . . . or for a
> Rolls-Royce limousine like yours, Mr . . . They are asking only for
> a slim crust of bread.

The tough, hostile image that Lewis projected was something of an act.
When colleagues and friends such as Gardner Jackson suggested he
should frown less when photographed, Lewis replied, 'Why, Gardner,
my stock in trade is being the ogre. That's how I make my way.' He
told Frances Perkins, 'Madame Secretary, that scowl is worth $1 mil-
lion.' He and Perkins disliked each other. Lewis had demanded a 'real'
labour person as Secretary of Labor and dismissed Perkins, saying, 'She
would make a good housekeeper.' She never understood his posturing,
as when tense negotiations in 1939 prompted her to report that 'John
Lewis is very ugly today – very ugly'. She missed the point. As Lewis told
a business acquaintance who suggested he hire a public relations man
to improve his image, he was just going to have to be disliked and disrespected by most American people if he was to fight successfully for the
coal miners. While journalist Marquis Childs described Lewis as 'a pretty
aloof figure' and concluded that 'this is a very curious man', another
journalist (and UMWA employee), Ed Levinson, said that Lewis understood the psychology of making himself aloof. He played at scowling
for the cameras because it served to make him look more powerful and
therefore more formidable in negotiations.

The combination of his negotiating skills and the miners' willing-
ness to strike (with or without UMWA approval) enabled Lewis to negotiate frequent wage rises and shorter hours. In 1948, he won improved
safety measures and unprecedented medical and pension benefits. He
could change tactics and compromise when necessary, as in the 1950s
when both he and the mine operators recognised that the coal industry
was in decline and adjusted their negotiations to a more collaborative
process.

JOHN THE BAPTIST

During the bitter Harlan County War between strikers and operators in
the 1930s, striking coal miners would throw strikebreakers who tried to
cross picket lines into a stream, declaring, 'Baptised in the name of John
L. Lewis.'

While miners frequently felt their work and safety were undervalued and considered strikes a fair bargaining weapon, their industrial action often met with hostility from coal users, the law courts and politicians. Nevertheless, in 1964, President Lyndon B. Johnson awarded Lewis the nation's highest civilian honour, the Medal of Freedom, for his work on the UMWA Welfare and Retirement Fund. The citation described him as an 'eloquent spokesman of labor, [who] has given voice to the aspirations of the industrial workers of the country and led the cause of free trade unions within a healthy system of free enterprise'.

When Lewis died in 1969, influential Illinois union leader Reuben Soderstrom, who in 1940 had described Lewis as 'the most truth-twisting windbag that this nation has yet produced', nevertheless said that Lewis would be remembered for 'making almost a half million poorly paid and poorly protected coalminers the best paid and best protected miners in the world'.

Achievements – the industrial workers

John L. Lewis is a heroic figure to many of those who believe that worker representation and bargaining power constitute an important contribution to the making of America.

When Lewis began as a union man in 1908, the American labour movement was still in its infancy. Fewer than 10 per cent of the non-agricultural workforce was unionised, big business and the federal government were hostile to unions, and public opinion often associated labour activists with anarchist, communist and socialist immigrants. The labour unions struggled during the prosperous 1920s, but grew stronger under the pressure of the Great Depression and with the help of a more sympathetic President in Franklin D. Roosevelt (1933–45).

The miners were affiliated to the American Federation of Labor (AFL), and in autumn 1933, Lewis called on the AFL to offer membership to the mass-production workers in the automobile, steel, rubber, lumber and electrical industries. He told the AFL executive council that the federation needed far more members to acquire the political power that would bring about helpful legislation for workers. However, the craft unions that dominated the AFL did not want the less skilled mass-production workers to join. It therefore rejected Lewis's demand. Lewis responded with the establishment of what became the Congress for Industrial Organisation (CIO), which acquired millions of industrial workers as members and helped unionise them in the face of the unhelpful posture of the AFL and the traditional anti-union hostility of companies such as U.S. Steel and General Motors. When the CIO split from the AFL, Lewis became its first president. One of the advantages of Lewis's dictatorship was that he had unquestioned control of the UMWA's finances, and it was his UMWA that financed the CIO in its early days, giving $2.5 million to the steelworkers alone.

In 1933, there were 3 million union members. By 1939, it was over 8 million, and these unionised workers earned far more than the non-unionised. Lewis was the most powerful labour leader America had ever seen, and his CIO had helped millions of American families obtain a higher standard of living. He had created the modern American mass labour movement (by the time he retired in 1960, 25 per cent of the non-agricultural workers were unionised) and transformed it into a far more powerful force in the economy, with great influence in the Democratic Party.

What motivated John L. Lewis in his organisation of the industrial workers and his split from the AFL? His hostile biographers Dubofsky and Van Tine were not alone in thinking it was 'ambition, even egomania' that just possibly coincided with the interests of the working class.

JOHN L. LEWIS V. WILLIAM GREEN

When Lewis fell out with the AFL, the AFL president was William Green (1873–1952). Green was born in Ohio to the immigrant daughter of a Welsh miner and her English miner husband. Green worked as a coal miner from the age of sixteen, and was a union activist from 1891. From 1910 to 1914, he served in the Ohio state legislature and was influential in the production of legislation to benefit workers. From 1914, he focused on UMWA and AFL work. He was president of the AFL from 1924 to 1952. In the 1930s, he promoted workers' rights in collaboration with the federal government, but failed to prevail against the craft unions' determination to exclude industrial workers' unions from the AFL.

JOHN L. LEWIS V. BENJAMIN FRANKLIN FAIRLESS

Benjamin Franklin Fairless (1890–1962) was born to an impoverished Welsh-born coal miner and his wife, a Welsh miner's daughter. Fairless worked his way up from poverty to the presidency of U.S. Steel in 1938. That company owned coal mines, and as a result Fairless frequently clashed with John L. Lewis. There were several occasions on which Fairless was as unpopular with the general public as John L. Lewis. For example, he rejected the idea of pensions for steelworkers, despite the executives having generous ones. His U.S. Steel was the last steel company to give in on the issue.

Lewis did not play a particularly positive role in healing the divisions between the AFL and CIO, which might be taken to confirm 'ambition, even egomania'. However, when a friend asked Lewis why he got involved with the CIO, 'He told me that he did it because he was tired of the coal operators telling him whenever he tried to raise the wages of his miners, that he was asking for more than the workers of steel, auto and rubber were getting' (the steel companies owned their own coal mines). Lewis might well have been speaking the truth there: for him, it was always the miners.

'THE HUMP', THE MOB AND CHICAGO UNIONS

The Welsh tradition of union connections is further illustrated in the person of Llewelyn Morris Humphreys (1899–1965), whose parents were Welsh immigrants. Their son gained fame as 'The Hump'. Before The Hump reached his teens, he was involved in Chicago street gangs. During the Prohibition years, he stole bootleg, impressed and worked for Al Capone, performed several mob killings, and basically ran several Chicago labour unions. By the 1950s, he was recognised as the Mob's number-one brain. Although he called himself Murray Humphreys from the time that he was a teenager, he gave his daughter the Welsh-sounding name Llewella. Despite his dangerous life and career, he died of natural causes. He is a distant relative to Plaid Cymru politician Lord Dafydd Wigley

A new American Dream

The America in which John L. Lewis was raised was a nation in which individualism and self-help were essential elements of the American Dream his parents had pursued when they emigrated from Wales. Theirs was the dream of many immigrants, of a more affluent life that would be acquired through hard work. However, this American Dream had to be sought within a capitalist system in which there were great and inevitable inequalities of wealth and frequently painful boom and bust cycles.

During the economic depression that followed the end of the First World War, many were willing to work hard but unable to find employment. While federal government intervention in the economy was anathema to the Republican administration of Warren G. Harding and to many American voters, Lewis grew convinced of the need for it. When he stood for the AFL presidency in spring 1921, he advocated old age pensions and unemployment insurance. Lewis's candidacy was unsuccessful, because the conservative AFL remained steadfastly opposed to such social reform.

That post-war economic depression paled into insignificance when compared to the Great Depression of the 1930s. In a 1931 speech, Lewis urged the nation's political leaders to be more proactive in combating the depression, lest American society reach breaking point amidst the awful poverty that afflicted around one-third of Americans. He declared that the miners' diet was 'actually below domestic animals standards', a claim confirmed in 1933 by First Lady Eleanor Roosevelt's journalist friend Lorena Hickok. Hickok observed miners' families in West Virginia who 'had been living for days on green corn and string beans – and precious little of that. And some had nothing at all.' In his testimony before the Senate Finance Committee in February 1933, Lewis argued that the government should ensure employment and good wages because that would enable workers to buy goods and thereby stimulate the economy. He also demanded a greater say for organised labour and the right to collective bargaining, while assuring the committee that 'American labor stands between the rapacity of the robber barons of industrial America and the lustful rage of the Communists, who would lay waste to our traditions and our institutions with fire and sword'.

In March 1933, Franklin Roosevelt became President of the United States, having promised American voters a 'New Deal' to combat the unprecedented unemployment and despair. The new President introduced the revolutionary national economic planning for which Lewis had called. He created jobs and supported directives and legislation that confirmed union rights.

While there is no evidence that Lewis's advocacy of large-scale government intervention in the economy and/or his subsequent meeting with the new President influenced Roosevelt's policies, it is possible. It may be significant that Lewis's close friend and adviser Jett Lauck became a Roosevelt adviser.

Roosevelt's policies constituted a remaking of American society and the economy, and introduced a somewhat modified version of the American Dream. However, Lewis's campaign speeches in support of Roosevelt's 1936 re-election bid reflected a more revolutionary vision of the American Dream, a vision in which the federal government gave greater power and benefits to the unions.

In one of the speeches, Lewis claimed: 'My voice tonight will be the voice of millions of men and women unemployed in America's industries, heretofore unorganised, economically exploited and inarticulate.' He argued that a strong labour movement would free the United States from enslavement by the reactionary financial elite epitomised in

Figure 19. *John L. Lewis attracted large audiences in his capacity as the leader of the miners and as a famously dramatic and inspirational orator. Courtesy of the United Mine Workers of America Archives.*

John Pierpont Morgan Jr., an elite that sought to recreate the form of capitalism that had caused the depression. In a speech to 30,000 miners in Pottsville, Pennsylvania, Lewis blamed financial capitalists such as Morgan for the depression, for exploiting labour and for World War I (he insisted that investment bankers and munitions manufacturers had a vested interest in the United States entering that war). He said America faced a struggle over

> whether the working population of this country shall have a voice in determining their destiny or whether they shall serve as indentured servants for a financial and economic dictatorship which would shamelessly exploit our natural resources and debase the soul . . . and . . . pride of free people. On such an issue there can be no compromise.

Aware of accusations that unions were full of subversive left-wingers, he insisted that they were the 'best insurance against the spread of alien and subversive doctrines' such as communism.

THE WELSH ANCESTRY OF J. P. MORGAN JR

Miles Morgan (1616–99) of Llandaff, near Cardiff, emigrated to America in 1636 and settled in Massachusetts. In 1869, his descendant Junius Spencer Morgan (1813–90) was the lucky inheritor of the childless George Peabody's bank. Junius renamed the bank J. S. Morgan and Company. Junius's son, John Pierpont Morgan Sr (1837–1913), demonstrated his gift for making money during the Civil War. He bought 5,000 rifles from an army arsenal at $3.50 each and sold them on to a commander in the field at $22 each. He avoided military service by paying $300 for a substitute, and went on to develop and finance a great railway empire. During the great panic of 1907, when many New York City banks were on the verge of bankruptcy, it was Morgan who stabilised the nation's financial system. He was important in assisting the formation of several great industrial giants, including General Electric and U.S. Steel. He had a great deal of influence over Congress, but from the late nineteenth century there was growing public concern about the ruthless acquisition of wealth by businessmen such as Morgan, who came to be called 'robber barons'. It was believed by many that the robber barons represented corruption, monopolistic practices and rampant individualism. That prompted President Theodore Roosevelt (1901–9) to promote legislation to curb their activities. In contrast, conservatives praised Morgan for strengthening the national economy when he financed railroads, canals, steel mills and shipping lines.

J. Pierpont Morgan Jr (1867–1943) was deeply involved in the financing of the combatants of the First World War, as demonstrated by his loans of $12 million to Russia in 1914 and $500 million to Britain and France in 1915. He was a director of U.S. Steel, which was famously anti-union. Such policies earned him the undying hatred of John L. Lewis.

The Glass–Steagall Act (1933), designed to prevent another Great Depression, separated investment and commercial banking and thereby decreased the influence of the robber barons such as Morgan.

JOHN L. LEWIS'S VERDICT ON ROOSEVELT'S REPUBLICAN RIVAL FOR THE PRESIDENCY IN 1936

Lewis told 30,000 cheering miners in Pottsville, Pennsylvania that the Republican candidate Alf Landon was 'just as empty, as inane, and innocuous as a watermelon that had been boiled in a bath tub'.

Figure 20. *John L. Lewis (right of the lectern) campaigning with President Franklin D. Roosevelt (left) in coal country, Wilkes-Barre, Pennsylvania, in 1936.*

Lewis campaigned for liberal state governors and for Roosevelt in the coal states of Ohio, Kentucky, Indiana and Pennsylvania, and the UMWA spent an unprecedented $600,000 on Roosevelt's election. It is difficult to assess the extent to which this contributed to Roosevelt's landslide, but Roosevelt won Pennsylvania's industrial towns decisively and UMWA funding certainly contributed to the election of pro-union governors in the industrial states.

In a December 1936 radio speech, Lewis said:

> Labor demands a new deal in America's great industries . . . Labor demands legislative enactments making realistic the principles of industrial democracy . . . The time has passed in America when the workers can be either clubbed, gassed, or shutdown with impunity . . . Labor will . . . expect the protection of the Federal Government in the pursuit of its lawful objectives.

Here, Lewis was thinking not only of what he thought Roosevelt owed the union members who had voted overwhelmingly for him, but also of the anti-union Supreme Court, led by another of Welsh descent, Charles Evans Hughes.

CHARLES EVANS HUGHES (1862–1948)

Born to a Welsh immigrant in Glenn Falls, New York, Charles Evans Hughes held an exceptional number of significant offices. After a successful legal career, he was elected Governor of New York (1907–10). As Governor, he promoted legislation that curtailed the exploitation of child workers and introduced the first workers' compensation legislation in American history.

After Republican President Taft (1909–13) appointed him to the Supreme Court (1910–16), Hughes supported laws that set minimum wages and regulated work hours, and opposed laws that discriminated against black Americans. The Republican Party persuaded Hughes to stand for the presidency in 1916, but he was defeated by the Democrat Woodrow Wilson. Republican President Warren G. Harding (1921–3) appointed Hughes as Secretary of State (1921–5), and Hughes proved the driving force behind the administration's promotion of international naval disarmament, respect for the territorial integrity of China, and the stabilisation of the German economy. In 1930, Republican President Herbert Hoover appointed Hughes chief justice of the Supreme Court.

The conservative majority on the Hughes Supreme Court struck down several of the Democrat Roosevelt's New Deal laws, including the Wagner Labor Relations Act of 1935, which guaranteed workers' rights to organise and required employers to bargain with union representatives. It also prohibited 'unfair labor practices' such as employer discrimination against union members, refusal to bargain, and the creation of and support for company unions. As far as union men such as John L. Lewis were concerned, Hughes was on the wrong side again when the Guffey Coal Act (1935) and New York state's minimum wage law were ruled unconstitutional. When an exasperated Roosevelt threatened to 'pack' the Supreme Court with more liberal justices, Hughes managed the court so that it became less hostile to the New Deal measures. The Hughes court then upheld legislation on the minimum wage, the new social security system, and labour union rights. It also upheld anti-racial discrimination rulings of lower courts.

Charles Evans Hughes retired from public life in 1940. In his capacity as Supreme Court justice and Secretary of State, he had for the most part supported far greater government intervention in the economy and society and in international affairs – the two most pronounced developments in the remaking of America in the twentieth century.

Roosevelt was not an overly enthusiastic supporter of labour unions – the pro-union legislation passed by Congress during his presidency was initiated by others. This was but one of the areas in which Lewis and Roosevelt had differing views of what constituted the American Dream, and by 1940 they had openly fallen out.

Lewis versus Roosevelt – two American Dreams

Some attribute the split between Lewis and Roosevelt to personalities, but although Roosevelt's wife Eleanor told a Lewis aide that both were 'prima donnas', it is more convincing to argue that their clash was an ideological one that centred upon their differing interpretations of the American Dream. While Franklin Roosevelt was keen to have working-class votes and to give the workers employment, collective bargaining powers and a basic welfare safety net, he was not as fully committed to workers' rights as Lewis. That alienated Lewis, who had other grievances. He resented Roosevelt's apparent disregard for mine safety, rejection of advice from labour about federal appointments such as Secretary of Labor, and failure to support striking steelworkers against management. In 1937, Lewis's frustration with Roosevelt was such that he dropped hints about the establishment of a new political party based on labour.

Lewis believed much more needed to be done to make a better America. In December 1937, he made speeches demanding more New Deal measures such as federal expenditure on subsidised housing, a social security system that would allow senior citizens to retire with dignity and in comfort, and job creation schemes. However, Roosevelt had lost congressional support for further economic and social reform and was increasingly focused on the expansionist ambitions revealed by Japan (1931), Italy (1935) and Germany (1936).

In a March 1937 speech, Lewis declared:

> Europe is on the brink of disaster and it must be our care that she does not drag us into the abyss after . . . Safety and security for Americans lie in non-participation in this conflict and the addressing of ourselves to the major problem now confronting us in our internal economy and domestic establishment.

In 1940, Lewis lamented Roosevelt's continuing focus on foreign policy: 'Let him turn his face to cabins where [black] American people are being lashed by white-robed [Ku Klux Klan] powers.' Lewis and labour leaders could not forget how another President, Woodrow Wilson, had been distracted from further reforms by the First World War. Lewis considered that war an unnecessary one in which conservative businessmen and politicians had repressed labour and radicals. While Lewis's American Dream required a focus on domestic issues, Roosevelt believed that the preservation of the American Dream necessitated aid to the opponents of expansionist powers because those powers were likely to threaten American interests.

WELSH VERSUS ENGLISH

When Britain's King George VI and his wife Queen Elizabeth visited Roosevelt's Hyde Park home in spring 1939, John L. Lewis rejected an invitation to meet them there. Later in life, he would refer disapprovingly to 'English imperialism'. Many of Welsh descent in America resented the English conquest of Wales and disliked the pro-Empire stance of the English elite, and this probably helps explain Lewis's isolationism.

Lewis made a dramatic intervention in the 1940 election because he was convinced that Roosevelt's re-election would result in US entry into the war in Europe, the development of an imperial presidency, American imperialism, the erosion of democratic liberties and the facilitation of the corporate financial elite's control of US economic policy (anti-labour corporations were receiving government defence contracts). Lewis's fears were justified, but so too was Roosevelt's assessment of the threat that expansionist powers posed to American security.

As far as Lewis was concerned, it was not only Roosevelt's foreign policy that endangered American democracy. In a radio speech of 25 October 1940, Lewis criticised Roosevelt's unprecedented bid for a third term in the White House, regretting 'the spectacle of a President who is disinclined to surrender that power, in keeping with traditions of the Republic'. Lewis endorsed the Republican candidate, Wendell Wilkie, even though many in the CIO and some in the UMWA favoured Roosevelt (dummies of Lewis were hanged in effigy in Ohio coalfields with placards saying JUDAS, TRAITOR, DICTATOR). Lewis's had been a brave stance for a man supposedly power-mad. He had promised to resign as CIO chief if CIO members voted for Roosevelt, and he kept his word when most of them did so. Lewis was not the only American patriot to fear the repeated re-election of a President. When Roosevelt stood for a fourth term in 1944, his candidate for Vice President, Harry Truman, was one of many others who felt uneasy, and congressional legislation after Roosevelt's death ensured a two-term limit in future. In Roosevelt's defence, he believed he would be the most able master-mind of US foreign policy during a time of war and crisis – and he was probably right.

Lewis's predictions should Roosevelt get re-elected in 1940	Results of Roosevelt's re-election
The United States would enter the war in Europe	Roosevelt's aid to Hitler's opponents encouraged Hitler to declare war on the United States after Pearl Harbor, which brought America into the war in Europe
An imperial presidency and American imperialism would develop	The Second World War laid American isolationism to rest and confirmed the United States as by far the most powerful nation in the world. From the late 1940s, America was involved in a Cold War with the Soviet Union. As is always the case in wartime, the power of the President greatly increased, so that there was much talk of an 'Imperial presidency' in the 1970s in particular. The United States had always been an expansionist state, as demonstrated by late nineteenth-century acquisitions such as the American West, Hawaii, Puerto Rico and the Philippines. During the Cold War, the United States made a series of alliances and interventions (most famously in Vietnam) that some perceived as imperialist.
Democratic liberties would be eroded	The emphasis on national security during the Second World War and the Cold War rendered dissent unpopular and some dissenters suffered for their beliefs
The financial elite would gain control of US economic policy	US government defence requirements and contracts greatly benefited big business during the Second World War and the Cold War, and resulted in what President Eisenhower (1953–61) called the 'military-industrial complex'. Eisenhower feared that the military-industrial complex had a vested interest in continuing conflict, and warned against it in his final speech as President.

Lewis v. Roosevelt – wartime strikes

When the miners went on strike in 1941, Roosevelt publicly criticised Lewis as unpatriotic and endangering national security. Lewis was fast developing into one of the nation's most hated men, even though he emphasised his support for the war effort after the Japanese attacked Pearl Harbor in December 1941, and told some wildcat strikers in July 1942, 'Our nation is at war and coal production must not cease.'

The height of Lewis's unpopularity came in 1943. The pressure for greater production in wartime had made mining more dangerous than ever, the federal government was curtailing collective bargaining, and wages were being kept down to combat inflation. As a result, many miners ignored the no-strike pledge made at the outbreak of war and engaged in wildcat strikes. Most Americans considered this unpatriotic. An air force pilot was quoted as saying, 'I'd just as soon shoot down one of those strikers as shoot down Japs – they're doing just as much to lose the war for us.' A Gallup poll revealed an 89 per cent disapproval rating for Lewis. Many agreed with veteran labour reporter Louis Stark's claim that Lewis was 'craving power for its own sake', and a *Stars and Stripes* editorial said, 'Speaking for the American soldiers John L. Lewis, damn your coal-black soul.' While Lewis contended that the government was trying to 'economically disembowel' the miners, the rank and file walked out. Although the UMWA ordered the 558,000 striking miners to return, Roosevelt refused to acknowledge that it was rank-and-file militancy and told the press it was Lewis's fault. Eventually, the dispute was settled, although on terms less favourable than the miners desired. While production did not really suffer, the miners encouraged other workers to go on strike, distracted the government from the war effort and aroused great anti-union feeling. Did John L. Lewis care? One old friend said he was a union man 'from his toes to the top of his head'. He wanted what his miners wanted and the rest could say what they liked. However, he had miscalculated: the wartime miners' strikes contributed to the anti-labour sentiments that led to the 1943 and 1947 congressional legislation that greatly restricted union freedom.

Saint or sinner?

Lewis recognised that he aroused conflicting views and once asked himself, 'What makes me tick? Is it power I'm after, or am I a St Francis in disguise, or what?' The views of his contemporaries and historians have varied in line with the individual's political, economic and social position.

Those who disapproved of trade/labour unions – and the *Druid* demonstrated that their number included some of Welsh descent – loathed Lewis because he was such a committed union man. There were some who believed in labour unions but disliked Lewis and his methods, some who regretted his methods but revered him and some who considered his methods justified. There were some who apparently changed their minds: when Lewis died, even passionate Lewis-hater David McDonald said that 'in the field of labour he was the greatest Roman of them all'.

Lewis biographers Melvyn Dubofsky and Warren Van Tine (1986) were pro-union but concluded that Lewis was, 'A practitioner of the theory that power is the only morality', a man who used 'brutality, bullying, deceit, and bluff' to get to the top and stay there. They were disgusted by what they considered to be Lewis's abhorrent social climbing, assessing him as a 'striver, climber, a man driven by ambition and perhaps eager to compensate for his lowly social origins', a man who from the 1920s listed his occupation as 'executive' on his passport. Lewis integrated well with the Washington elite, many of whom found him courteous and gentlemanly, and it seems that he may indeed have been sensitive about those lowly origins, because he had apparently left one gullible society matron convinced that he was 'very well connected in Wales'.

While Dubofsky and Van Tine were sympathetic to labour unions but not to Lewis, Ron Roberts's 1994 biography was far more sympathetic to Lewis, as might be expected from someone with similar Welsh mining roots. Arguably, John L. Lewis can be better understood if placed in a Welsh context. While an emphasis on mutual aid was a characteristic of Lewis's parents' Mormon religion, it was also a characteristic of influential Welsh politicians such as David Lloyd George and Aneurin Bevan, and of Welsh and Welsh American mining communities. During the 1900 presidential election, the settlement at Hiteman near Lucas was the only precinct in America where a majority of voters opted for the left-wing Social Democratic Party candidate. In 1906, Lewis had helped organise a cooperative from which miners could buy supplies cheaper than in regular stores. Most telling of all, he risked unpopularity with his own CIO and UMWA members when he criticised President Roosevelt for abandoning the New Deal. Lewis had a genuine commitment to social improvement and working-class welfare: his friend Saul Alinsky recalled, 'I saw him weep at the plight of others,' and Lewis ended his retirement speech with the words, 'The business of keeping a person alive is the number and obligation of every person.' Of course, that was a genuine commitment which was not necessarily in conflict with personal ambition.

WELSH SOCIAL REFORMERS

In 1923, former British Prime Minister David Lloyd George visited the United States. He nearly left Scranton, Pennsylvania, off his itinerary because the city was in decline, as was its Welshness. However, crowds of 15,000 greeted Lloyd George and his wife and daughter when they arrived at Lackawanna Station. It seems likely that Lloyd George's Welsh American admirers such as Frank Lloyd Wright's Welsh-born mother were aware that he had enthusiastically promoted social reforms such as old age pensions and unemployment insurance while he was a member of the great pre-war Liberal reforming government.

Another Welsh social reformer, Aneurin Bevan, played an important role in the Labour government's introduction of Britain's National Health Service. John L. Lewis read a great deal, and one would imagine that he knew of these two Welsh promoters of revolutionary social programmes.

Lewis won much for the miners and the industrial workers, although sometimes by undesirable methods. He had tried to promote an alternative version of the American Dream, but this workers' vision of a remade America was one that never prevailed against the American belief in individualism, acceptance of corporate influence, and rejection of anything that seemed to smack of socialism or communism. Lewis's vision owed much to his Welsh background, but he considered himself a proud American. Union leaders and their members were often criticised as un-American, but Lewis always emphasised their patriotism. When criticised over a miners' strike in 1919, Lewis responded:

> I am an American, free born, with all the pride of my heritage. I love my country with its institutions and traditions. With Abraham Lincoln I thank God that we have a country where men may strike. May the power of my government never be used to throttle and crush the efforts of the toilers to improve their material welfare and elevate the standards of their civilisation.

In his trumpeting of his Americanism, he was trying to deflect criticisms that the version of the American Dream to which he and others in the labour movement subscribed was unpatriotic. He thought himself an American, but his mining background, his social reform ideas and his fears of imperialism made him a very Welsh American, whose vision of the future and whose fears of the direction Roosevelt's

America was taking after 1936 went against the tide. In that sense, he was not fully assimilated, which was something that he did not understand and that only some of his more sympathetic chroniclers have grasped.

'TWO GREAT AMERICANS'

In 1940, the Museum of Modern Art in New York City put on an exhibition entitled 'Two Great Americans'. Both had Welsh ancestry: Frank Lloyd Wright was adjudged 'the greatest American architect of all time' by the American Institute of Architects (AIA) in 1991, while D. W. Griffith was a great movie maker of the silent era. He introduced dramatic close-ups, fade-outs, cross-cutting, tracking shots, exceptionally coordinated crowd scenes and the revolutionary use of a full musical score to accompany the epic movie, a genre that he pioneered.

Griffith was made very aware of his Welsh ancestry by his mother. She frequently reminded him that his name meant 'dearly beloved' in Welsh, and tried to discourage him from becoming an actor by reminding him of his descent from Welsh kings. Others were aware of his Welsh ancestry. Screenwriter Anita Loos found him 'secretive', a trait she thought characteristic of the Welsh, whom she considered 'very peculiar people'. Griffith got on well with Welshmen such as the politician David Lloyd George and the singer-actor-composer Ivor Novello (a stage name). He was also very close to his press agent, Gerit Lloyd, who was of Welsh descent.

FRANK LLOYD WRIGHT (1867–1959)

The Welsh family background

Frank Lloyd Wright's maternal grandparents, Richard Lloyd Jones and Mary (Mallie) Thomas, emigrated from Llandysul on the Cardiganshire–Carmarthenshire borders in 1844. Their motivation was probably to acquire land and to escape the social ostracism that resulted from their Unitarian religion's rejection of the idea of the Holy Trinity. The Lloyd Joneses settled in a Welsh community near Spring Green, Wisconsin, where three of Richard's siblings already resided. Richard and Mallie attended a union church that welcomed a variety of Protestants, but voluntarily departed when threatened with eviction because of their Unitarian beliefs. Amongst Richard's children was Welsh-born Anna, Frank Lloyd Wright's mother.

THE WELSH IN WISCONSIN

The 1900 US census listed 3,356 people born in Wales and 7,866 children of Welsh people in Wisconsin. The early Welsh settlers in Wisconsin settled in close-knit rural communities centred on their churches. Their descendants were frequently using the Welsh language in church services, newspapers and magazines into the 1920s and 1930s. Perhaps third-generation Welsh American and Professor of English Phillips G. Davies was being a little harsh when he contended that, with the exception of Frank Lloyd Wright, 'they made no really substantial impact upon the face of Wisconsin'.

The Lloyd Jones family retained a strong attachment to their Welsh heritage and connections. Anna married Massachusetts minister Richard Carey Wright, but Frank's sister Maginel subsequently recalled, 'It was a disadvantage . . . something not quite right . . . for . . . my mother to have married a New Englander' with no Welsh connection. When Frank's aunts commissioned additions to their school, they told the architect that they wanted 'a Welsh feel' for the assembly room. Anna remained interested in Wales into her old age, at which time she possessed photographs of David Lloyd George and of a meeting celebrating Welsh hymn writer Ann Griffiths.

THE ADVANTAGES OF MARRYING WITHIN THE WELSH COMMUNITY

In 1871, a Welsh miner opined that 'the clean, rosy-cheeked, hard-working Welsh girls' were far preferable to Yankee girls who spent their time reading novels and boasted that they knew no more about cooking or baking 'than a mole knows about knitting socks'.

Frank was adored by his possessive Welsh-born mother. She assured him from an early age that he was destined for greatness and told him of Welsh history, culture and traditions, including the story of Taliesin, an ancient Welsh poet-prophet.

After the failure of her marriage, Anna focused even more on her children, and especially on Frank. He was christened Frank Lincoln Wright, but with the departure of his father he attached himself even more firmly to the Lloyd Jones clan, calling himself Frank Lloyd Wright and adopting the Lloyd Jones family motto, 'Truth Against the World'.

In his autobiography, Wright recalled that his mother chose his profession because 'there was nothing quite so sacrosanct' as architecture. He wrote that she 'lived much in him'. She also wanted to live with or at least near him, but she did not get along with his women, and he declared her 'impossible to live with quietly', adding that 'when Aunt Nell enters into the proposition then there is perfect hell'.

Frank Lloyd Wright loved the Wisconsin valley in which his maternal grandparents had settled. All the Lloyd Joneses were buried there. It was something akin to sacred ground to the family. Wright had to leave the valley for his career as an architect, but he always came back and it was there that he would build the home that he christened Taliesin.

THE MAN AND HIS GENIUS

While a young architect in Chicago, Frank Lloyd Wright married Catherine Lee Tobin. Amongst their seven children, Robert Llewellyn seems to have valued the Welsh connection, because he always called himself Llewellyn. Wright quickly made a name for himself in Chicago, buoyed by his great self-confidence: 'Early in life I had to choose between honest arrogance and hypocritical humility. I chose honest arrogance.'

In 1909, in the face of almost universal opprobrium, Frank Lloyd Wright abandoned his Chicago practice, wife and six children, and went to Europe with his mistress Mamah. 'I am a wild bird and must stay free,' he explained. The press, already fascinated by his behaviour, devoted many pages to the tragedy that befell him in 1914. His servant Julian Carlton calmly served up a meal at Wright's Wisconsin valley home, Taliesin, then went berserk. He murdered seven people and set the whole place on fire. Mamah was the first he attacked, perhaps because she had given him notice of termination of employment. He cut open her head with one hatchet blow.

While still devastated by Mamah's death, Wright fell in love with wealthy, weird Miriam Noel. A disgruntled housekeeper reported him under the 1910 Mann Act for transporting Miriam from Chicago, Illinois, to Spring Green, Wisconsin, but he was not charged (the Mann Act was the congressional response to agitation about the so-called 'white slave trade', under which prostitutes were forcibly taken from one state to another).

In 1923, Wright married Miriam, but the marriage only lasted six months. She had mental health issues: she pulled a gun on Wright and threatened to kill a friend of hers to whom she thought he had taken a fancy. The divorce proceedings were bitter and the press enjoyed the scandal.

Wright's last great love was Olga, who was thirty years his junior and hailed from Montenegro. She moved into Taliesin in 1925, along with Svetlana, her daughter from her first marriage. Miriam was loath to let Wright go. She chased Olga and her new-born baby out of a Chicago hospital, and reported her to the immigration authorities. Wright and Olga had travelled frequently between Taliesin and Chicago, and Miriam reported this as an offence against the Mann Act. At one point, Miriam turned up at Taliesin, found all the entrances barred, and destroyed two NO VISITORS ALLOWED signs to the delight of the watching press. Miriam sued Olga for 'alienation of affection' and Olga's first husband sued Wright for the same. Wright and Olga then fled to Minneapolis, which gave the Justice Department new evidence under the Mann Act, about which there would have been no problem if Olga had simply got out of the car and walked over the state line. Miriam obtained a writ that gave her legal access to Taliesin, but when she entered, two bankers entered with her in the hope of getting some of the money Wright owed them. When they threatened her with foreclosure, Miriam swiftly left. The Justice Department found it easy to track Wright: he used a false name, but retained his distinctive broad brimmed hat, swirling cape and dramatically wielded cane. Wright and Olga were arrested and jailed under the Mann Act, but the charges were quickly dropped. They spent the winter of 1926 in a rented beach house in La Jolla, California, where Miriam found them, entered their home and smashed up everything on which she could lay her hands. By this time, American public opinion was beginning to turn against Miriam. Her words and actions had become increasingly bizarre. She admitted that she had drawn a knife on Wright and had threatened to use a gun. She had publicly berated the Governor of Wisconsin. She was charged with writing an obscene letter and was given a thirty-day suspended sentence for having wrecked Wright's Los Angeles house. She was insistent that she was in Los Angeles for a Hollywood screen test, and that she was expecting the baby of a Crown Prince in Europe – at the age of fifty-nine years.

Wright lived happily ever after with Olga, whom he married in 1928. He recognised his own weaknesses, describing himself in one letter as a selfish individual who made everyone else suffer, a 'crooked' man capable of self-deceit who would never hesitate to 'always slip and slide and cheat' in order to avoid censure, someone willing to 'slay or betray or desert', and a weak, vain hypocrite. His cousin Richard Lloyd Jones no doubt agreed. When Wright struggled to get commissions during the Great Depression, Richard felt sorry for him and commissioned him to design a house in Tulsa, Oklahoma, but scolded him for his 'I-own-the-world' behaviour, his selfish determination always to have his own way whatever the cost, his contempt for society, his lack of sympathy for others, his self-centredness, arrogance, intolerance and vainglorious character. Frank seems always to have been unmoved. The house gave Richard problems. The flat roof leaked almost immediately and Richard complained: 'Damnit, Frank, it's leaking on my desk!' Frank responded, 'Richard, why don't you move your desk?' During one cloudburst, Richard's wife and family rushed around with buckets to catch the rain. She said, 'Well, this is what we get for leaving a work of art out in the rain.' Richard found his cousin amazing in many ways, not least because he proved that 'a man does not need any money' – Frank Lloyd Wright simply begged and borrowed it or obtained credit! He blamed his great extravagance on those who made it so easy for him to borrow money and he had little sense of decency about it. For example, despite having received vast amounts from one of his several indulgent patrons, Darwin Martin, he basically swindled Martin's heirs of what he owed. Wright remained in debt for most of his life, congratulating himself that his 'gift' for increasing his debt 'amounts to genius'.

The architect Richard Neutra described Wright as 'truly a child but not a well-behaved one', while the English writer C. S. Nott also felt that 'in essence he was a boy. Perhaps this was one of the reasons why we all loved him.' Wright won over many with that childlike quality, his ability to exercise considerable charm and his sense of humour. It was not always easy to tell when he was joking. He once referred to himself in court as the world's greatest architect, and when asked if that was not a rather inflated opinion, he answered, 'Well, I was under oath, wasn't I?' He probably was the world's greatest architect, which explains why so many remained patient with him. One of his nieces commented, 'Of course he was vain. He'd be talking to me and if there was a mirror in the room he'd be look- ing into that the whole time and not at me . . . He had to believe in himself. Nobody else did for a long time.' Critics frequently wrote him off. During Wright's struggles in the Depression years of the 1930s, intellectual and collector Philip Johnson declared him America's greatest nineteenth-cen- tury architect, which infuriated him, and one Chicago wag christened him 'Frank Lloyd Wrong'. When the art critic Henry-Russell Hitchcock wrote in an essay that Wright was 'the greatest architect and perhaps the greatest American' of the early twentieth century, Wright was incandescent. 'I warn Henry right here and now, that having a good start, not only do I fully intend to be the greatest architect who has yet lived – but the greatest Architect who will ever live.'

As Richard Neutra' s wife said, 'He can't be measured with the yard- stick of the ordinary citizen. Those who condemn him are incapable of understanding his art.' 'I am what I am,' said Wright. 'If you don't like it, you can lump it.'

The architect and the making of America

Wright believed that what he had contributed to the making of America was the creation of an American architecture. For much of the early part of his career, which began in the late nineteenth century, most other American architects were emulating old and new European styles. In contrast, Wright would increasingly insist that his creations were organically integrated within, and reflective of, the American landscape and spirit.

Wright's first 'American' creations were the 'prairie houses' of the first decade of the twentieth century. The Robie House is generally considered to be the best example of the 'prairie style' home, of which Wright wrote: 'We of the Middle West are living on the prairie. The prairie has a beauty of its own, and we should recognise and accentuate this natural beauty, its quiet level. Hence, gently sloping roofs, low proportions, quiet skylines... and sheltering overhangs.'

The low, horizontal lines of his prairie houses reflected the open American prairie landscape, and their ribbons of windows brought the wide-sky expanses characteristic of that external landscape into the spacious central rooms. American individualism was reflected in the spacious, unique homes he built for private individuals.

In the 1930s, what he called his 'Usonian houses' were aimed at making beautiful designs affordable to ordinary Americans. These houses were the ancestors of the subsequently ubiquitous single-storey American ranch-style homes, with their spacious, open-plan interiors, abundant natural light, exterior patios and carports.

'AWARE OF HIS WELSHNESS'

When Gethin Scourfield produced and directed a Welsh-language documentary on Frank Lloyd Wright in 2006, he recounted that 'people seemed to be aware of his Welshness' in Chicago. Much of Wright's work was done in Chicago and its environs, including the Robie House.

Inevitably, though, Wright's best work was for wealthy patrons. When in the year 2000 the American Institute of Architects took an unofficial poll on the top twentieth-century buildings, only Frank Lloyd Wright had more than one on the list. The four of his listed were the Robie House (1909), Fallingwater (1934), the Johnson Wax Building (1936) and the Guggenheim Museum (1943–59). Fallingwater was perhaps his best example of the organic integration of a private home into the surrounding landscape, while the Johnson Wax Building and the Guggenheim were characterised by carefully managed natural light for work/spectating, coupled with soaring stone work for the beauty and inspiration that could lift the heart of the appreciative.

'How much of a Welshman he really was'

In the first edition of his autobiography (1932), Frank Lloyd Wright emphasised the joys of his Welsh family's life, beliefs and traditions, and

Figure 21. *Frank Lloyd Wright's Fallingwater, Mill Run, Pennsylvania.*
(https://en.wikipedia.org/wiki/File:Wrightfallingwater.jpg. Attribution:
Sxenko)

of responding to nature in the Lloyd Joneses' Wisconsin valley. One joker said that it was as if the book had been translated from the Welsh, because there were so many verb-free descriptive passages about the valley. His sister Maginel called the family's valley 'the Valley of the God-Almighty Joneses' and it was there in 1914 that Frank Lloyd Wright first built Taliesin, his primary residence for the rest of his life. Even after his beloved Taliesin burned down (twice), Wright simply rebuilt it. As he said,

> I turned to this hill in the Valley as my grandfather before me turned to America – as a hope, and a haven . . . I feel that I belong to this region . . . My grandfather began my life here. My mother and her people continued it and . . . loved the valley to which I have come back as the third generation in a struggle to develop, on old family soil, some of the finer elements of what we call civilisation.

That emphasis upon the Welsh contribution to American 'civilisation' or culture was quite common amongst Welsh Americans: it could be literary or musical as in an eisteddfod, or artistic as in Wright's architecture.

Wright's biographer Meryle Secrest (1998), argued that his attachment to the valley of his ancestors 'ought to settle the issue of how much of a Welshman he really was'. Wright identified himself strongly and maybe even exclusively with his Welsh heritage. Perhaps half-jokingly, he admitted that, like most Welshmen, he was a convincing liar. Maginel described him as typically Welsh and a worthy descendant of his Unitarian ancestors. When designing the Unitarian Meeting House at Shorewood Hills, Wisconsin, in 1947, Wright said that 'there you see the Unitarianism of my forefathers find expression in a building by one of the offspring . . . I tried to build a building here that expressed that over-all sense of unity.' Even when that church ran out of money, he continued and completed that work. The outsider status that Frank Lloyd Wright believed in, cultivated and relished, has been attributed by some to his Welsh and Unitarian background. Some consider his reverence for place to be typically Welsh. He certainly surrounded himself with references to Wales. He placed a Welsh motto over the fireplace in the playhouse in Taliesin and had a Welsh harp in one of the rooms. In some ways it almost became an affectation: he continually urged his friend and admirer Lewis Mumford to spell his name Llewis in the Welsh fashion, while one non-Welsh individual groused that anyone named Jones got preferential treatment at Taliesin. Those close to Wright were well aware of the Welsh preoccupation. In 1926, his long-suffering patron Darwin Martin sent him a handbook about Wales. Wright thanked him and said the book gave him

interesting details about the name Taliesin. Wright was greatly critical
of Britain in both world wars, because he felt the country was involved
in the war to serve British imperialism. The FBI concluded that he was
not anti-American, just anti-English. The Lloyd Joneses long remembered
and resented English landlords back in Wales and shared the traditional
anti-English sentiment of many Welsh non-conformist émigrés.

Figure 22. *Frank Lloyd Wright (right) with Clough Williams-Ellis at
Portmeirion, during Wright's sole visit to Wales (1956)*. (Reproduced
courtesy of Portmeirion Ltd)

Despite Frank Lloyd Wright's attachment to what was Welsh, Maginel seems to have visited Wales long before her brother. He made his first and only visit in 1956. He visited the architecturally interesting Portmeirion, where some of the construction echoed Fallingwater, and drove all over the country with his wife and daughter. There is no record of his visiting the areas from which his ancestors came. Portmeirion's Welsh architect, Clough Williams-Ellis accompanied them some of the way. They visited Lloyd George's tomb together, which suggests the son may have shared the mother's reverence for that Welsh-born politician. Williams-Ellis declared himself 'startled' to find Wright 'much more impractically Welsh than I was myself'. Wright received an honorary Ph.D. from the University of Wales on this visit, but perhaps it was intimations of mortality rather than that doctorate that accounted for this belated pilgrimage to the land of his fathers.

TAFFY AND HOLLYWOOD

Wright called his daughter Kathryn 'Taffy'. Her daughter was Academy award-winning Hollywood actress Anne Baxter, who adored her grandfather and on occasion described herself as Welsh.

When Frank Lloyd Wright died in 1959, he was buried in the grounds of the family chapel in the Wisconsin valley where lay Richard Lloyd Jones ('Ein Tad' or 'Our Father'), Mallie ('Ein Mam' or 'Our Mother') and all the other Lloyd Joneses. That had been his wish. However, when his wife Olga died in 1989, those close to her respected her last wishes and had Wright dug up (still 'marvellously intact' after twenty-six years according to the undertaker), cremated and reburied alongside her at their winter home in Arizona, Taliesin West. Wright's children by his other marriages were furious, as were most Wisconsin residents. When he said, 'I was born in Wisconsin and I belong in Wisconsin,' it was the Wisconsin of the valley of the God-Almighty Joneses, the Wisconsin of the Welsh. That the family graveyard there had a powerful resonance for him is evident from his autobiography, where he told of how he imagined himself walking through the family graveyard and hearing the voices of family ghosts telling him to look at the symbol on the gates – TRUTH AGAINST THE WORLD. Perhaps the truth was that, while the Wisconsin valley represented the Welsh of him, the desert home of Taliesin West in Arizona represented the inexorable pull of the New World. His biographer, Ada Louise Huxtable, said that Wales was 'the land to which he was so deeply tied by family and temperament' – but, if somewhat forcibly, his mortal remains had been assimilated to American soil.

BEYOND JOHN L. LEWIS AND FRANK LLOYD WRIGHT

After the influx of the second half of the nineteenth century, Welsh immigration to the United States was greatly reduced. Some still came: there were those who came to Hollywood to work in the motion picture industry, amongst them my cousin's uncle; there were yet more economic immigrants, including my paternal grandparents; there were those who married American military personnel, including my great-aunt. She could count amongst her children, grandchildren and great-grandchildren a war veteran, an anaesthetist, a diplomat and a novelist. But by that time, America had already been made.

CHAPTER ELEVEN

WALES, THE WELSH AND THE MAKING OF AMERICA – CONCLUSIONS

A SPECIAL PEOPLE?

IT HAS LONG been common for the Welsh and Welsh Americans to claim that those with Welsh blood contributed something special to the history of America. This is well illustrated by Pennsylvanian examples. In 1892, Scranton-born Pennsylvania Governor Louis Arthur Watres assured his Scranton audience on St David's Day that no history of Pennsylvania or America that omitted the role of the Welsh could be considered complete. Of course, Watres may have had Welsh ancestry himself and even if he did not, it was only good manners to emphasise the importance of the Welsh before an audience of Welsh descent, especially as they were prospective voters. Regardless of his motivation, Watres was surely correct. The Welsh *had* been particularly important in the foundation and growth of Pennsylvania.

In 1893, the Rev. Ebenezer Edwards of Minersville, Pennsylvania, won the essay competition at the International Eisteddfod at the Chicago World's Fair. The essay was entitled 'Welshmen as civil, political, and moral factors in the formation and development of the United States Republic' and was published in 1899. Edwards went beyond Pennsylvania to other colonies/states in search of 'Welshmen', although many of his inclusions were less than one-eighth Welsh. He argued that the Welsh were vital to the establishment of the United States:

> the US Government enjoys the heritage of the ancient Kymry . . .
> The memory of Welsh free institutions still lingered in the hearts of
> Welshmen, they came hither to escape the tyranny of the English
> church and state and to plant the standard of freedom upon this
> Western Hemisphere . . . The laws of ancient Britons . . . guaran-
> teed the equality of civil and religious rights and served the pursuit
> of life, liberty and happiness. The 'free' principles – civil, political
> and moral – which distinguished these colonies did but reflect
> what had for ages existed and flourished among the Cymry.

Edwards admitted that the purpose of the essay was to ensure that the Welsh people were given appropriate recognition for their contribution. He said that the essay title 'has been placed on the International Eisteddfod program because this fact has lacked the full recognition it deserves'. Carl Wittke described the essay as 'a veritable hodgepodge of names . . . without scientific merit or organisation' in his *We Who Built America*, published in New York in 1939, but Edwards's claim of Welsh support for the principle of 'escape from tyranny' had been significantly demonstrated in the American Revolution years.

It was not only Pennsylvanians who insisted on the importance of the Welsh. Governor Arthur Thomas of Utah, who had Welsh ancestry, told the *Druid* in 1911 that Welsh American unity needed to be preserved, for every Welsh American should be 'proud of his race, for every page of American history, from the day of the first settlement down to the time of the Revolution, and during and since the Revolution, is illumined by the work accomplished by Welshmen'. Like Governor Watres, Thomas probably had his eye on Welsh votes, but being 'proud of his race' was no doubt his main motivation in praising the Welsh contribution to the making of America. Another example was John Sharp Williams, who represented Mississippi in the US Senate from 1911 to 1923. His claim that no nation in proportion to its size contributed more to the development of the United States than had the Welsh was entered in the Congressional Record.

From at least the Civil War onwards, it was typical of both the Welsh and immigrants of all nationalities to declare themselves admirable and worthy of greater recognition by others. National pride was no doubt combined with an uneasy awareness that native Americans were often critical and resentful of immigrants, and these presentations of a distinguished pedigree were designed to try to help combat such prejudice.

'IT IS A PITY . . .'

In the late nineteenth century, William Davies wrote from Youngstown, Ohio, 'It is a pity that the Welsh have not as much emigrating spirit as the Germans and the Irish.'

Welsh immigration was reduced to a trickle during the early twentieth century, but after the general revival in pride in one's ethnicity in 1970s America, History Professor Edward G. Hartmann produced his *Americans from Wales: A Treasure Chest of Information for People Interested in their Welsh Heritage* in 1983. Hartmann lamented that 'much has been written about the coming and achievements of many of the other ethnic groups, particularly those numerically strong', but 'the story of most of the smaller groups . . . remains to be written'. He felt that studies of the smaller groups 'must also be told if a true picture of the evolution and amalgamation of the American people is to be achieved'. He recognised that 'studies of this sort in the past have been marred through bias and

exaggeration' and said that while he had tried to be 'objective throughout', he thought it should be noted that he was 'the son of a Welsh
immigrant mother' who 'quite naturally takes pride in the achievements'
of the Welsh:

> Thousands of Welsh immigrants and their descendants played mod-
> est roles pioneering and developing large sections of America's
> agricultural lands; thousands more played important roles as skilled
> workmen and supervisors in the key fields of steel production,
> coal mining, other extractive industries, and in slate production.
> Many others played various roles as workers in other economic
> activities, in politics and statecraft, in the professions, in the arts
> and sciences, in the field of entertainment, and in a variety of mis-
> cellaneous ways. These formed part of the solid core of American
> citizenry upon which our great civilisation rests. Many others of
> Welsh stock, however, rose from the ranks to acquire respected
> and even renowned fame in virtually every field of endeavour in
> the American environment . . . Some statistics might prove helpful
> at this point to illustrate the Welsh contribution of distinguished
> Americans. The monumental scholarly study, the Dictionary of
> American Biography, restricted to biographical data concerning
> America's deceased outstanding leaders, includes 328 people of
> Welsh extraction and perhaps some others with Welsh names
> about whom ethnic origin is lacking but who may have been of
> Welsh blood. Of the 328 listed as being definitely Welsh, forty-eight
> were immigrants, twenty-six children of immigrants, twenty-nine
> grandchildren of immigrants, and the remaining two hundred and
> twenty-five of Welsh stock. Broken down these include four pres-
> idents of the United States, thirty governors, twenty-two United
> States Senators, nineteen leading jurists, twenty-seven other high
> public officials, thirty-nine ministers of the gospel, sixteen physi-
> cians, three composers, twenty engineers and inventors, seventeen
> scientists, seven educators, ten artists, five actors, twenty-one busi-
> ness and industrial leaders, fifteen scholars, thirty-seven military
> leaders, eleven authors, and twenty-two miscellaneous. Surely this
> is no mean record for an ethnic group of the size of the Welsh!

The systematic evaluation of the relative contributions of differing ethnic
groups is most likely an impossible task, but the 328 in the Dictionary
of American Biography constituted 1/45 of the 15,000 entries – a high
proportion in the context of the numbers of those of Welsh descent.

HOW THE UNITED STATES NEARLY HAD A 31.2 PER CENT WELSH PRESIDENT IN 2016

Hillary Clinton was America's First Lady from 1993 to 2001, after which she was elected to the US Senate in 2001. In 2008, Senator Clinton was narrowly defeated by Barack Obama in the race for the Democratic presidential nomination, but as president he appointed her as his Secretary of State. In 2016, she gained the Democrat nomination and won the popular vote by 3 million. However, due to the historic role of the electoral college, she lost the election to Republican presidential candidate Donald Trump. Had Mrs Clinton been elected president, the nation would have had a president whose ethnic breakdown has been calculated by genealogists as 31.2 per cent Welsh in origin. Mrs Clinton has told of how some of her ancestors emigrated from industrial south Wales in the second half of the nineteenth century.

'NAUSEATING' WELSH WRITERS

Just as there is a long tradition of Welsh and Welsh Americans claiming that the Welsh constituted a particularly notable ethnic minority in the United States, so has there been a long-standing awareness of the dangers of reading Welsh writers on Welsh achievements in the United States.

In an 1876 article in the *Atlantic Monthly*, the Rev. Erasmus W. Jones wrote: 'I am aware that this subject in the hands of native Welshmen is in danger of suffering injustice, owing to the natural tendency we have of over-estimating the excellences of our own nation, and of cherishing undue zeal for its peculiarities.'

Druid, the English-language Welsh American newspaper published from 1907 to 1937, was extravagantly boastful about Welsh American achievements, one example being its frequent insistence that Abraham Lincoln was a great Welsh statesman. In 1909, William Howells wrote from Garfield, Utah, to the *Druid*, saying that he found 'this ever constant overwhelming praise of the Welsh' to be 'nauseating', and 'not warranted by facts', because 'the various "Dago" countries have produced men and are producing men of greater international renown'. He felt the praise that Welsh Americans were giving themselves 'practically amounts to God's chosen race'. The editor of *Druid* responded that Howells needed to take indigestion medicine.

The awareness of the dangers of ethnic pride continued. In 1979, the eminent Welsh historian Glanmor Williams warned of 'the besetting sin of the historiography of American emigration: excessive praise of the feats and merits of one particular group or nation'. What then can be safely and objectively concluded?

Every group made some contribution to the making of America, although not all were resident there from the seventeenth century. Early arrival gave the Welsh and their descendants greater opportunities to shape early American history than some other ethnic minority groups. Welsh blood was frequently diluted by intermarriage, but first-generation Welsh immigrants surely contributed more than many other minority ethnic groups to both the establishment and the industrialisation of the United States. Like all the pioneers, of whatever origin, the Welsh helped open up the new lands, and in so doing demonstrated how much immigrants can contribute to a nation.

Studying the Welsh contribution to the making of America evoked in this Welsh author a sense of the loss and of the missed opportunities for a nation that loses people to emigration. An 1892 editorial in *Y Drych* claimed the Welsh in America were superior to the Welsh in Wales in that they were more egalitarian, tolerant, broadminded, practical, adventurous, ambitious for material success, polite – and less servile. Were they? The editorial was probably accurate in claiming that the emigrants were more adventurous and ambitious, and there one cannot help but feel that Wales lost many it could ill afford to lose and many that America was lucky to have gained.

BIBLIOGRAPHICAL
ESSAY

~~~~~~

INTRODUCTION

THERE IS as yet no general history of the Welsh contribution to American history, although books by Professor David Williams and Professor Edward G. Hartmann have come quite close. Williams's all too brief *Cymru ac America: Wales and America* was written in 1946 and then reprinted in 1975 by the University of Wales Press, Cardiff. In 1941, Professor Williams also delivered a lecture entitled, 'The Contribution of Wales to the United States of America'. This can be accessed at *https:// www.genuki.org.uk/big/wal/Archives/NLWjournals/USA*.

There is far more detail in Hartmann's *Americans from Wales: A Treasure Chest of Information for People Interested in their Welsh Heritage*. This was first published in 1967 and reprinted several times, most recently in 2001 by the National Welsh-American Foundation. Elwyn Ashton's *The Welsh in the United States* (Caldra House, 1984) follows in Hartmann's footsteps in emphasising Welsh settlements and culture in America rather than the Welsh contribution to the making of America. Retired postman W. Arvon Roberts's *150 Welsh-Americans* (Gwalch, 2008) is a collection of brief biographies that encourage the reader to consider the eternal question as to the point at which an American's Welsh ancestry becomes so distant that claiming him (or her) as a Welsh American perhaps ought to be avoided.

1. THE MADOC LEGEND

Gwyn A. Williams, *Madoc: The Making of a Myth* (Eyre Methuen, 1979) is a scholarly, exhaustive academic study of the Madoc myth, upon which this book's chapter 1 relies heavily. There is further material on the impact of the Madoc legend on immigration in Hywel M. Davies, *Transatlantic Brethren: Rev Samuel Jones (1735–1814) and His Friends: Baptists in Wales, Pennsylvania, and Beyond* (Lehigh University Press, 1995).

2. THE WELSH AND THE COLONISATION OF NORTH AMERICA

There are several recent excellent books on colonial America: Alan Taylor, *American Colonies: The Settling of North America* (Penguin, 2001) and Richard Middleton and Anne Lombard, *Colonial America: A History to 1763* (Wiley-Blackwell, 2011). These books reflect the new scholarly consensus that studies of colonial America must go beyond the British colonies and give due weight to French and Spanish colonisation and the interconnectedness of the Atlantic world. There are some who may argue that the rejection of an Anglocentric narrative of the birth of the United States could conceivably go too far.

Relations between William Penn and the Welsh Quakers are covered in Penn biographies such as Mary K. Geiter, *William Penn* (Longman, 2000), John A. Moretta, *William Penn and the Quaker Legacy* (Pearson Longman, 2007) and Andrew R. Murphy, *William Penn: A Life* (Oxford University Press, 2019). If further proof were needed that Welsh immigrants had an independence of spirit whch sometimes made them awkward to deal with, see Hywel M. Davies, *Transatlantic Brethren*.

There are two useful reprints of books on the early Welsh settlers: Thomas Allen Glenn, *Merion in the Welsh Tract: With Sketches of the Townships of Haverford and Radnor* was originally published in Norristown, Pennsylvania in 1896, then reprinted by the Genealogical Publishing Company of Baltimore, in 1970, 1992, 1994, 1999 and 2001; *Welsh Tract of Pennsylvania: The Early Settlers,* published by Heritage Books in 2007, is a facsimile reprint of the first 276 pages of *Welsh Settlements of Pennsylvania* by Charles H. Browning, published by William J. Campbell in Philadelphia in 1912. A letter from the Quaker Thomas Ellis advocating that other Welsh Quakers join their brethren in Pennsylvania can be accessed at *https://journals.sas.ac.uk/fhs/article/view/2754/2712.*

3. RICHARD PRICE AND THE AMERICAN REVOLUTION

The third chapter in this book relies heavily on Paul Frame, *Liberty's Apostle: Richard Price: His Life and Times* (University of Wales Press, 2015). Roughly half of this biography is devoted to Price's views of America and his communications with Americans.

For John Adams's mastery of Welsh history, access three of his *The Letters of Novanglus*:

https://founders.archives.gov/?q=%20Author%3A%22Adams%2C%20John%22%20%20%20%20%20Welsh&s=1111311111&r=5 (20 March 1775)

https://founders.archives.gov/?q=%20Author%3A%22Adams%2C%20John%22%20%20%20%20%20Welch&s=1111311111&r=4 (3 April 1775)

https://founders.archives.gov/?q=%20Author%3A%22Adams%2C%20John%22%20%20%20%20%20Welsh&s=1111311111&r=6 (10 April 1775)

4. THE WELSH AMERICAN MILITARY CONTRIBUTION TO THE AMERICAN WAR OF INDEPENDENCE

The American background is covered in great and scholarly detail in the volume in the reliable Oxford History of the United States series by Robert Middlekauff, *The Glorious Cause: The American Revolution, 1763–1789* (Oxford, 2005). For a briefer and useful overview of the birth of the United States, see Alan Farmer, *The American Revolution and the Birth of the USA, 1740–1801* (Hodder, 2015).

While biographers are inclined to become excessively fond of their subjects, biographies are amongst the easiest of reads and a useful introduction to a period such as the Revolutionary War. Phillip Papas, *Renegade Revolutionary: The Life of General Charles Lee* (New York University Press, 2014) and Mary Stockwell, *Unlikely General: 'Mad' Anthony Wayne and the Battle for America* (Yale University Press, 2018) are sympathetic, balanced treatments of their subjects. Both Don Higginbotham, *Daniel Morgan: Revolutionary Rifleman* (Omohundro Institute and University of North Carolina Press, 1961), and Lawrence E. Babits, *A Devil of a Whipping: The Battle of Cowpens* (University of North Carolina Press, 1998), were understandably full of admiration for Daniel Morgan. James Graham's 1856 *The Life of General Daniel Morgan* can be accessed at *https://quod.lib.umich.edu/cgi/t/text/text-idx?c=moa;idno=ABJ2761.*

Daniel Boone's exceptionally exciting life has inevitably elicited several interesting biographies, amongst which are John Mack Faragher, *Daniel Boone: The Life and Legend of an American Pioneer* (Henry Holt, 1992) and Robert Morgan, *Boone: A Biography* (Algonquin Paperbacks, 2007). Morgan begins with a very useful date list of Boone's whereabouts at different times.

5. THE WELSH AMERICAN POLITICAL CONTRIBUTION TO THE AMERICAN REVOLUTION

Charles Rappleye, *Robert Morris: Financier of the American Revolution* (Simon & Schuster, 2010) is very detailed on Morris's financial dealings. Colin Gwinnett Sharp, B*utton Gwinnett: Failed Merchant, Plantation Owner, Mountebank, Opportunist Politician and Founding Father* (You-Caxton Publications, 2015) is a short, fascinating read.

While Francis Lewis and William Floyd appear not to have attracted biographers, there are numerous biographies of Thomas Jefferson. Chapter 1 of R. B. Bernstein's short biography, *Thomas Jefferson* (Oxford, 2003) covers his youth and background. Joseph J. Ellis, *American Sphinx: The Character of Thomas Jefferson* (Vintage, 1998) focuses on Jefferson's public life, while Kevin R. C. Gutzman, *Thomas Jefferson Revolutionary: A Radical's Struggle to Remake America* (St Martin's Press, 2017) focuses on Jefferson's ideas.

While it seems unlikely that John Adams had Welsh ancestry, and that if he did it was far distant, David McCullough, *John Adams* (Simon & Schuster, 2001) is an excellent biography.

6. MERIWETHER LEWIS, JAMES MONROE AND THE AMERICAN WEST

The American background to the Lewis and Clark expedition is covered in two volumes in the Oxford History of the United States series: Gordon S. Wood, *Empire of Liberty: A History of the Early Republic, 1789–1815* (Oxford, 2009) covers both domestic and diplomatic issues, while George C. Herring, *From Colony to Superpower: U.S. Foreign Relations since 1776* (Oxford, 2008) focuses on expansion and foreign affairs.

Stephen Ambrose, *Undaunted Courage: The Pioneering First Mission to Explore America's Wild Frontier* (Simon & Schuster, 1996) is a good read that is sympathetic to Lewis but also realistic on his faults and issues.

Thomas C. Danisi and John C. Jackson, in *Meriwether Lewis* (Prometheus Books, 2009), are amongst those who find it difficult to accept that this heroic figure committed suicide. They focus on his life and career after the expedition, and construct a detailed argument to counter the more commonly accepted belief that Lewis killed himself. In John D. W. Guice (ed.), *By His Own Hand? The Mysterious Death of Meriwether Lewis* (University of Oklahoma Press, 2006), the scholarly arguments for and against suicide read like a good mystery or detective story.

There is a very pro-Monroe biography by Harlow Giles Unger, *The Last Founding Father: James Monroe and a Nation's Call to Greatness* (Da Capo Press, 2009).

7. The Welsh go West

A useful source for the experience of the transatlantic voyages is Ronald D. Dennis, *The Call of Zion: The Story of the First Welsh Mormon Emigration* (Brigham Young University, 1987).

Alan Conway (ed.), *The Welsh in America: Letters from the Immigrants* (University of Wales Press, 1961) is a wonderful collection of letters that bring the Welsh immigrant experience to life.

Gwyn A. Williams, *The Search for Beulah Land* (Holmes & Meier, 1980) expands upon his *Madoc* book, with extra detail on Morgan John Rhys and the Cambria settlements, and on John Evans's exploration of the West under Spanish auspices. There is further insight into Morgan John Rhys in Hywel M. Davies, *Transatlantic Brethren*. John Thomas Griffith's *Rev. Morgan John Rhys: The Welsh Baptist Hero of Civil and Religious Liberty of the 18th Century*, Classic Reprint Series (Forgotten Books, 2018) contains a biography of Rhys, along with his sermons and writings.

John Humphrys, *The Man from the Alamo* (Wales Books, 2004), is densely argued with regard to the career of John Rees, and fascinating for those who enjoy a good detective story.

The National Library of Wales's digitising of the archive of the Welsh in Ohio can be accessed at *https://www.webarchive.org.uk/wayback/archive/20130415142856/http://ohio.llgc.org.uk/*. The National Library's brief introductory videos based on the Wales-Ohio Project show contemporary photographs and use quotations from contemporaries: 'Who emigrated from Wales?' (*https://www.peoplescollection.wales/items/24149*), 'Why emigrate?' (*https://www.peoplescollection.wales/items/24150*) and 'Leaving Wales' (*https://www.peoplescollection.wales/items/24151*).

William E. Van Vugt, *British Buckeyes: The English, Scots, and Welsh in Ohio 1700–1900* (Kent State University Press, 2006) gives generous recognition to the Welsh contribution to the development of Ohio, with details on individual Welshmen who succeeded in Ohio and merited mention in Ohio County histories.

There is a great deal of invaluable information on the Welsh in Oneida County in the 1914 Cornell MA thesis by Paul Demund Evans, which can be accessed at *http://sites.rootsweb.com/~nyunywh/oneidawelsh/*.

The disgruntled Evan Evans living in Lewis County, New York, can be accessed at *https://www.peoplescollection.wales/items/8062*. The People's Collection contains a considerable amount of material about Welsh emigrants.

Cherilyn A. Walley, *The Welsh in Iowa* (University of Wales Press, 2009) covers both agricultural and mining communities.

Phillips G. Davies, *Welsh in Wisconsin* (Wisconsin Historical Society Press, 2006) explores Welsh agricultural settlements and their culture, and reprints several letters by the Wisconsin Welsh. There is a more detailed account focused on one area of Wisconsin in Robert Humphries's University of Wales Trinity St David's 2012 thesis, 'The settlement and assimilation of the Welsh in Iowa County, Wisconsin, 1840–1920'.

The letters of William Davies Evans, who explored Welsh settlements across America, have been translated by Margaret Morgan Jones in two books: *Travels of a Welsh Preacher in the USA: Peregrinations of William Davies Evans during the Late Nineteenth Century* (Gwasg Carreg Gwalch, 2008) and *From Aberystwyth to San Francisco: The Welsh Community in America in the Late Nineteenth Century* (Gwasg Carreg Gwalch, 2013).

There is an overview survey of Welsh immigration in Stephan Thernstrom (ed.), *Harvard Encyclopaedia of American Ethnic Groups* (Harvard University Press, 1981). The sole individual contribution that Thernstrom made to the Encyclopaedia was this entry on the Welsh, an ethnic group that he did not seem to find appealing or significant.

Inevitably, there are few works that focus on the activities in the United States of women from Wales or with Welsh ancestry. However, there is a biography of Martha Hughes Cannon by Mari Grana, *Dr Martha:*

The Life of a Pioneer Physician, Politician, and Polygamist (Taylor Trade Publishing, 2015). The Utah TV channel KUED produced a documentary on Martha Hughes Cannon in 2012, which can be accessed at *https:// video.kued.org/video/utah-history-martha-hughes-cannon/*. The unusual opportunities afforded to Mormon women in Utah are covered in Patricia Lyn Scott and Linda Thatcher (eds), *Women in Utah History: Paradigm or Paradox?* (Utah State University Press, 2005).

8. WELSH AMERICANS AND THE AMERICAN CIVIL WAR

For the background on the American Civil War, Alan Farmer, *United States Civil War: Causes, Course and Effects 1840–77* (Hodder, 2012) has the clarity of exposition that characterises that Hodder series. For greater detail, see James M. McPherson, *Battle Cry of Freedom: The American Civil War* (Oxford University Press, 1988).

William J. Cooper Jr, *Jefferson Davis, American* (Vintage, 2001) is a detailed biography of the Confederate President, which emphasises Davis's ideological motivation. The focus of Herman Hattaway and Richard E. Beringer, *Jefferson Davis, Confederate President* (Kansas, 2002) is Davis's presidency, as is James M. McPherson, *Embattled Rebel: Jefferson Davis as Commander in Chief* (Penguin, 2014). Davis's wife, Varina Davis, was more 'Welsh' than her husband, and Joan E. Cashin, *First Lady of the Confederacy: Varina Davis's Civil War* (Belknap Press, 2006) gives an interesting insight into an unusual woman.

Jerry Hunter, *Sons of Arthur, Children of Lincoln: Welsh Writing from the American Civil War* (University of Wales Press, 2007) is an investigation of letters and literary endeavours written by Welsh-speaking soldiers who fought for the Union. The issue of the ethnic contribution during the Civil War is covered by William L. Burton, *Melting Pot Soldiers: The Union's Ethnic Regiments* (Fordham University Press, 1998), and by Dean Mahin, *The Blessed Place of Freedom: Europeans in Civil War America* (Brassey's, 2002). It is interesting to compare the Welsh American with the Irish American experience, which is traced in the 2005 *Columbia Guide to Irish American History*, by Timothy J. Meagher. James Webb's *Born Fighting: How the Scots-Irish Shaped America* (Mainstream Publishing, 2009) is a somewhat frightening example of the dangers of writing about the contribution of an ethnic group to the making/shaping of America. Webb's generalisations about the nature and impact of the Scots-Irish require greater substantiation.

THE COLUMBIA GUIDE TO IRISH AMERICAN HISTORY
(COLUMBIA UNIVERSITY PRESS, 2005)
BY TIMOTHY J. MEAGHER . . .

. . . traces the Protestant 'Scotch-Irish' emigration and assimilation during the seventeenth and eighteenth centuries, followed by the mid-nineteenth-century Catholic Irish immigration. The Catholic Irish immigrants
and their descendants somehow managed to combine American patriotism and Irish nationalism. The book traces the greater difficulty faced
by Irish Catholics in gaining acceptance in the United States, in contrast
to the experience of the Scotch-Irish and the Welsh. Another difference
between Irish Catholic and Protestant Welsh immigrants was that Irish
enthusiasm for the American Civil War proved less long-lasting than the
Welsh. That seems to have been due to heavy military losses, and perhaps even more to the freeing of slaves. Unlike the churches frequented
by Americans with Welsh ancestry, the Irish-dominated Catholic Church
in mid-nineteenth-century America did not encourage churchgoers to
support abolition. Given the trajectory adopted by the current author in
this book, it is interesting to read Meagher's account of the early twentieth-century Scotch-Irish societies, and especially that the Pennsylvania
Scotch-Irish society supported the publication of books

> promoting the Scotch-Irish role in American history . . . Empha-
> sis was on the importance of the Scotch-Irish in winning the
> American Revolution, securing the Constitution, taming the
> West, and providing leadership in higher education. Scotch-
> Irish individuals of particular note were celebrated, including
> presidents Andrew Jackson, James Polk, James Buchanan,
> William McKinley, and Woodrow Wilson; politicians James G.
> Blaine and Marc A. Hanna; banker Thomas Mellon; inventor
> Cyrus McCormick; architect Charles F. McKim; and musician
> Stephen Foster.

For those who believe in the Welsh ancestry of Abraham Lincoln,
James M. McPherson, *Abraham Lincoln* (Oxford University Press,
2009) is a very brief introduction. Eric Foner, *The Fiery Trial: Abraham
Lincoln and American Slavery* (Norton, 2010) explores the politics
of slavery.

Professor of Surgery Ira Rutkow's biography, *James A. Garfield*
(Times Books, 2006) not surprisingly emphasises the fascinating medical
history after the shooting.

9. THE WELSH AND THE INDUSTRIALISATION OF AMERICA

The Oxford History of the United States volume that covers the period of rapid industrialisation is Richard White, *The Republic for Which It Stands: The United States during Reconstruction and the Gilded Age, 1865–1896* (Oxford, 2017).

Unfortunately, Oliver Evans seems to lack a biographer, but other Welsh contributors to industrialisation are well covered. The first few pages of Nathan Vernon Madison, *Tredegar Iron Works: Richmond's Foundry on the James* (The History Press, 2015) are devoted to the relatively recent discovery of the importance of Welsh immigrants in the establishment of these great ironworks of the South. Some of the chapters in Peter N. Williams, *From Wales to Pennsylvania: The David Thomas Story* (Wales Books, 2002) cover the contribution of Thomas to the growth of the iron industry in America. The story of William R. Jones has been written by his descendant Tom Gage in *American Prometheus: Carnegie's Captain, Bill Jones*. This can be downloaded without cost at *https://digitalcommons.humboldt.edu/monographs/4/*. Bill Jones's role in the Johnstown flood is covered in David McCullough, *The Johnstown Flood* (Simon & Schuster, 1968). This chapter makes extensive use of William T. Jones, *Wales and America: Scranton and the Welsh 1860–1920* (University of Wales Press, 1993), which explores the work and culture of the Scranton Welsh, and their gradual assimilation. James J. Davis's autobiography, *The Iron Puddler: My Life in the Rolling Mills and What Came of It*, can be accessed at no cost at *https://archive.org/details/ironpuddlermylif00daviiala/page/n8*.

Eirug Davies, *The Welsh of Tennessee* (Y Lolfa, 2012) is very much in the tradition of detailing Welsh individuals and groups who contributed to the economic development of a particular area, often making considerable fortunes for themselves.

Anne Kelly Knowles, *Calvinists Incorporated: Welsh Immigrants on Ohio's Industrial Frontier* (University of Chicago Press, 1997) is a systematic scholarly investigation. Knowles's article on 'Migration, Nationalism, and the Construction of Welsh Identity', in Guntram H. Herb and David H. Kaplan (eds), *Nested Identities* (Rowman & Littlefield, 1999), puts Welsh emigration to the United States in a wider context.

There is a lively narrative of Welsh participation in the Wild West in Dafydd Meirion, *Welsh Cowboys and Outlaws* (Y Lolfa, 2003).

10. THE ASSIMILATION OF THE WELSH

Daniel Jenkins Williams, *The Welsh of Columbus, Ohio: A Study in Adaptation and Assimilation* (Oshkosh, Wisconsin: Published by the Author, 1913) has been reproduced in a digital file created at the Library of Congress, and is available free of charge online, and in a reprint by Amazon.

References to Wales and the Welsh in Professor Ewing Summers (ed.), *Genealogical and Family History of Eastern Ohio* (1903) can be accessed at *https://babel.hathitrust.org/cgi/pt?id=inu.32000014429445&view=1up&seq=630&q1=Welsh*.

Ronald L. Lewis, *Welsh-Americans: A History of Assimilation in the Coalfields* (University of North Carolina Press, 2008) traces Welsh emigration and life in the coalfields, with less emphasis on assimilation than the title suggests.

Robert Llewellyn Tyler, *Wales and the American Dream* (Cambridge Scholars Publishing, 2015) investigates the Welsh in four towns: Bevier, Missouri; Sharon, Pennsylvania; Poultney, Vermont; Emporia, Kansas. He traces the process of assimilation and evaluates the frequent claim that the Welsh were very upwardly mobile.

Aled Jones and Bill Jones, *Welsh Reflections: Y Drych & America 1851–2001* (Gomer Press, 2001) covers (amongst other issues) the process of assimilation through the pages of *Y Drych*.

Melvyn Dubofsky and Warren Van Tine, *John L. Lewis: A Biography* (University of Illinois Press, 1986) is rather critical, but Ron E. Roberts, *John L. Lewis: Hard Labor & Wild Justice* (Kendall Hunt, 1994) is far more sympathetic.

Richard Schickel, *D. W. Griffith: An American Life* (Limelight Edition, 1996) explores Griffith's cinematic innovations, and mentions the Welsh connections.

Meryle Secrest, *Frank Lloyd Wright: A Biography* (University of Chicago Press, 1992) is a detailed but fascinating read, with a persuasive emphasis on the influence of Wright's Welsh family background. There is a similar emphasis on the Welsh influence in Ada Louise Huxtable, *Frank Lloyd Wright: A Life* (Penguin, 2004). Bruce Brooks Pfeiffer, *Frank Lloyd Wright*, ed. Peter Goessel (Taschen, 2015) contains hundreds of illustrations that demonstrate Wright's genius.

11. WALES, THE WELSH AND THE MAKING OF AMERICA: CONCLUSIONS

Hillary Clinton mentioned her Welsh ancestry on p. 4 of her *Living History: Hillary Rodham Clinton* (Simon & Shuster, 2003).

For reasons of comparison, a book that might be considered a Scottish parallel to this book is Michael Fry, *'Bold, Independent, Unconquer'd and Free': How the Scots Made America Safe for Liberty*, Democracy and Capitalism (Fort Publishing, 2003). Fry includes Welshman Robert Owen's communistic experiments at New Harmony, Indiana, on the grounds that Owen married a Scot and managed New Lanark, and counts the Scots Irish as Scottish . . . There are several parallel claims, such as Scottish sailors on board Viking voyages that discover America, and Scottish philosophers influencing the Declaration of Independence and the Constitution.

SOME SIGNIFICANT WELSH AMERICAN PERIODICALS

Dates of publication	Place of publication	Owner, publisher, editor	Focus
Y Drych (The Mirror) [weekly then monthly newspaper]			
1851–2003, when it merged with *Ninnau*	Utica, New York, then Milwaukee, Wisconsin, from 1962	Initially owned and edited by Caernarvonshire-born John W. Jones. Published by Thomas J. Griffiths for over fifty years.	News of Welsh American communities and of Wales. Increasingly written in English from the 1930s.
Baner America (Banner of America) [newspaper]			
1868–77, then merged with *Y Drych*	Scranton, Pennsylvania	Owned by Henry M. Edwards, editors included the Rev. Morgan A. Ellis	Similar to *Y Drych*
The Druid [weekly, fortnightly, then monthly newspaper]			
1907–37	Scranton until 1912, then Pittsburgh		Similar to *Y Drych*, but in English

Dates of publication	Place of publication	Owner, publisher, editor	Focus
Cyfaill or Hen Wlad yn America (Friend of the Old Country in America) [monthly magazine]			
1838–1933	New York City	Established/edited by the Rev. William Rowlands until 1866	Intended to serve all Welsh religious denominations, but eventually solely Calvinist-Methodist
Y Cenhadwr Americanaidd (The American Missionary) [magazine]			
1840–1901	Steuben, New York	Founded by the Rev. Robert Everett	Welsh Congregationalist magazine, characterised by militant anti-slavery and pro-temperance stance
Y Seren Orllewinol (The Western Star) [monthly magazine]			
1844–67	Utica, New York, then Pottsville, Pennsylvania, from 1854	Edited by the Rev. W. T. Phillips	Baptist magazine
The Cambrian [fortnightly then monthly magazine]			
1880–1919	Cincinnati, Ohio, then Remsen, New York, from 1886, then Utica, New York	Owned/edited by the Rev. D. J. Jones of Cincinnati, Ohio, then from 1886 by the Rev. Edward C. Evans of Remsen, New York, then by Thomas G. Griffiths of Utica, New York	General content of interest to those with Welsh connections

BIBLIOGRAPHY OF WORKS REFERRED TO IN THE TEXT

INTRODUCTION

Hartmann, E. (2001). *Americans from Wales.* fourth edn (Trucksville: National Welsh-American Foundation).

Lewis, R. L. (2008). *A History of Assimilation in the Coalfields: Welsh Americans* (Chapel Hill: University of North Carolina Press).

Williams, D. (1975). *Cymru ac America/Wales and America*, fourth edn (Cardiff: University of Wales Press).

CHAPTER 1

Peckham, G. (1583). *A True Reporte, of the Late Discoueries, and Possession, Taken in the Right of the Crowne of Englande, of the New-found Landes: by that Valiaunt and Worthye Gentleman, Sir Humfrey Gilbert Knight: Wherein is Also Breefely Sette Downe, Her Highnesse Lawfull Tytle Therevnto, and the Great and Manifolde Commodities, that is Likely to Grow Thereby, to the Whole Realme in Generall, and to the Aduenturers in Particular. Together with the Easines and Shortnes of the Voyage. Seene and Allowed* (London: John Charlewood).

Powel, D. (1584). *A Historie of Cambria now called Wales* (London: Rafe Newberie and Henrie Denham).

Williams, G. A, (1979). *Madoc: The Making of a Myth* (London: Eyre Methuen).

Williams, J. (1791). *An enquiry into the truth of the tradition, concerning the discovery of America, by Prince Madog ab Owen Gwynedd, about the year, 1170* (London: J. Brown).

CHAPTER 3

Adams, J. (1774; 1819 edn). *Novanglus, and Massachusettensis or Political Essays, Published in the Years 1774 and 1775, on the Principal Points of Controversy, between Great Britain and Her Colonies* (Boston: Hews and Goss).

Evans, L. (1755). *General Map of the Middle British Colonies in America* (London: Robert Dodsley).

McCullough, D. (2001). *John Adams* (New York: Simon & Schuster).

Paine, T. (1776). *Common Sense; Addressed to the Inhabitants of America, on the Following Interesting Subjects* (Philadelphia: R. Bell).

Price, R. (1758). *Review of the Principal Questions in Morals*, first edn (London: A. Millar).

Price, R. (1776). *Observations on the Nature of Civil Liberty, the Principles of Government, and the Justice and Policy of the War with America* (London: T. Cadell).

Price, R. (1784). *Observations on the Importance of the American Revolution and the Means of Making It a Benefit to the World* (London: T. Cadell).

Price, R. (1787). *Sermons on the Christian Doctrine* (London: T. Cadell).

CHAPTER 4

Jones, D. (1775). *Defensive War in a Just Cause Sinless* (Philadelphia: Henry Miller).

Lee, H. (1812). *Memoirs of the War in the Southern Department of the United States* (Philadelphia: Bradford and Inskeep).

CHAPTER 5

Jefferson, T. (1781). *Notes on the State of Virginia*, first public edn (London: John Stockdale, 1787).

Rappleye, C. (2010). *Robert Morris: Financier of the American Revolution* (New York: Simon & Schuster).
Sharp, C. G. (2015). *Button Gwinnett: Failed Merchant and Plantation Owner, Opportunist Politician, Mountebank, and Founding Father*, second edn (Oxford: YouCaxton Publications).

CHAPTER 6

Danisi, T. C., and J. C. Jackson (2009). *Meriwether Lewis* (Amherst, New York: Prometheus Books).

CHAPTER 7

Chidlaw, B. J. (1840). *Yr American* (Llanrwst: John Jones).
Conway, A., (1961). *The Welsh in America: Letters from the Immigrants* (Cardiff: University of Wales Press).
Davies, D. J. (1987). *Mormon Spirituality: Latter Day Saints in Wales and Zion* (Logan: Utah State University Press).
Haydon, J. R. (1932). *Thomas Owen: Chicago's True Founder* (Lombard, Illinois: Owen Memorial Fund).
Humphrys, J. (2004). *The Man from the Alamo* (St Athan, Vale of Glamorgan: Wales Books).
Jones, D. (1847). *Hanes Saint y Dyddiau Diweddaf, o'u sefydliad yn y flwyddyn 1823, hyd yr amser yr alltudiwyd tri chan mil o honynt o'r America oherwydd eu crefydd, yn y flwyddyn 1846 (History of the Latter-day Saints, from their establishment in the year 1823, until the time that three hundred thousand of them were exiled from America because of their religion, in the year 1846)* (Rhydybont: John Jones).
Jones, D. (1852). Llyfr Mormon (Merthyr Tydfil: J. Davies).
Thomas, R. D. (1872). Hanes Cymry America (History of the Welsh in America) (Utica: T. J. Griffiths).

CHAPTER 8

Burton, W. L. (1998). *Melting Pot Soldiers: The Union's Ethnic Regiments* (New York: Fordham University Press).
Channing, S. (1987). *Confederate Ordeal: The Southern Home Front* (New York: Time Life Books).

Donald, D., J. Baker and M. Holt (2001). *The Civil War and Reconstruction* (New York: W. W. Norton).

Hunter, J. (2007). *Sons of Arthur, Children of Lincoln: Welsh Writing from the American Civil War* (Cardiff: University of Wales Press).

Mahin, D. (2002). *The Blessed Place of Freedom: Europeans in Civil War America* (Washington, DC: Brassey's).

Potter, D. (1968). *The South and the Sectional Conflict* (Baton Rouge: Louisiana State University Press).

CHAPTER 9

Davis, J. J. (1922). *The Iron Puddler: My life in the Rolling Mills and what Came of it* (New York: Grosset & Dunlap).

Dean, J. W. (2004). *Warren G. Harding* (New York: Times Books).

Gibbons, P. E., 'The miners of Scranton', *Harper's New Monthly Magazine* (November 1877).

Hansen, M. L. (1940). *The Atlantic Migration, 1607–1860: A History of the Continuing Settlement of the United States* (Cambridge, Massachusetts: Harvard University Press).

Jones, W. D. (1993). *Wales and America: Scranton and the Welsh 1860–1920* (Cardiff: University of Wales Press).

Knowles, A. K. (1997). *Calvinists Incorporated: Welsh Immigrants on Ohio's Industrial Frontier* (Chicago: University of Chicago Press).

Lewis, R. L. (2008). *A History of Assimilation in the Coalfields: Welsh Americans* (Chapel Hill: University of North Carolina Press).

Madison, N. V. (2015). *Tredegar Iron Works: Richmond's Foundry on the James* (Charleston: The History Press).

Summers, E. (1903). *Genealogical and Family History of Eastern Ohio* (New York and Chicago: The Lewis Publishing Company).

Tyler, R. L. (2015). *Wales and the American Dream* (Newcastle upon Tyne: Cambridge Scholars Publishing).

Van Vugt, W. E., (2006). *British Buckeyes: The English, Scots, and Welsh in Ohio, 1700–1900* (Kent, Ohio: Kent State University Press).

White, E., and H. Taylor (1910). *General History of Macon County, Missouri* (Chicago: Henry Taylor & Company).

Williams, G. (1979). *Religion, Language and Nationality in Wales* (Cardiff: University of Wales Press).

Williams, P. N., (2002). *From Wales to Pennsylvania – The David Thomas Story* (St Athan, Vale of Glamorgan: Wales Books).

CHAPTER 10

Davies, P. G. (2006). *Welsh in Wisconsin* (Madison: Wisconsin Historical Society Press).

Dubofsky, M., and W. Van Tine (1986). *John L. Lewis: A Biography* (Urbana: University of Illinois Press).

Lloyd Wright, F. (1943). *Frank Lloyd Wright: An Autobiography* (New York: Duell, Sloan and Pearce).

Roberts, Ron E. (1994). *John L. Lewis: Labor and Wild Justice* (Dubuque, Iowa: Kendall Hunt).

Secrest, M. (1992). *Frank Lloyd Wright: A Biography* (Chicago: University of Chicago Press).

Sulzberger, C. L. (1938). *Sit down with John L. Lewis* (New York: Random House).

Summers, E. (1903). *Genealogical and Family History of Eastern Ohio* (New York and Chicago: The Lewis Publishing Company).

Thomas, R. D. (1872). *Hanes Cymry America (History of the Welsh in America)* (Utica: T. J. Griffiths).

Williams, D. J. (1913). *The Welsh of Columbus, Ohio: A Study in Adaptation and Assimilation* (Oshkosh: Published by the Author).

CHAPTER 11

American Council of Learned Societies (1928–36). *Dictionary of American Biography* (New York: Charles Scribner).

Edwards, Rev. Ebenezer (1899). *Welshmen as Factors* (Utica: T. J. Griffiths).

Hartmann, E. G. (1983). *Americans from Wales: A Treasure Chest of Information for People Interested in their Welsh Heritage* (New York: Octagon Books).

Williams, G. (1979). *Religion, Language and Nationality in Wales* (Cardiff: University of Wales Press).

Wittke, C. (1939). *We Who Built America: The Saga of the Immigrant* (New York: Prentice-Hall).

INDEX

꧁꧂